MORMONISM, MAMA and ME!

"Come and hear, all ye that fear God,
and I will declare what He hath done for my soul."
Psalm 66:16

Thelma Geer
Rt. 2, Box 723
Safford, Arizona 85546

Third edition of

Mormonism, Mama and Me!

Published by Calvary Missionary Press, P.O. Box 13532, Tucson, Arizona 85732. Printed in the U.S.A.

Library of Congress Cataloging in Publication Data
Geer, Thelma.
  Mormonism, Mama and Me!

  Library of Congress Catalog No. 81-146846
  ISBN 0-912375-00-0

Bibliography:
  1. Mormons and Mormonism—Controversial literature.
  I. Title.

TABLE OF CONTENTS

LIST OF ILLUSTRATIONS

The illustrations used in this book originally appeared in early books, both Mormon and non-Mormon.

iv

DEDICATED

Lovingly and Prayerfully to:

My Mormon Singing Mother
and
Singing Mothers Everywhere

That all may sing with Mama and Me
Our New Song:

"Thou art worthy to take the book,
And to open the seals thereof:
For Thou wast slain,
And hast redeemed us unto God
by thy blood."

(Rev. 5:9)

AUTHOR'S PREFACE

This is a singing love story. Perhaps it should have been entitled "Our New Song—Mama's and Mine." In it I hope to impart to you my love for Jesus, for Mama, and for my beloved Mormon people. But, most of all, I would have you know the love of Jesus and how much God "so loved..."

This book is my sincere attempt to explain the complex subject of Mormonism and the very hallowed experience I had of salvation by grace through faith in the Lord Jesus Christ. As you read this mixture of testimony and refutation of false doctrine, please bear in mind that this book is prompted by my deep love and concern for my beloved Mormon people. As a fourth generation Latter-day Saint who was born in the "Mormon country" area of Eastern Arizona, I grew up loving the Mormon people, their heritage, customs and way of life. For this very reason, I want all of them to know the assurance of salvation through the Lord Jesus Christ and to acknowledge His divine right to be pre-eminent in every way and in everything. As the Apostle Paul cried out from the bottom of his heart for his people, Israel, to be saved (Romans 10:1-4) so do I cry out to my people (who *think* they are literally a modern Israel) that they too, might be saved!

For every assertion and disclosure of Mormon doctrine discussed, I have attempted to furnish ample documentation from reliable Mormon leaders and General Authorities. Every reference has been carefully checked and rechecked for accuracy and proper context. These men (whom the Mormons really believe "speak for God Himself": *Doctrine and Covenants,* 21:4-5, 68:4, *et al.*) have made their doctrine clear to Mormon and non-Mormon alike. Even though my basic presupposition is that the system known as the Church of Jesus Christ of Latter-day Saints is not a Christian communion, it remains for each of you to weigh the evidence and decide for yourselves. I pray that each of you, Mormon or non-Mormon, approach the subject with an open mind and heart.

I will not deny, nor even apologize for the fact that my heritage as a descendant of Mormon pioneer stock has "flavored" my approach in this book. The stories I grew up with about my forebears have made them seem like well-known friends, and since one cannot really divorce modern Mormonism from its pioneer influences, I may have seemed to "dwell in the past" as far as their doctrines are concerned. To some this may seem unfair or unnecessary; however, *just the opposite is true!* If Joseph Smith, Brigham Young and the other early prophets did not know and understand *true* Mormonism, who amongst their successors can? Therefore it is necessary to know the "roots" of Mormonism. It is not only fair to call forth the sayings of Joseph and Brigham for examination, it is demanded by the Mormon church itself every time they proclaim these men as *true* prophets of the living God!

For my Christian reader, I hope that I have given you sufficient information in this book that you will see for yourself that Mormonism is not compatible with the true gospel of Jesus Christ. For my Mormon reader who is determined (as I was for the first 30 years of my life) to remain in Mormonism, you will, at least, be acquainted with all the Mormon gospel, the secreted basic "meat" of Mormonism rather than the veiled, watered-down "milk" allowed the vast majority of Latter-day Saints and the public. I plead with you to face up today and prove whether "these things [the teachings of the Latter-day prophets] be so": "...Jesus was not begotten by the Holy Ghost...the Father came himself and favored that spirit with a tabernacle [body] instead of letting any other man do it..." "the God-given power of procreation...is one of the chief means of man's exaltation and glory..." "...No man or woman of this dispensation [YOU!] can enter the celestial kingdom of God *without the consent of Joseph Smith...*"!

Preface to the 3rd Edition

As this third edition of my "love story about Jesus and for my Mormon people" goes to press, I make further acknowledgement of my responsibility to God, to my Mormon people and to Christians everywhere to continue to honestly represent Mormonism for what it really is and to stand steadfastly, but lovingly, against its errors and hidden doctrines. But I have an added responsibility: the responsibility to assure all readers—Mormon and non-Mormon—that in spite of Mormon charges to the contrary, I have not misrepresented Mormonism in any way. As proof of my sincerity and honest presentation, and in answer to Latter-day Saints' charges against me, I do hereby pledge and give notice: my original (1830 1st Edition) Book of Mormon (valued at $7,000) will be surrendered to the first Mormon able to prove that any Mormon doctrine discussed in this edition of *Mormonism, Mama and Me!* has not been taught by Mormon authorities.

Actually in my writing of this book, I had withheld some of Mormonism's teachings, which range from the blasphemous to the ludicrous. But they are not unimportant; in fact, several represent foundation stones of Mormon belief ...false doctrine built upon false doctrine resulting in a theological house of cards:

> "...it required the male and female, united, to make one image of His [God's] own body, and that male and female [God and one of His purported wives] were necessary to form one Adam...it required male and female to make an image of God."[1]

Apostle Orson Pratt estimated that

> "...the vast family of spirits who were [sexually] begotten before the foundation of the world...amounts to one hundred and five thousand million which was the approximate number of sons and daughters of God in Heaven...

> "If we admit that one personage was the father of all this great family, and that they were all born of the same mother, the period of time intervening between the birth of the oldest and the youngest spirit must have been immense [based upon a nine-month gestation period]. If we suppose, as an average, that only one year intervened between each birth, then it would have required over one hundred thousand million of years for the same mother to have given birth to this vast family...

"If the father of these spirits, prior to his redemption [death and resurrection], had secured to himself, through the everlasting covenant of marriage, many wives... the period required to people a world would be shorter... with a hundred wives, this period would be reduced to only one thousand million years."[2]

The reason that Mormon authorities teach that God and His wives and Jesus and His wives (and all resurrected, temple Mormons) have spirit babies in heaven is because they eat spirit food instead of earthly food:

"When the world is redeemed, the vegetable creation is redeemed and made new, as well as the animal; and when planted in a celestial soil, each vegetable derives its nourishment therefrom;... This is the origin of spiritual vegetables in Heaven... Thus the spirits of both vegetables and animals are the offspring of male and female parents which have been raised from the dead... The celestial vegetables and fruits... constitute the food of the Gods... Celestial vegetables, when digested, form a spiritual fluid which gives immortality and eternal life to the organization in which it flows."[3]

My dear reader, may I ask you this question: Would you want to trust your soul's eternal destiny to such foolishness as this? God's Word, the Bible, warns us to give no heed "to fables and endless genealogies" and to "refuse foolish and ignorant speculations," but rather, "retain the standard of sound words in the faith and love which are in Christ Jesus."

To Christians everywhere, I covet your prayers and encouragement as I witness of Jesus' undying love for my beloved Mormon people.

February 2, 1983
Safford, Arizona

1. Little, James A. and Franklin Richards, *A Compendium of the Doctines of the Gospel,* "The best available material for the use of the Elders," 1882, p.120

2. Pratt, Orson, "Figure and Magnitude of Spirits," *The Seer,* Vol. 1, No. 3, March, 1853

3. Ibid. and op. cit. "The Pre-Existence of Man."

ACKNOWLEDGEMENTS

To name all of those who have aided in the production of this book would require a book itself! However, you all know who you are—and I bless God for the contribution that each of you made. Special thanks must go to my dear loving and patient husband, Ernest. Most of all, I am beholden to the Holy One who brought them into my life, and who convicted me of my sin and need for salvation, brought me up out of the horrible pit and set my feet upon a rock and established my goings (Psalm 40:2). To Him I became indentured when He caused my name to be written in the Lamb's Book of Life. To Him, the author and finisher of all faith, I give all honor and glory and praise, now and forever!

AMEN

FOREWORD

Mormonism, Mama and Me is a most timely book, appearing, as it does, at a time when the women of Mormonism are beginning to question their status as equal members of society and to speak out about it.

The plight of womanhood in Mormonism has been an unenviable one ever since the days of Joseph Smith and the doctrines created under Section 132 of *Doctrine and Covenants*. Under these doctrines a man cannot get complete elevation to godhood without a wife/wives sealed to him in the temple, and a woman's only salvation in the celestial world is to be sealed in the temple to a Mormon husband in good standing.

If a wife apostatizes, her husband has a perfect right, according to the church, to divorce her and with the divorce withdraw all of her celestial rights—she will be left in the grave on resurrection morning. Mormon women have a great fear of such a fate.

Thelma Geer was born and raised in a fourth generation Mormon home, the great-granddaughter of Mormon pioneer John D. Lee, one of the bodyguards of Joseph Smith and Brigham Young. Lee had nineteen wives (all taken to "save their souls") and sixty-four children. No one would have a more comprehensive knowledge of the Mormon plural wife system than Mrs. Geer.

Happily, Thelma Geer came to know the Lord Jesus as Saviour as a young woman. In her biography she combines a very complete depiction of the role of women in Mormonism (and its peculiar doctrines) with an impeccable application of Christian doctrine. It is all charmingly told.

This book should be read by Mormon women so that they would lose their fears of retribution should they defect. It should be read by all Christian women who have any contact with Mormon people. Pastors should read the book so that they could have direction in counseling.

Gordon H. Fraser
Woodburn, OR, May 1980

Chapter One

BORN A MORMON

Reminiscing is such fun when you've finally reached the golden age of grannyhood. The best part is remembering when I was a chubby-cheeked (no wrinkles or creases), eager, loved and loving youngster. Every bit of me was in love . . . with everything and everybody, especially Mama. My life and home radiated around Mama.

Doesn't everyone long to write an "I Remember Mama" ode? To set down the everlasting impressions of childhood? To relive the happenings and happiness of life on the old homeplace? My recollections center around gentle, loving Mama and Papa, Lula May and Cecil Lehi Smithson.

At work or play, we were a fun family, a zealous, fourth-generation Mormon family. We pulled together just as our pioneer ancestors had as they pushed and pulled their homemade handcarts across mountains and plains to the Zion of the West . . . The Great Salt Lake Basin. There with Brigham Young, they proclaimed, "This is the place!"

We, too, had a piece of Zion to occupy. Led by Mama, we sang as our ancestors had sung,

> Put your shoulder to the wheel. Push along.
> Do your duty with a heart full of song.
> We all have work, let no one shirk,
> Put your shoulder to the wheel.

And so, during the Great Depression, we "grubbed" alongside Mama and Papa and kept grub on the table. In our tight-knit Mormon community of Cactus Flat, Arizona

[1]

(more properly designated Lebanon on the map, though no cedars flourished there, only mesquite, catclaw and cacti), Mama's songs and Mama's stories of our Mormon ancestors encouraged us and kept us proud to be Smithsons ... proud to be Mormons.

Mama used to tell us, "Even though we're as poor as Job's turkey [however poor that was], we can be thankful that we're not as poor as church mice, nor as dumb. They're born and raised in a Mormon church house and never learned to sing "Count Your Blessings!" We all knew what was coming next. With Mama leading we lustily sang,

> Count your blessings, name them one by one
> Count your blessings, see what God hath done.

Then we'd listen as Mama recounted our blessings, especially the blessing of being born white Mormons.

Just to have been born a Mormon—especially a light white one—was the greatest of all earthly blessings. An earnestly-sought special privilege, an earned-in-heaven reward, a mark of distinction.

As a white Mormon, I proudly accepted the teaching that my fair skin and Mormon parentage signified that I had been one of God's most intelligent and obedient born-in-heaven spirit children. There in a primeval childhood I had diligently applied myself to all the mandates and instructions of the heavenly Father and my own heavenly mother.

As a reward for my superior attributes and attitudes, I had been singled out, trained and qualified to be born a white Latter-day Saint, deserving of emulation, adulation and eventual deification. All dark-skinned people, even darker-complexioned Caucasians, and members of all other religions had been inferior spirits in heaven. (Our family still wonders what celestial mischief one of our favorite Aunties got caught in to cause her to be born so dark.) Moreover, they would probably remain inferiors on earth and again in the resurrection. Superior intelligent spirits such as mine would naturally and inherently choose to be born white and delightsome Latter-day Saints, while the more ignorant, ignoble spirits neither earn nor know better than to be born into inferior, false religions.

As a white Mormon, I heartily endorsed these teachings of our Latter-day Saints' authorities, especially those of Mormon prophet/presidents and apostles such as Apostle Melvin J. Ballard, who declared that:

> Of all the thousands of children born today, a certain portion of them went to the Hottentots of South Africa; thousands went to Chinese Mothers; thousands to Negro Mothers; thousands to beautiful white Latter-Day Saints Mothers. Now you cannot tell me that all these spirits were just arbitrarily designated, marked, to go where they did ... I am convinced it is because of *some things they did before they came into this life.*

Melvin J. Ballard
Crusade for Righteousness, Page 218

**CHOICE SPIRITS GIVEN
THE FAVORED LINEAGE**

Mormon President Joseph F. Smith asked of the Mormon people:

> Is it not a reasonable belief, that the Lord would select the choice spirits to come through the better grades of nations? Moreover, is it not reasonable to believe that less worthy spirits would come through less favored lineage? Does this not account in very large part, for *the various grades of color* and degrees of intelligence we find in the earth?

Joseph Fielding Smith
The Way to Perfection, Page 48

Delighting in Mormonism's assessment that whiteness denoted righteousness, I early gloried in my lovely white skin, my Latter-day Saints parentage and presumptive pre-eminence, counting myself worthy indeed and most fortunate.

In tender-hearted, wide-eyed wonder I marvelled, as did all Mormon youngsters, that God the Father had once been a tiny human baby, born aeons ago on another planet to white "Mormon" parents. Since all Mormons are carefully shielded and sternly cautioned against contamination with so-called Christian churches and their doctrines, I readily embraced the Latter-day Saints' delusion that this "baby god" had grown from babyhood to manhood. And that while living on that earth as a Mormon, God the Father had been required to fulfill all the Mormon gospel requirements including celestial marriage in the Mormon temple and the siring of a multitude of *mortal* offspring, followed by His death and resurrection! In heaven myraids more spiritual offspring reportedly were—and still are—born to God the Father and His wives through celestial procreation and gestation. Thus, God the Father had progressed from a celestial pre-existence to babyhood, to manhood, and on to godhood just as I would do too if I were an obedient, diligent Latter-day Saint.

Just as my grandparents long ago had set themselves to do, my parents, too, would follow God the Father's purported gospel pattern. They would "practice their religion," obeying the commandments and ordinances of the Mormon church paying their tithes, church and temple assessments in full. Then they, too, could be married and sealed for eternity in a Mormon temple and wear the authorized holy undergarments of the Mormon priesthood. And most certainly Mama and Papa would "live their religion" by providing *earthly* bodies for God's purported millions of spirit children, as many as they possibly could.

PAPA PROVOKED TO PARENTHOOD

"Who are we to deny God's little spirit children earthly bodies and a Mormon home?" Mama, with eyes glinting determination, demanded of the world at large and Papa in particular. "You know as well as I do that we're failing our religious duty. After all, we've been up there too, begging for bodies, wanting to come to earth. I can't help feeling sorry for God's poor little spirit children and ashamed of us for not doing more to help."

"Whoa up now, May," Papa patiently soothed. "You know we've heard about the little spirits in heaven all our lives and that I know about their needs and feel just as sorry for them as you do. But why get so rambunctious about it this morning? Simmer down and finish your biscuits; I'm hungry."

"You talk about hungry! What about all those little bodyhungering spirits in heaven? I'm trying to tell you that we ought to be religious enough to provide as many bodies for them as we possibly can."

"I've told you before that you don't need to coax and convince me," Papa smirked. "They can come as fast and as often as they want. I'm with them and you all the way. After all, as I've heard so many of our Mormon elders say, this is one Mormon commandment that we Mormon men don't mind keeping. Just holler when you're ready."

"You really shouldn't joke about so sacred an obligation, Chunk. But I am grateful that you're such a good family man, able and willing to provide a home and bodies for God's little needy spirits, just as our parents did for us. Just as our church authorities insist that God commands us to do. And besides all that my empty arms hanker for another tiny wee one to hold and to mold."

And so, even though Mama and Papa were as poor as the Arizona desert dirt from which they scraped out a meagre living, they ushered me, their third born, royally into their already crowded two-room Mormon home. They verily believed that true royalty—a sexually begotten-in-heaven spirit baby of God—had come down from heaven to bless and ennoble their lives. On that cold and blustery twelfth of March more than half a century ago, they, with hearts and hearth aglow, humbly and proudly made room for this tiny, newborn Mormon.

Together Mama and Papa named their newest daughter Thelma Rachel Smithson. They determined that I should early learn that the Church of Jesus Christ of Latter-day Saints is the only true church and that Joseph Smith was a true prophet of God.

From them I learned such other Mormon "gospel truths" as these:

- God is an exalted man with a physical body, parts and passions.

- Men may become Gods.

- Jesus is merely one of God's billions of sexually begotten-in-heaven sons and the only one sexually begotten by Him on earth.

- Satan is a full spirit brother of Jesus. He could have been the Saviour if his plan of salvation had surpassed that of Jesus.

- Adam's "sin" was a blessing and *not* a curse.

- It was just as necessary for Adam to sin as it was for Christ to be crucified.

From early childhood these Mormon teachings were an important part of me. Easily and naturally they had possessed my very soul, mainly through Mama's singing.

MY MORMON SINGING MOTHER

Early and late, sad or glad, Mama was forever singing. She had a song to suit every occasion and a special one, I believe, for my "birthing."

I've always fancied that Mama must have been singing as I was aborning and that Mama infused me with a melody at my birth, for always I've had a bent and a yen to sing just as Mama did. Now wouldn't it have pleasured both Mama and me mightily if I could have claimed the distinction of coming into this world singing instead of squalling? However, I surely must have learned to sing (though wordlessly) before I learned to walk, for I seem to have always known the hymns and ballads she sang to me.

My earliest remembrance of Mama—the first, and I believe, the greatest impression of her life on mine—was the enchantment and pleasure of hearing her sing such tender ballads as "Just Plain Folks." In God's providence it was a very special song. It lastingly instilled in me a tender regard for just plain ordinary folks and led to the greatest blessing of all my life.

Mama's "Just Plain Folks" ballad is about a prodigal son, but unlike the Biblical one . . . in every way. The prodigal son of Jesus' parable portrays God's willingness to pardon and welcome the repentant, confessing sinner. He was a rich boy who left his father's country estate to seek freedom but found want, ending up in the pigpen of sin, slopping hogs. He then humbly sought forgiveness for his sins from his loving, forgiving father.

But the poor-folks country lad in Mama's ditty was an ornery, mean-spirited maverick who evidently never did realize his sinful unworthiness and seek his father's forgiveness. Consequently he never experienced the joy and peace that pardon affords.

I wish I could sing to you the sad story of Mama's poor country lad who had left his plain folks' simple, country way of life and had gone not only to the city, but to the dogs. There in the big city where he soon struck it rich, he was, instead of feeding swine, living "high on the hog." One Saturday night while he was throwing a whing-ding of a Sodom and Gomorrah-Belshazzar party, his poor gray-haired, hard-working parents unexpectedly came to visit him.

I remember the words and tune so well, and especially the tender pathos in Mama's lovely, soft voice as she crooned:

But cooly did he greet them
For rich friends were by his side,
Who'd oft times heard him boast of home so grand.
As the old man sadly looked at him
He said with modesty,
As he gently took his dear wife by the hand,
We are just plain folks, your mother and me,
Just plain folks as our own folk used to be.
Since our presence seems to grieve you,
We will go away and leave you
We are sadly out of place here,
For we're just plain folks.

Mama's pining song left me pining too . . . pining for all poor forsaken parents whose wayward, ungrateful children turned out to be loose livers. Its manipulative message packed a mighty wallop, sending prickles up and down my spine.

Even though I knew that Mama was deliberately preaching to me in her intriguing songs, I enjoyed most of them anyway, especially "She's Only a Bird in a Gilded Cage" and "After the Ball Is Over." But "Baby Your Mother as She Babied You" always left me miserable and ashamed. Every one of her persuasive folk songs implanted their purposed lessons in my heart and directed my life, just as Mama planned them to. But most influential of all were the

Mormon hymns we sang about Joseph Smith, the first prophet of Mormonism.

We sang "Oh, How Lovely Was the Morning" when Joseph Smith, as a fourteen-year-old farm lad "saw the Father and the Son." We truly believed that in answer to young Smith's prayer as to which church to join, God and Jesus had appeared to the questioning youth in their once earthly, now bloodless resurrected human bodies of flesh and bones. Both God and Jesus had, according to Joseph Smith, sojourned in these bodies while living on earth as mortal men.

In the ensuing conversation, God supposedly commanded Joseph Smith to "join none of them [*the churches*], for they were *all* wrong . . . all their creeds were an *abomination* in His sight; that those professors [*all church members and ministers*] were all corrupt.

Because of these Mormon teachings I had early learned to disdain all other churches, mistrust their members, and most especially their ministers. I labeled their doctrines as lies and arrogantly denounced their beliefs that God was a Spirit.

GOD, A POLYGAMOUS MARRIED MAN

Along with all other informed Mormons I believed in a "Father in heaven who was begotten on a previous heavenly world by *His* Father."[2] The God of Mormonism was once a helpless, burping baby—born to Mormon parents who brought Him up to "live worthy of the Gospel" and to obey all the mandates that Mormon gospel proposes. And so at the age of eight, the child-God supposedly had to undergo baptism by immersion for the remission of His sins, imposition of hands for the reception of the Holy Ghost and confirmation of His church membership. All of which supposedly placed Him in the kingdom of *His* God! After having thus been cleansed of all His sins, "born of water" by baptism, and "born of the Spirit" by the imposition of hands, our fledgling God was ready for further advancement.

At about the age of twelve, God the Father was ordained a deacon, just as all worthy twelve-year-old Mormon boys are. This, the first of several degress of the Latter-day Saint priesthood, was a giant step in His progress to godhood. On and up He struggled through the offices of teacher and priest until finally He merited the coveted prestigious power and authority of becoming a Mormon elder, which granted His initial admission into the inner sanctum of the Mormon temple.

At last, He was allowed to learn Mormon priesthood secrets which hitherto had been withheld because only mature, worthy "Temple Mormons" can bear the "strong meat" of Mormonism's secret doctrines and practices. All of this practically guaranteed His godhood for He could now have His wives and children sealed to Him for His eternal glory. Therefore, in special temple rites the newly enlightened future God was married and sealed for eternity to numerous wives, just as all Mormon men must do in order to eventually become gods.

The multiplication of God's wives and children and children's children plus the amassing of great knowledge and intelligence supposedly determined the greatness of the developing God. He therefore set about earnestly extending His kingdom of wives and children, gaining extensive experience and knowledge along the way. The enormity of His vast and various family duties and the tides of time naturally took their toll.

Our future God must have known that the time for His departure was at hand. Another expedient step must be taken on His "Glory Road," one more milestone in His progression to godhood. Patiently and feebly the infirm God-man awaited His death and resurrection, just as any other aged, enfeebled Mormon patriarch would do.

And thus, the God of Mormonism who was "once a man in mortal flesh as we are" and "has once been a finite being"[3] having limits and bounds and subject to *death* and was "once in a fallen state,"[4] "passed through the experiences of mortal life, including death and resurrection."[5]

After God sickened, died and was resurrected, He resurrected his numerous wives. God and His wives now have resurrected bodies of flesh and bones. The primary difference between their bodies and ours is that they no longer have blood in their veins. They reportedly live together as husband and wives and by procreation (generation) beget children in the same way and gestation period (the celestial equivalent of nine months) as all humans do. Mormon historian B.H. Roberts put it this way:

> When in our literature we say, "God created the spirits of men," it is understood that they were begotten. We mean "generation" not "creation."

B.H. Roberts
Mormon Doctrine of Deity, Page 260

The God of the church of Jesus Christ of Latter-day Saints is still not yet perfect. He is still progressing from one degree to a higher level of perfection, still advancing in wisdom and knowledge, still busily and unceasingly sexually impregnating His wives. Ever and anon God must keep progressing, building up a greater kingdom and exaltation for himself, making room for the developing of lesser gods—the devout, large-familied Mormon elders of this world.

They, too, are busily climbing Mormonism's ladder of exaltation, ever pressing hard on the heels of God, ever climbing up behind Him, steadily pushing Him on ahead so that they can take His lately vacated station and become gods themselves. We Mormons truly believed that "As man is now, God once was. As God is, man may become."

Apostle Orson Hyde summarized this doctrine when he said:

> Remember that God, our Heavenly Father, was perhaps once a child, and mortal like we ourselves and rose step by step in the scale of progress, in the school of advancement; has moved forward and overcome, until He has arrived at the point where He now is.

Orson Hyde
Journal of Discourses
Volume 1, Page 123

A little simple reasoning makes us to understand that God's further advancement to greater heights of perfection depends partly on the clambering, zealous Mormon elders and, to a greater degree, on His numerous obliging wives and their offspring, and therefore, even partly on me. For I, along with God's other more obedient spirit children in our pre-earthly "primeval childhood," had reportedly aided God in inspiring and cajoling, organizing and controlling the ill-starred, second-rate disobedient spirits, my weak little brother and sister spirits. Most of them are presumably only my half brothers and half sisters, all having been sired by the same heavenly Father, but borne by different heavenly mothers.

In such a hodgepodge of spirit children, there are the obedient and disobedient, the super intelligent and the intellectually defective, the ambitious and the dawdlers, the righteous and also those who prefer to follow Satan, all of whom are in need of the heavenly Father's correction, supervision, and presence. However, God, with His hindering body of flesh and bones can be in but one place at a time. God, therefore, must have a pressing need for proficient spirits such as I to take over the lesser celestial kingdom affairs, leaving Him free to effectuate the two major requirements on which His continued advancement hinges and which none but He can do.

Foremost are the time-consuming, debilitating procreative visits to each of His thousands of wives, which surely must leave him worn and weary, drained in spirit and in body with very little time and energy to spend in advancing in knowledge and wisdom. He must garner ever greater stores of learning, for according to the first prophet of The Church of Jesus Christ of Latter-day Saints, "the glory of God is intelligence."[6] But surely the extension of God's intelligence, as important as it is, does not compare with the strength and fervor poured into the multiplication of His progeny, which keeps God and His queens as busy as the proverbial bees around the honey pot.

In the highest realms of heaven, "drones" are inexcusable, even me. As God the Father, "the directing Intelligence of the universe," keeps striving for ever-greater godhood, my heavenborn, not-yet-mortal spirit assertedly kept working, learning and progressing. At all costs I had to earn the right to leave heaven and be born on earth, for without the experiences and circumstances of an earth life I could never achieve my highest potential—that of becoming a celestial queen and goddess, a heavenly mother. Assuredly, more than anything else that could be given to me and most earnestly sought for was the privilege of leaving heaven.

As a rule, most false religions have their members working their way up to heaven, but Mormonism had me *first working my way out and down.* However, my prestigious performance in heaven caused God to keep me there longer. Through the aeons of eternity God had reserved me in heaven so that I could receive the ultimate of all eternal blessings. I was to be born in Joseph Smith's dispensation, the "greatest dispensation of all times," which he ushered in on April 6, 1830, when he established what eventually became known as The Church of Jesus Christ of Latter-day Saints.

LATTER-DAY "SAINTS"

I, too, delighted in the teachings of the high officials of the Mormon Church that there

> ... are many spirits that are *more noble, more intelligent* than others ... among the Saints is the most likely place for these spirits to take their tabernacle [bodies], through a just and righteous parentage. They [the more noble, more intelligent] are to be sent to that people that are the most *righteous* of any other people upon the earth ... This is the reason why the Lord kept sending them here ... The Lord has not kept them in store for five or six thousand years past, and kept them waiting for their bodies all this time to send them among the Hottentots, the African negroes, the idolatrous Hindoos [sic], any other of the fallen nations that dwell upon the face of this earth. They are not kept in reserve in order to come forth to receive such a degraded parentage upon the earth ..
>
> Orson Pratt
> *Journal of Discourses*
> Volume 1, Pages 62-63

Whereas disapprobation and disgrace are said to be the just portion of the purported "lesser spirits," deference and high esteem are thought to be the just dues of the Mormon authorities and their wives. They presumably were of the elite set in heaven; the outstanding leaders and organizers of God's spirit children, set apart and coached in heaven for their leading roles and specific high offices in the Mormon kingdom in these "latter days."

To these, our Latter-day high priests and prophets, we Mormons gave all due honor and unthinking loyalty, being constantly reminded at home and in sacrament meetings to "obey the counsel of the authorities of the church." Moreover, we must never challenge their edicts nor envy their high status, never resent being their underlings. For before leaving heaven we had agreed to continue as their subordinates on earth. There we had promised to "sustain" them as our leaders in the priesthood and in all earthly affairs.

After all, we were told, it was because of our own faults that we were not of the heavenly "upper crust." We should have applied ourselves as diligently in heaven as the "authorities" had. Therefore, we now must be content with our lower status on earth. We felt duty bound to honor the agreements we had made in heaven, and to submit to their higher priesthood powers.

Neither were we to lament the fact that the same ruling families of early-day Mormonism are still the leading families of The Church of Jesus Christ of Latter-day Saints (for explanation we were again referred to the premortal spirit world).

We all believed the romantic notion that aeons ago in heaven our Mormon spirits had wooed and won our earthly "intendeds," and that together our affianced spirits had strolled down heaven's lover's lane seeking still other spirits to become our earthly children. They in turn had wooed and won their own true-loves, who chose and trained other spirits to become *their* earthly children. And so on, *ad infinitum.* These, we were told, were truly "made in heaven" marriages!

And, of course, the spirits of our Mormon church authorities had judiciously chosen their brides-to-be from the cream of the spiritual crop. This they were entitled to do, for they held high priestly positions and long tenure in the church of heaven. They and their super-special spiritual fiancees had, of course, chosen and trained ultra-elite spirits to perpetuate the family's prestigious powers in the earthly priesthood, ecclesiastical politics and the elite inner circle of what would become Mormonism.

Since the authorities of the church had been trained in heaven and I had "sustained" them there, I was to support their earthly endeavors and edicts in these latter days. I felt obliged to take counsel of the authorities in every area of life, especially their "spiritual" reasonings concerning God's wives and my own heavenly mother, for whom I felt a special love and affinity, fascination and gratitude.

ADORATION OF HEAVENLY MOTHER

Along with other well-intentioned Latter-day Saints, I loved to sing one of Mormonism's most popular hymns, "Oh My Father," which further developed our belief in and adoration for a heavenly mother as well as a heavenly Father. The heavenly mother doctrine was enhanced as we sang:

> In the heavens are parents single?
> No, the thought makes reason stare.
> Truth is reason, truth eternal
> Tells me I've a Mother there.

In conclusion we sang this petitionary prayer begging for the blessings and permission of both the heavenly Father and heavenly mother to re-enter heaven and live with them there:

> Then at length when I've completed
> All you sent me forth to do
> With your mutual approbation
> Let me come and dwell with you.

My heavenly mother was just as real and important to me as my heavenly Father. She seemed more intimate and dearer to me, for I presumed that God the Father was away much of the time from our particular mansion. Jealously I fancied Him striding masterfully across His vast heavenly domain, visiting and making love to His other wives, begetting other spirit children, sternly correcting and instructing His other oft-time wayward offspring, while my heavenly mother lonesomely waited at home religiously tending her home and children, especially, me!

In prayer and in song I thanked God for sending the "Latter-day prophet," Joseph Smith, to teach us these astounding doctrines and "to guide us in these latter days."

JOSEPH SMITH'S BLOOD PLEADS UNTO HEAVEN

I sang of the blood of my "martyred" Mormon prophet who had died in a wild exchange of gunfire while fighting for his life in the Carthage, Illinois, jail. There, he was shot through the heart by a bullet from an angry frontier mob as he awaited trial on charges of treason, which stemmed from his destruction of the *Nauvoo Expositor*. This newspaper had been issued by disgruntled Mormons to expose the prophet Joseph Smith and to accuse and reprove him for, among other evils, teaching many gods, polygamy, adultery and secret temple marriages for eternity with *other* Mormon men's wives and daughters.

We Mormons never allowed our minds to dwell on the fact that these disaffected Mormon men had a right to challenge the Latter-day prophet. Never did we even consider that Mormons themselves had instigated, and to a great extent comprised, the mob that killed our prophet. Most certainly we never admitted that our prophet may have been *guilty* of the charges leveled against him; our prophet could do no wrong.

Even though Joseph Smith had died an inglorious death in a common jail cell, charged as a traitor, an adulterer and a horse thief, we Mormons glorified him and laid the blame on other churches and their ministers. We sang vindictively of how "The Priests of Baal" (ministers of other denominations), "desperate their crafts to save," had incited the mob that slew our prophet. In conclusion we intoned, "long shall his blood which was shed by assassins plead unto heaven. Earth shall atone for the blood of that man."

In still another glorifying Mormon hymn, "The Seer, Joseph, The Seer," we related how Joseph Smith:

Of noble seed, of Heavenly birth
Came to bless the Saints on earth . . .

The Saints, the Saints his only pride
For them he lived, for them he died ...

Unchanged in death with a Saviour's love
He pleads their cause in the courts above ...

He died, he died for those he loved
He reigns, he reigns in the realms above ...

He waits on Zion's shore
To welcome the Saints forevermore.

I knew the songs and stories of Joseph Smith and I knew them well. I had heard them day and night for half a lifetime. Whereso'er Mormon people congregate, Joseph Smith's spirit seems to pervade the air as they tenderly talk of his lowly birth, his life, his ministry, his death, his worth. But I knew very little about Jesus' birth, and I was too embarrassed to ask for there seemed to be something clandestine about Jesus' conception.

One night before I was old enough to understand the hows and wherefores of childbirth, as I sat quietly in the fireplace corner, I overheard the visiting Mormon missionary telling my father about when "God overshadowed Mary." When Papa discovered my presence, he sternly ordered me from the room. Then I realized that the Mormon missionary's recital of Jesus' birth had not been meant for my little girl ears. I had overheard a Mormon priesthood secret.

JESUS AND SATAN—SEXUALLY
BEGOTTEN SONS OF GOD

For years, though I tried to forget the incident and my embarrassment and shame, the question was always there —how *was* Jesus conceived and why the mystery?

I believed, along with all other Mormons, that Jesus is merely one of Gods' billions of sexually begotten sons. He supposedly was the first one born in heaven to God and His wives, and "the Only Begotten in the flesh." I did not then know of Mormonism's secret teaching that God came to earth with a fleshly body and "overshadowed Mary causing her to conceive."

We Mormons believed also that Lucifer and Jesus were brothers; both had been sexually sired and born in heaven. ("The Devil is a spirit son of God who was born in the morning of pre-existence," says Bruce R. McConkie, *Mormon Doctrine,* p. 192.) And that at a "Council of the Gods," where plans were being made for the redemption of mankind, both Jesus and the devil offered to become the Saviour. Because Jesus' plan supposedly proffered freedom of choice and Satan's scheme did not, the Council elected Jesus to be the Redeemer of the world instead of Lucifer. However, even the devil could have been the Saviour if he had formulated a better plan.

We Latter-day Saints believed that in order to gain exaltation and become a god it was necessary for Jesus to come to earth, receive a body and be totally obedient to all Mormon ordinances and requirements, including temple marriage. Jesus, it was said, had come as one of God's spirit sons in the "meridian of time." Joseph Smith, another of God's choicest spirit sons, assertedly had come to usher in the greatest of all dispensations, "the fullness of time." He holds sway over the Church, earth, heaven and hell in this dispensation, all the while steadily advancing to greater godhood as Jesus and other gods assertedly did in their dispensations.

THE BIBLE—A POLLUTED, INSUFFICIENT GUIDE

I followed these Mormon beliefs and the Mormon authorities blindly; never reading the Bible for myself— seldom if ever hearing it read, even in Mormon services. This was in accordance with the Mormon apostles:

> The words contained in this Bible are merely a history of what is gone by; it was never given to guide the servant of God in the course he should pursue. *The Bible is not a sufficient guide,* it is only the history of the people who lived 1800 years ago.
>
> Orson Hyde
> *Journal of Discourses*
> Volume 2, Page 75

Moreover:
. . . there are many plain and precious things taken away from the book [Bible]. Because of these things which were

taken away out of the gospel of the Lamb, an exceeding great many do stumble, yea, insomuch that Satan hath great power over them.

Book of Mormon
I Nephi 13:28b, 29b

I was taught that the Bible causes "a great many to stumble and fall," and is "part the word of God, part the word of man, and part the word of the devil." Full of conflicts and errors with "much truth taken away and much error added," it had no real place in my life or in the life of any other Mormon I had ever met.

Apostle Orson Pratt asked, "Who knows that *even one verse of* the Bible has escaped pollution so as to convey the same sense that it did in the original?"[7] So I went haphazardly along following Mormonism's scheme, *which does not include* faith in the sufficiency of the blood of Jesus to cleanse our personal sins.

I never realized that I had not given Christ His rightful place in my heart and life until one day, because of the ingrained regard for just plain folks (instilled in me by Mama's folksy singing), I attended the Calvary Baptist Church services in my hometown of Safford, Arizona. I went that day out of love for my keen-witted, silver-haired "daddy-in-law." He was justly proud, I believed, of his heritage of being a humble, hard-working man of the soil. He was just a soft-spoken sharecropper, lately from East Texas, and presently an exultant charter member of this newly organized small band of devout Bible-believers.

It was then and there that I first learned (though I rebelled against it) that I not only had a natural "bent and yen" for singing but I had, as well, an innate hankering for *sinning!*

To say that I was surprised to hear that God's Word declared me to be a sinner, a child of the devil and not a favorite child of God—as I had always prided myself on being—does not half-way describe my reactions. I could not believe my ears and I most certainly would not believe that Baptist preacher!

For the first time in my life I began reading the Bible. I would prove to my non-Mormon husband, Ernest, and especially to his folks, that I was *not* born a sinner, but was as I had so often told them, God's begotten spirit child. I would also prove that I, a favorite spirit child of God, really had been born into this world with innate goodness, looking and acting as much like the heavenly Father and my heavenly mother as I did my earthly parents.

But to my dismay, as I studied the Bible to prove that I was not a sinner, I was convicted of sin! I began to feel uncomfortable. I was no longer satisfied with myself; bothered by my faults and failures (we Mormons never spoke of them as sins),I was no longer able to sugar-coat or water them down, nor wave them aside for a later perusal. I could no longer be satisfied to wait until after I had died and gone to Mormonism's world of departed spirits or to paradise to make things right.

I could not understand all this sudden awareness of my sinful inner self. Could it be that my conscience had suddenly aroused itself, was wide awake, more active than usual? But if it were my conscience, why should it after thirty years of near dormancy, suddenly stir up all this sudden volcanic activity? Why all this moiling and boiling? It was belching up ashes of the past that I had so easily put aside and practically forgotten—what in the world was happening inside of me?

But then, how *could* I realize or express what was happening to me when I had not even heard that it should and would happen? My Bible study had brought on these attacks. The Holy Spirit was reproving, convicting and convincing *me,* a Latter-day Saint, of *sin!* He was making me to hunger and thirst after righteousness, and to realize that I was a dirty, besmirched "nothing," needing a mighty Saviour. I saw myself as just a mangy coyote "critter" born with an innate yen for sinning, skulking wantonly and wearily in the desert of life, howling at the moon, as it were.

No one had ever told me that I needed to give my heart to *Jesus.* I had never even heard of Jesus' plea: "Give me thine heart." I had never before been made aware of my sinfulness, nor of my failure to allow Jesus his rightful and honored place in my heart and life.

There, that first Sunday of January, when for the third time I had accompanied my daddy-in-law to the Baptist services, I heard the minister read: " . . . and hath translated us into the kingdom of His dear Son: in whom we have redemption through His blood, even the forgiveness of sins . . . And He is the head of the body, the church: who is the beginning, the firstborn from the dead; that in all things He might have the pre-eminence." (Col. 1:13-18) As I listened to the message, I realized that the Bible speaks of Jesus as God's *only* Son, not merely one of His many sons as I had always been taught. "When the fullness of the time was come," the preacher continued reading, "God sent forth His Son, made of a woman, made under the law, to redeem them that were under the law, that we might receive the adoption of sons." (Gal. 4:4, 5)

Then I began to realize that God had sent His only Son "in the fullness of time" (Gal. 4:4, Eph. 1:10) and *not* in the meridian of time as Joseph Smith had claimed. By claiming that he had ushered in the fullness of time and opened up the greatest dispensation of all times, Joseph Smith had stolen honor from Jesus and confiscated it to himself. Now I knew that in the fullness of time, when all things were right and ready, Christ had come to redeem me, who was under the law of sin and death, that I might become God's adopted child.

According to the Bible we had not been born God's children in heaven but "were dead in trespasses and sins,"

> . . . and were by nature the children of wrath. But God, who is rich in mercy, for His great love wherewith He loved us, even when we were dead in sins, . . . hath quickened us (made us alive) together . . . with Christ, (by grace ye are saved) . . . For by grace are ye saved through faith; and that not of yourselves: it is the *gift* of God: *not of works*, lest any man should boast.
>
> Eph. 2:1-9

The Holy Spirit brought me to the knowledge and conviction that I was a sinner, even though I was a Latter-day Saint. He made me realize that I was guilty of many, many sins, but the *greatest* sin was in not giving Christ first place in my heart and life. I seemed to hear Him saying, "Give me first place in your heart. Make *me* pre-eminent in your life."

I felt Him at my heart's door. I heard His pleading: "Behold, I stand at the door, and knock: if any man hear my voice, and open the door, I will come in to him, and will sup with him, and he with me." (Rev. 3:20)

The minister's invitation to accept Christ as Saviour was seemingly directed at me. As he asked, "Why won't you accept my Jesus?" I looked about for a Baptist who was accepting Jesus. I wanted to know how it was done. Surely that Baptist minister did not mean me—I was already a church member!

I had been baptized when I was eight years old to have my sins washed away. Shortly thereafter I had been "confirmed" and supposedly "born of the Spirit" when three Mormon elders had laid their hands on my head and commanded me to receive the Holy Ghost.

I had been taught that the Holy Ghost cannot be received any other way and I believed it. All my life I had trusted that these "men who hold the Mormon priesthood possess divine authority thus to act for God, and by possessing part of God's power they are in reality part of God."[8]

My name was already on the Mormon Church roll and so was supposedly entered in the Lamb's Book of Life. I knew that my works and ordinances were recorded in the Mormon Ward record books by our Mormon Ward clerks.

FOOTNOTES

1. Smith, Joseph, *Pearl of Great Price,* Writings of Joseph Smith, 2:19.

2. Pratt, Orson, *The Seer,* page 132.

3. Young, Brigham, *Journal of Discourses,* Vol. 7, page 333.

4. Pratt, Orson, *The Seer,* page 23.

5. Talmage, James, *Jesus The Christ,* page 39.

6. *Doctrine and Covenants,* Section 93:36.

7. Pratt, Orson, *Divine Authenticity of the Book of Mormon,* page 47.

8. B. H. Roberts, *New Witness for God,* page 187.

MORMON BAPTISM.

CEREMONY OF CONFIRMATION.

Chapter Two

BORN AGAIN

No, that Baptist minister didn't mean me—I was a Mormon. But God meant me! Even though I was a Latter-day "Saint," I was still a sinner in need of salvation. It was for my sake that—

> God so loved the world, that He gave His only begotten Son, that whosoever believeth in Him should not perish, but have everlasting life ... He that believeth in Him is not condemned, but he that believeth not is condemned already, because he hath not believed in the name of the only begotten Son of God.
>
> (John 3:16, 18)

As the missionary pleaded "Oh, *why won't you* accept my Jesus?" God spoke to my heart saying, "Why don't you accept my Son? He died for Mormons the same as He died for Baptists."

Then I knew that even though I was a Latter-day Saint, I must rest my all on Jesus. Gladly I yielded myself to Him too wide-eyed with the wonder of it all to close my eyes and bow my head. I was happy to know that God and Jesus so loved *me.* My heart thrilled with rapture and ached with shame and sorrow as I sought forgiveness for taking Christ for granted. I thanked Him for continuing to love me when I had never really loved and worshiped Him. I now knew that Jesus had been willing to leave heaven and come to earth to be made sin because of His love and concern for me. He had not come seeking an exaltation to godhood for Himself, as I had always been led to believe. Jesus was *already* God. God the Son had come to seek and save me, a Latter-day Saint.

[23]

I now knew myself to be a sinner and not a saint, not a begotten child of heavenly parents, but an unworthy sinner whom God had "so loved." I knew it because I had read it in God's Holy Word and because God the Holy Spirit had brought the convicting knowledge to my heart. I asked Jesus to forgive me for not loving Him when He had loved me enough to die for me. Christ, who knew no sin, had left His glory in heaven to come "to be sin for us that we might be made the righteousness of God in Him." (II Cor. 5:21) I thanked Him for taking my place on the cross and vowed to take my place at the foot of His cross that other Mormons might give Jesus first place in their hearts and lives.

Now, I no longer sing about Joseph Smith, for when I took Jesus as my personal Saviour, I no longer needed Joseph Smith "the prophet." Now I sing about Jesus, of how when I received Him as my Saviour and Lord, He gave me a new heart, a new life, a new purpose. I rejoice as I sing my new song of praises to our God and claim this matchless promise "now many will hear of the glorious things He did for me, and stand in awe before the Lord, and put their trust in Him." (Psalm 40:3, Living Bible)

If there had been a "Mrs. Universal Ectasy Contest" on that once-in-a-lifetime Sunday when I received Jesus in my heart—with all the attendant joys and wonderful surprises His Holy Presence still occasions—I would have been declared the most enchanted, gladsome woman of the year.

Christ's indwelling had instantaneously elevated me to the straight "E Class." All at once I was enlightened, excited, elated, enriched, enthusiastic, encouraged, edified, eager, energetic, and exhilarated—all because I had been elected and straight-away expedited to go forth and tell *all* that the Lord had done for me, just as the Samaritan woman at Jacob's well had done!

I hurried off to Mama's house, confident that when I exclaimed and proclaimed to her Jesus' incomparable love and sacrificial death, she too would receive Him as readily and joyfully as I had.

MAMA'S REACTION

I felt as though "I had the world by the tail with a downhill pull all the way," as Papa used to say. The only cloud on my sunny horizon that lovely magical Sunday afternoon was that I could not tell Papa, too, about my newfound Saviour. Papa had been dead twelve years and I still missed him so.

He died expecting to go to hell, believing the Mormon teaching that hell is only a *temporary* place for the disobedient spirits. We all believed that Papa could be released to paradise after he had served at least a two-year prison term. This is, according to some local Mormon authorities, the very minimum penal punishment the dead may expect to receive. After he had "paid the uttermost farthing," Papa was expected to begin progressing on toward heaven and eventual godhood . . . providing Mama journeyed to one of the Mormon temples to have vicarious temple washings and anointings, endowments and ordinances performed in his name, in his stead, and on his behalf.

Because of ill health, lack of money and other family involvements, Mama had to wait, conscience-stricken and wearied, ten long years before she was able to attend to Papa's "works for the dead." She eventually had these vicarious endowments performed (hoping for Papa's release from the spirit prison and his progress to future glory) in the Arizona Temple. There she was duly married and sealed for eternity to Papa by enlisting a Mormon elder to act as proxy for her dead mate. Papa and Mama's civil wedding ceremony, performed by a Mormon bishop some forty years earlier, had been for this life only.

But now, as a new-born babe in Christ, I was beginning to realize that there was nothing anyone could do for Papa. I was beginning to have doubts that Joseph Smith and his priesthood subordinates, alive or dead, could help Papa either. I just left that up to God and hurried on to Mama's house, still confidently aglow with my new-found joy and the heart-heated (not just warmed) assurance that all things from now on would go just right for me and for Mama.

However, I had not reckoned on Joseph Smith's pull with Mama nor the power of the devil. I knew much about Joseph Smith, but very little about Satan. The devil was now playing havoc with Mama and me.

But instead of blaming the devil, Mama blamed that "chicken eatin' Baptist preacher" for leading me away from Mormonism, the one true church. She heartbrokenly pleaded, "Our Mormon church has been good enough for your grandparents and their parents, for your poor dead Daddy and for me. It surely ought to be good enough for you."

Prior to that glorious day of my new birth, I would have been ashamed as well as grieved to so disappoint, hurt and humiliate Mama. But now, having learned of all that Jesus had suffered on my behalf and having committed myself to Him as a thank offering, I owed *Him* total allegiance—even above my beloved mama.

Gently and tearfully I tried to tell Mama so, but the more I spoke of Jesus, the more she reminded me of the sufferings and sacrifices in my behalf of Joseph Smith, not to mention hers and Papa's, and of my obligations to uphold the Mormon church and its authorities. She implored me to keep the family ties intact on earth lest they (according to what we were taught by Mormonism) be broken in heaven, causing heartbreak and loss of status in heaven for Papa and other relatives "gone on before" and eventually even for my dear, dear mama.

Never before had I seen Mama so broken-hearted and beaten down as she begged me to forsake "this Jesus saves foolishness" and return to my former faith and allegiance to Mormonism. Never before had I deliberately, knowingly pierced her heart so deeply as I knew I must that day as I held adamantly to the stand I had taken for Jesus. Our tears mingled together as I knelt at Mama's knees pleading with her to understand my love for Jesus and for her, begging her to forgive me for the grief I was causing her, but most of all imploring her to consider Jesus' brokenhearted grief and His just claim over both of our lives.

Even today, my loneliness for Mama makes it impossible for me to convey further details of our shared grief and tender compassion for each other. Nor can I tell of the dreadfulness of the wall of partition which separated us that day as we tried vainly to comfort and convince each other.

I should have known that Mama would not easily put aside a busy-bee lifetime of eulogizing and honoring Joseph Smith in unstinting personal service and rapturous song. Her humming and poignant singing of popular Mormon hymns such as "We Thank Thee, Oh God, for a Prophet to Guide Us In These Latter-Days," "Hail to the Man Who Communed with Jehovah" and "Oh, Give Me Back My Prophet Dear" were too deeply imbedded in the very fibers of Mama's loving heart, as well as her tune-filled voice box, to be so easily dislodged.

In spite of the recriminations and insults I knew I must face, my concern for Mama's happiness and assurance of her salvation kept sending me back regularly to witness to her of Jesus' power to save. She was both hurt and disappointed in me. She intended to stay that way.

She was religiously riled, as angry as a charging bull as she accused me, saying, "You think you are so smart. How can you believe that the mother who bore you, then tenderly tended and raised you, is just an old hell-bound sinner, not good enough for heaven and, I suppose, for that matter, not good enough for you either?"

What she did not understand—nor would she listen to my reasoning—was: " ... that they are all under sin ... There are none that seeketh after God ... none that doeth good, no, not one . . . for all have sinned and come short of the glory of God." (Romans 3:9-23) Nor did she know that I had judged myself a thousand-fold more severely than I would ever judge anyone else, least of all my own precious mama.

Had not I, while believing and following Mormon doctrines, come under the convicting power of the Holy Spirit? Had not He, through God's Holy Word, caused me to realize that I was guilty of treading under foot the precious blood of Jesus, and counting the blood of the Covenant an unclean thing? And so, I reasoned that Mama, still believing and trusting in the same false Mormon teachings and practices, must also be lost. Desperately I tried to convince Mama that I was not judging, just loving.

"Oh Mama," I pleaded, "please try to understand that it's my love for you and my regret for the enfeebling heartache my leaving Mormonism has caused you. That's what keeps spurring me on. I want you well and happy again."

I stopped to regain my composure and waited for Mama's encouragement. None was forthcoming. Mama sat ramrod straight, fire in her eyes, and tears trickling down her cheeks. She had had her "say." Now it was all up to me to bridge the gap.

"I know you don't want to talk about it ever again, but please, Mama, listen one more time. Have you ever heard that faith in Jesus and repentance brings well-being to the body as well as to the soul? God's Word promises us that if we be not wise in our own conceits and sure of our own wisdom, but love and fear the Lord and 'depart from evil it shall be health to thy navel, and marrow to thy bones.' (Proverbs 3:7,8) Then a deep-down all enveloping peace enfolds us, bringing health to both spirit and body. Even to the very innermost part of us—the marrow of our bones— we'll have renewed health and vigor, a brand-new love and zest for life. And for each other."

I kept on praying and visiting. Surely any day now, my heart kept saying, Mama must realize that it is love for Mama and Jesus—not pious judging—that keeps bringing me back day after day to pray and to plead again for Jesus' sake and for Mama's sake. Urgently I begged her to publicly confess Jesus as her Saviour for:

> The word is nigh thee, even in thy mouth, and in thy heart: that is, the word of faith, which we preach; that if thou shalt confess with thy mouth the Lord Jesus, and shalt believe in thine heart that God hath raised Him from the dead, thou shalt be saved. For with the heart man believeth unto righteousness; and with the mouth confession is made unto salvation.
>
> (Romans 10:8-10)

The Living Bible paraphrases this same passage of confession unto salvation thus:

> God's message of Salvation is near you, on your lips and in your heart, not in good works, dietary laws, baptism, church membership and temple rituals. That is the message of faith that we preach. If you declare with your lips, 'Jesus is Lord,' and believe in your heart that God raised Him from the dead, you will be saved. For we believe in our hearts and are put right with God. We declare with our lips and are saved.

I studied the Bible and tried to pray enough for both Mama and me. Then one momentous day God answered my prayers with the assurance of victory in Jesus for my Mama. Someday she, too, would yield herself without reservation to the One who had died for her. Continuously I prayed: "God hasten the day . . . Let this be the day that Mama accepts Jesus. If not today, give me the grace of patience."

A NEW SONG

Since Mama would not listen to me talk about Jesus, I tried her own singing tactic—the one she had long used on me. It was now my turn to star in the preaching-teaching role. I sang often. I sang *loud and clear* so that everyone could hear, even the neighbors across the way.

God had "put a new song in my mouth, even praise unto our God," that was just itching to get out into the open so that "many shall see it, and fear, and shall trust in the Lord." (Psalm 40:3) But first I had to learn some new songs.

I had vowed never again to sing the Mormon songs Mama had taught me, not even our favorite, "Whispering Hope." I did not then know that it is truly a genuine Christian hymn borrowed by the Mormons from Christ-honoring faiths. When its melody kept singing in my heart, God gave me these new words of devotion and dedication to sing to Mama, to you, and to the world:

> Strong be my faith and as steadfast
> As the love which Thou givest to me,
> Strength and the will to serve Thee
> This will my prayer ever be.
> Then, in the time of temptation,
> Teach me to watch and to pray
> Oh, may I hear thy sweet whisper—
> "Lo, I am with thee alway."
> O Glorious Promise
> With Christ by my side
> Christ as my comfort
> And Christ as my guide

Mama listened as I sang my new songs of Jesus, just as she had always listened with motherly pride to my Mormon songs. After some time the sacred melodies finally fanned embers of remembrance and longing in Mama's heart. These were the same Christ-honoring hymns Mama's mother had sung to her; sacred, melodious messages learned "back home" in my grandmother's quiet hills of West Virginia. Little-by-little, Mama's resistance melted as she began softly humming and eventually singing along with me my new songs, the songs *her* mother had sung to her. One day as we sang "Softly and Tenderly Jesus is Calling," Mama talked tenderly of her mother's faith and dedication, of arduous service to her husband and fourteen children out here in the harsh, raw desert wastes of the West.

As the years passed slowly, I rejoiced that Mama was beginning to draw nigh unto Jesus, who had so long been patiently waiting that He might draw nigh unto her. My hopes soared anew! Surely any day now Mama would turn it all over to Jesus and my years of prayers and fears would be fulfilled in her complete surrender unto salvation and subsequent well-being.

Mama's life of hard work, coupled with more than her share of everyday family trials of sickness, sorrow and hard times had taken its toll. She nearly slipped away into eternity one day as I stood by her bedside, too frightened, too numbed to pray. Seconds later as a sense of peace and assurance enveloped me I realized that the Holy Spirit Himself was praying for me when I was not able, as promised in Romans 8:26.

Ever after, having thus been awakened to a consciousness of God the Holy Spirit's benevolence toward me and a need to express my gratitude to Him, I have thanked Him for His powerful comforting influence that day and all others. Especially have I thanked Him for His convicting regenerative power that had brought me to Jesus and to peace. I yearningly bade Him to please help me pray more effectively, fervently and unceasingly for Mama and my other beloved Mormons.

With every warming sunrise my heart glowed with hope and gratitude that God the Father had spared Mama's life through the night, that He had lengthened her days that I might still delight in her love and the comfort and joys of her presence. I thanked God that once again, Mama had a bright, brand-new day before her in which to respond to God's sin offering, another day of promise in which to yield herself completely to Christ so that He might shower upon her this blessed new life and joyous new song which He had so graciously given me.

Except for God's promise, my spirits would have waned with each passing sunset. Another day had come and gone; Mama had still not confessed Jesus publicly. She had denied herself yet another day of the unsearchable riches and pleasures, the blessed peace and solace of His presence. Again I thanked Him for His tender mercies and long-suffering toward us both, and for having allowed Mama and me this additional day of fulfilling companionship.

I ended each day praying, "Tonight Mama is all alone. There in the long and lonely dark midnight hours, help Mama to feel her need to surrender her all to Jesus the Light. Before the dawn of another day may the Light of the World dawn upon her soul that she need never be alone in darkness again. For this I pray. Not for my own sake, even though I long for this dreadful, dividing middle wall of partition to be broken down that Mama might understand and be proud of me again. Nor just for Mama's sake, but for Jesus' sake I pray because I love Him so."

My coveting Mama's salvation and her influence for the glory of Jesus made me more eager and zealous, but it made Mama more mule-headed and resentful! Life for me in my hometown among my estranged loved ones and Mormon friends was the hardest I had ever known. But it was also the happiest. Sometimes I longed to move away and never come back. However, I had vowed to witness and to win, and quitters never win, not even a puny marble game. This time *I must win,* for I was playing and praying for the highest stakes in the world—the eternal salvation of the priceless souls of my loved ones, who daily made it plain that they no longer loved me as they once had.

Do you ask how I could know that Mama had not trusted in the blood of the Lamb, God's only offering for sin? I knew because she told me so! Mama and every Mormon to whom I have ever witnessed have insisted, "Christ cannot save me by Himself. I must help him by keeping the commandments, obedience to the church's laws and ordinances and a life of good works."

I had to wait thirty long, wasted years in that same spiritual ignorance for someone courageous and honest enough, fervent and concerned enough, to tell me that Jesus had died because I was a sinner in need of a Saviour who could *really* save.

I vowed to unhesitatingly share Jesus with others so that they need not wait, as I had waited, to hear of Jesus' power to save. This sacred vow specifically included my mama. And so, I witnessed at every opportunity in word and in deed, then waited confidently for God's promise of Mama's salvation to be brought to fruition. I grieved for each moment's unclaimed joys and the consolation and comfort of God's presence that she was missing, ever zealous that Mama's old-time, heart-warming folksiness be set to work for the glory of the One True and Holy God, not misused to promote Mormonism's god. Mama's pert persuasiveness, I was sure, could then bring many other loved ones to the matchless Saviour, God's only begotten *unique* Son.

In between God's promise to me of Mama's salvation and its fulfillment twenty years later, I was to learn the joys and duties of prayer, patience and perseverance. These proved to be, for me, the heart of soul-winning, as well as the avenues, most times shaded and pleasant though oft-times rough and wearisome, of my daily walk with Jesus, who escorted me right up to heaven's portals the day Mama committed her soul to Him.

VIEW OF MAIN STREET, SALT LAKE CITY.

Chapter Three

MAMA LOOKS TO HEAVEN

As the years went by, Mama grew weaker and more feeble; so did her smiles; so did her beloved, gnarled, work-worn hands that refused to be idle. Nonetheless, she doggedly set herself to the task of braiding precious woolen rugs for each of her four children. Then as a continuing expression of her motherly love and care for us, colorful quilts were pieced together from the remaining wool scraps to keep our hearts as well as our bodies warm and comforted, for we all knew, especially Mama, that these were to be her parting gifts to us. Mama's life here on earth was drawing to a close.

Each ringing of the phone quivered my heart with fear for Mama. Then one day Mama's "Macedonian Call" came by phone. In a tired, little voice she said, "I'm not feeling at all well today, honey. Can you come over and help me?"

And I had just two weeks left in which to "baby my mother as she'd babied me." I would also try to do the impossible: to make up to Mama for all the mountains of accumulated hurts, disappointments and tears that I had caused her, but most of all, to talk to Mama again about heaven and how to get there.

Lately and frequently Mama, realizing that she soon must come to the river of death, had been asking Ernest, my fine Christian husband, about life after death, especially of what heaven will be. How proudly, humbly and prayerfully I had listened to him pointing Mama to the crucified Christ of Calvary, to Him who saith, "I am the way, the truth, and the life; no man cometh unto the Father, but by me." (John 14:6) How grateful I was that Mama was finally agreeing, not with Ernest, but with the powerful, precious Holy Bible, God's only word to man, a word that is so perfect and complete that nothing must be added to nor taken from its sacred message.

Even if these blinding tears would cease to flow and even though I had complete control of my limited faculties and the English language—the dearth of which you have recognized from the first sentence of this "singing" love story—I could not convey to you the poignant sweetness and sadness of the last few days before Mama left us, for we were in Immanuel's ground.

Suffice it to say that Mama and I (and I'm sure it was the same for my beloved sister and two stalwart brothers) loved and enjoyed each other in a greater capacity than we had ever known before. We were crowding into fleeting moments enough joys and tenderness to perfume the rest of our lifetimes. We were constructing, under God's guidance, a refreshing, sheltering bower to which I could return when my heart hungered for Mama as it does even now.

You who may have watched at a loved one's deathbed know both the joy and the pain I experienced in doing the little things for Mama; tenderly combing her silvered hair, smoothing her bed, giving drink and nourishment just as she had continued doing for me long after I was grown and married and had a delightful daughter of my own. And have you, too, experienced one of the greatest joys of all earthly ministries: that of assuring your loved one, whose soul seems to be hovering—anxious to take its flight—of the glorious life everlasting that is just a breath and a sigh away for those who will trust solely in Jesus?

Together, Mama and I considered Jesus' willingness to leave heaven and become sin for us, asking only in return that "we believe on him." (John 6:29) Quietly we discussed Mama's need to respond to Jesus' plea, to commit to God's will and keeping not only herself but her beloved younger son, for whose sake she fought death, desperately determined to remain on earth as long as she could.

Exultation at death-time, especially that of one's own beloved mother, may seem unnatural, even heartless and impious. Nevertheless, pure and holy jubilation permeated that hospital room as Mama and I talked of heaven as she *finally gave her heart to Jesus,* who waited so patiently for her to come to Him! We talked of how, when it came time for her soul to take its triumphant flight to heaven's glory, there, Jesus would rise to welcome her to her heavenly mansion. (John 14:2) And surely it would be a magnificent one.

There was no need to mention that there would be no stop-overs in a crowded, intermediate Mormon spirit world "prison place," . . . just a direct, straight-through, non-stop flight to heaven. No need to say that no one except Jesus—not Saint Peter nor the prophet Joseph Smith—must or could admit her. To do so would have been trivial. We were looking to Jesus, the Alpha and Omega, the Beginning and the End, the Author and Finisher of our faith, talking about God's true heaven, not man's vain, earthly imaginings. We were not only talking, but singing of heaven.

This time it was me leading the singing, choosing the songs and Mama singing ever so faintly at first, finally inaudibly. Words cannot express the blessedness of seeing her lips moving soundlessly in songs of praise to Jesus, her eyes fixed on mine and mine lost in the depths of hers that for many years had mirrored her love, her concern, her empathy for me. Nor can I begin to explain the gratification of the clasping of our hands, one final and last time on this earth. This time it was the strength of my hands that comforted and caressed, that undergirded.

And so I sang with and for Mama, songs of praises to Jesus and marvelous songs of heaven, "Beautiful Isle of Somewhere," "There's a Land That is Fairer Than Day," "Rock of Ages," and felt the brush of angels' wings as they hovered around us, waiting for God to call my dear mama home to be with Jesus and her own mama. "Up there," Mama, consoling, whispered to me, "your mama will be waiting with her mama, waiting for you to join us."

Then I heard Mama quietly and calmly surrender herself

to God and to death, "Heavenly Father, receive my soul. In Jesus' name and for His sake, Amen." As Mama prayed in the "sweetest name on mortal tongue," the angels sang and rejoiced in heaven. (Luke 15:10)

Together, with our hearts and eyes fixed on heaven, we sang "Whispering Hope." "Sing it often to your baby brother for me. It's his favorite, too. You can stop now," she whispered and went quietly to sleep to awaken in heaven to sing with her mama our New Song, Mama's and mine, dedicated to my singing mama who, as the angels sang, went on home to be with Jesus . . . and to all Mormon singing mothers everywhere, that they too will . . .

> Listen to the voice of the Saviour
> Coming from heaven above,
> Filled with a message so tender,
> Filled with the message of love,

the message that:

> God so loved the world, that He gave His only begotten Son, that whosoever believeth in Him should not perish, but have everlasting life.

> John 3:16

Chapter Four

BACK TO THE BEGINNING

Every story has a beginning, a middle and an end. I have already told you the middle and the end of my story. Now it remains for me to tell you something of the beginning of it. The beginnings are rooted, of course, in Mormonism itself. The sketchy outline of Mormon doctrine I have given you so far must certainly have you wondering about what we as Mormons really believed.

I will not attempt a deep theological expose nor go into every phase of Latter-day Saints' doctrine. I want to convey to you, my reader, what I know to be a few of the leading items of Mormon doctrine, as well as point out to you some hidden doctrines that are basic Mormon beliefs which I (and many other modern Mormons) were not allowed to know. It will remain for you to weigh the evidence and determine if my proposition that Mormonism is not Christian is a valid one.

UNDERGROUND MORMONISM

In order to get the full picture and not just a bird's eye view of Mormonism, one must go back to the early frontier days of the Church of Jesus Christ of Latter-day Saints. There, in her sought-for isolation and voluntary exile in the West, most doctrines and practices were out in the open—

not hidden away and secretly taught and practiced as now. These Mormons chose to leave Illinois rather than accept the stipulations of the state officials that they cease voting as a block, abandon ecclesiastical communal living, disperse themselves in other neighborhoods and cities, and forsake polygamy and all other unlawful practices.

Those of the Latter-day Saints who chose to remain in Illinois were able to live peaceably with their "Gentile" neighbors after the influence of Joseph Smith and Brigham Young was withdrawn. Many of these "Saints" became members of the Reorganized Church of Jesus Christ of Latter-Day Saints with headquarters in Independence, Missouri. Their doctrines have never included Adam-God worship, polygamy and blood atonement as did those of the Utah "Saints."

There were about 10,000 Latter-day Saints who eagerly followed Brigham Young to Utah. For a look at them we must journey back a hundred years or more, back to the early days of Utah Mormonism before its basic beliefs were shunted underground, back to the time when real Mormonism was publicly preached, without hedging and deceit, in every hamlet in the Territory of Utah. Back before—if there were such a time—the Mormon priesthood bearers were taught to guard their secret doctrines, even by lying if necessary, and back before Mormons were cautioned:

> Give not that which is holy unto the dogs, neither cast ye your pearls before swine, lest they trample them under their feet, and turn again and rend you.
>
> (Matt. 7:6)

And this was exactly the treatment rendered the Mormon elders when they had publicly and openly advanced such Mormon gospel notions as:

- The Bible is a mixture of truth and error, an insufficient guide, with many plain and most precious parts taken away.

- God himself was once a man, and men may become gods.

- Adam is God of this world and the only God with whom we have to do.

- The everlasting covenant of plural marriage.

- Heavenly mothers and baby-making in heaven.

We must journey to the time—if ever such a time existed in Mormonism—that all Mormons could know all their doctrines and practices, back before new converts and the immature, unstable Latter-day Saints' queries regarding hidden doctrines were shunted aside by a hedging Mormon elder thus: "Remember that Christ has many things to say to the children, but ye cannot bear them now. You have need of the milk and not of the strong meat of the [Mormon] gospel."

We must journey to the time when Mormonism's doctrines were made public and an investigator of Mormonism could "like it or lump it, take it or leave it" if he chose to accept or reject the Latter-day gospel. Later, according to just about every expose written by "apostate" Mormons, such secret doctines as human blood sacrifices, polygamy, Adam is God and Christ is a polygamist were withheld from them until they were able to abide these "meats" of Mormonism. I guess that converts are more susceptible to shock than we who had been born into it.

It was no shock to me, as it would be to a non-Mormon, to be taught that God is an exalted, married man who once lived on earth with His numerous wives. That was all I had ever known and heard. The Mormon doctrine that God has had, and still does have, sexual intercourse with his wives was no shock to those of us who were life-long Latter-day Saints. In fact, the opposite notion would have astounded us. Sexuality among "the gods" is taken for granted and was always depicted as a beautiful, high and holy sacred relationship.

This most important, basic Mormon doctrine is no longer taught openly. It can only be found, subtly worded, in a few current publications and then couched in such modern terminology as "eternal families." Even so, Mormons understand that sexual intercourse for God and man is the steppingstone to godhood.

MORMON VIEW OF MAN

There are now over four million of my beloved Mormon kinfolks and friends, who most desperately need the testimony of Jesus' power to save. They await the Christian's concern and prayers, for they have yet to be told that ... "the blood of Jesus Christ His Son cleanseth us from *all* sin." (I John 1:7)

Mormons need to be told that salvation and redemption are *synonymous terms*, that right here on earth the marvelous grace of God "makes alive" the soul "dead in trespasses and sins." We are "born again" (saved from our sins and redeemed) when we believe in Christ, and confess Him as our personal Savior. Having realized that our righteousness is as filthy rags in God's sight (Isa. 64:6), we call upon Him who died for our sins to save us from sin and to *impute* unto us His righteousness. Then (and only then) we "pass from death unto life."

The second chapter of Ephesians describes what we are by nature and what we may become by God's grace.

> And you hath He quickened, who were dead in trespasses and sins;
>
> Wherein in time past ye walked according to the course of this world, according to the prince of the power of the air, the spirit that now worketh in the children of disobedience:
>
> Among whom also we all had or conversation [lived] in times past in the lusts of our flesh, fulfilling the desires of the flesh and of the mind; and were by nature the children of wrath, even as others.
>
> But God, who is rich in mercy, for His great love wherewith He loved us,
>
> Even when we were dead in sins, hath quickened us together with Christ, (by grace ye are saved;)
>
> And hath raised us up together, and made us sit together in heavenly places in Christ Jesus:
>
> That in the ages to come He might show the exceeding riches of His grace in His kindness toward us through Christ Jesus.
>
> For by grace are ye saved through faith; *and that* not of yourselves: it is the *gift of God:*

Not of works, lest any man should boast,

> For we are His workmanship, created in Christ Jesus unto good works, which God hath before ordained that we should walk in them."
>
> *Ephesians 2:1-10*

The supposition that the Church of Jesus Christ of Latter-day Saints and its doctrines are based on the Bible and its truths is herein denied. Romans 1:16 declares that "the Gospel is the power of God unto salvation to everyone that believeth" in the blood mediated by Christ's everlasting priesthood. The Gospel of Jesus Christ is not a set of church rules, rites and regulations administered by any earthly priesthood. God's Word demolishes Mormonism's claim that "the Gospel consists of laws and ordinances for man's obedience, by which he is redeemed from his own sins."[1]

> Knowing that a man is not justified by the works of the law, but by the faith of Jesus Christ ... for by the works of the law shall no flesh be justified.
>
> *Galatians 2:16*

Chief among the Mormon requirements of the gospel is faith in the prophet Joseph Smith and his divine calling, membership in the Latter-day Saint Church, acknowledgement of "Jesus as the Christ," total submission to the authorities of the church, and reliance on the powers of the Mormon priesthood.

Mormon elders supposedly can seal upon both the living and the dead the ordinances of baptism to wash away all sins, impart the Holy Ghost by the laying on of hands and bestow for time and eternity the power and authority of the Mormon priesthood. Thereafter, each worthy Mormon elder can be married and sealed for eternity in a Mormon temple, resurrect his wife and children, procreate countless offspring in heaven, and eventually build and rule a world of his own—provided he staunchly tithes all his annual salary, pays his fast offerings, church and temple assessments and endures "true to the end."

Most Mormons reject the fact that we are ... "by nature the children of wrath" ... "shapen in iniquity and conceived in sin" as Ephesians 2:3 and Psalms 51:5 declare us all to be. They still maintain that they are God's sexually procreated heaven-born offspring who, according to Apostle Bruce R. McConkie, naturally "begin their mortal life in a state of innocence and purity without sin or taint . . . ."[2]

In avowing that children begin their mortal life innocent and free from sin, Mr. McConkie was upholding Mormonism's century-old doctrine of the natural goodness of man. President Brigham Young declared that man is *not*

> naturally opposed to God . . . Paul says in his Epistle to the Corinthians "but the natural man receiveth not the things of God" . . . but I say it is the unnatural man that receiveth not the things of God . . . the natural man is of God."

Brigham Young
Journal of Discourses
Volume 9, Page 305

A year later, Brigham Young, again discussing the subject of the innate goodness of man, exhorted his followers:

> They say that man is naturally prone to evil . . . but if man had always been permitted to follow the instincts of his nature, had he always followed the great and holy principles of his organism they would have led him into the path of life everlasting.

Brigham Young
Journal of Discourses
Volume 10, Page 189

If Brigham Young had been truly led of the Spirit, he would have known by personal experience, as did Paul, that he himself was a natural-born sinner, prone to do evil. Moreover, Prophet Young, if he really had been a man of the Scriptures as true prophets are, would have agreed with the Apostle Paul. Prophet Young should also have known that the *Book of Mormon* agrees that:

> the natural man is an enemy to God and has been from the fall of Adam and will be forever and ever unless he yields to the enticings of the Holy Spirit, and putteth off the natural man.

Book of Mormon
Mosiah 3:19a

Through the years other Mormon leaders have continued to disregard their own Mormon Scriptures. For instance,

Brigham Young's successor, John Taylor, chose to uphold Brigham's inferior sin notions thusly: "In fact, as the President stated here not long ago, *it is not natural for men to be evil.*"³

These and other successive Mormon leaders and their followers, who still refuse to accept the Biblical teachings regarding man's natural tendency to sin, have not only exposed their spiritual condition but their spiritual ignorance as well. They have also gainsaid two of their four special books of Scripture, which despite Mormonism's claims to the contrary, manifoldly contradict themselves and each other. And yet, with all their Latter-day Scriptures—*Book of Mormon, Doctrine and Covenants, Pearl of Great Price,* plus the King James Version of the *Bible* (the only version they even partially accept as true)— Mormons still perilously deny this undeniable truth: To become a true saint, Latter-day or otherwise, one must first discover himself to be a sinner.

Because of Mormonism's doctrines of innate goodness and heavenly birth, few Latter-day Saints understand the deadly malady ravaging them. Few seek the divine remedy as prescribed by the Great Physician and His ABC's of Salvation. "All have sinned and come short of the glory of God." (Romans 3:23)

> All under the power of sin
> All gone wrong, no one does good, not even one
> All men have sinned and [because they]
> Are far away from God's saving presence. Their mouths
> Are full of bitter curses. They
> Are quick to hurt and kill, they leave ruin and misery
> wherever they go. They have not known the path of peace;
> nor have they learned to fear God."
>
> Romans 3:9-23
> *Good News Bible*

> But as many as received Him, to them gave He power to become [not already are] the sons of God.
>
> John 1:12

> Be it known unto you therefore, men and brethren, that through this man [Jesus] is preached unto you forgiveness of sins; and by Him all that believe are justified from all things, from which you could not be justified by the law of Moses.
>
> Acts 13:38,39

And the Blood of Jesus Christ His son cleanseth us from
all sin.

I John 1:7

Come now, and let us reason together, saith the Lord:
though your sins be as scarlet, they shall be as white as
snow; though they be red like crimson, they shall be as
wool.

Isaiah 1:18

If we confess our sins, He is faithful and just to forgive us
our sins, and to cleanse us from all unrighteousness.

I John 1:9

Come out from among them, and be ye separate, saith the
Lord, and touch not the unclean thing [false religion], and
I will receive you, and will be a Father unto you, and ye
shall be [not already are] my sons and daughters, saith the
Lord Almighty.

II Cor. 1:17, 18

[Nor do they know that] all we like sheep have gone
astray; we have turned every one [Latter-day Saints
included] to his own way; and the Lord hath laid on him the
iniquity of us all.

Isaiah 53:6

Instead of directing the poor, lost, blind Mormon sheep to
the True Shepherd that He might cleanse their sins and
forgive their iniquities, Mormon leaders have shepherded
them in the opposite direction, leaving them to "pay for
their own sins."

CHIEF MEANS OF MAN'S EXALTATION

One Mormon authority of the past century has bluntly
stated:

I wish to be perfectly understood here . . . Let it be
remembered that the prophet Joseph Smith taught that
man, that is, his spirit, is the offspring of Deity: not in any
mystical sense, but actually . . . instead of the God-given
power of procreation being one of the chief things that is to
pass away, it is one of the chief means of man's exaltation
and glory in that great eternity, which like an endless
vista stretches out before him! . . . Through that law

[*sexual increase*] in connection with an observance of all the other laws of the gospel, man will *yet attain unto the power of the godhead,* and like his Father, God, his chief glory will be to bring to pass the eternal life and happiness of his posterity.

B. H. Roberts
New Witness for God, Page 461
(1895 edition)

Note that the Mormon man's chief glory in heaven will be to procreate spirit children "like his Father, God."

This book, *New Witness for God,* was approved by a committee appointed by the First Presidency of the Church of Jesus Christ of Latter-day Saints as "orthodox and consistent with our teachings." It is still widely quoted by leading Mormons. Thus the brash assertion that man's attainment to godhood depends chiefly upon "his eternal God-given power of procreation" is still a vital and sanctioned teaching of Mormonism. There is no pausing (meno or otherwise) of sex and childbearing in eternity. By their "God-given power of procreation" Mormon men expect to evermore sexually sire multitudinous children in heaven and thereby become gods.

Their advancement to godhood by sexual procreation hinges upon special endowments and sealings performed by the Mormon priesthood in Mormon temples. These imposing edifices, erected sacrificially by hopeful, enterprising Latter-day Saints, are used expressly for priesthood ordinations, baptisms and confirmations for the dead, endowments, washings and anointings, marriages for eternity and sealings, for both the living and the dead.

Mormonism's vicarious work for the dead begins in temple basements. There millions of proxy baptisms and impartations of the Holy Ghost by the laying on of hands of the temple workers are performed. Mormon youth, in behalf of their dead relatives, are completely immersed in the large oval baptismal font, which rests on the backs of twelve bronze oxen. These youngsters have sometimes been "baptized and confirmed for the dead" as many as fifty or more times in one temple baptismal session for a like number of their dead kinfolk.

Following these initial basement rites, adult relatives of the dead or paid temple workers, in rituals several hours long, receive other vicarious temple blessings and ordinances for the dead. There in the holy temple chambers, the proxy Latter-day Saint must first allow his body to be washed in water, anointed with oil and blessed for and in behalf of the dead person.

Then the substitute for the dead person engages in various other ceremonies depicting the creation of this world, the making of Adam and Eve, their fall, the expulsion from the Garden of Eden, life in the lone and dreary world, rescue by the "Law of the Gospel," and the entrance beyond the veil. In these and other stages the participants receive necessary grips (special handshakes) and oaths which allow them to pass beyond the veil. As they progress, each person dons the various elements of the temple garments of the holy priesthood. (These are special suits of clothing made of white cloth.) Then the proxy couple, now fully attired in the special holy undergarments, wedding clothes, veil, cap, figleaf aprons, and robes, exchange vicarious temple wedding vows for "time and all eternity."

Next in line in these temple ordinances come the sealings of their children and the adoption of other kin. One by one each is credited and sealed to their parents "to come forth in the first resurrection" to exalt and further the kingdom of their parents. Every one of these temple ordinances must be performed for every family member, living or dead, until every family succeeding generation has been secured and sealed for eternity to the preceding one—family to family, line upon line, until eventually all are sealed to Joseph Smith, who seals them to "Father" Adam (who at one time was the "God of this world"). Genealogical information which cannot be acquired by researching Mormonism's vast genealogical libraries may perhaps be obtained by revelation from a church patriarch, or will have to wait until the millennium to be completed when all the books are opened.

During the Mormon version of the millennium, thousands of other Mormon temples will be erected. It was said to me that Christ will supervise those temples and workers of the Eastern world; Joseph Smith will direct those of all Western nations. Thus every person who has ever lived on this earth may receive these special ordinances which admit them to the celestial kingdom of God, provided, of course, that after death they had repented and received the Mormon gospel.

Mormons of this "greatest dispensation of all times" would be greatly advantaged by their head start in temple works and obedience to the gospel requirements. Mormons are warned that they must "be tithed," for "...he that is tithed shall not be burned at His [Christ's] coming." (D. & C. 64:23. See also 85:3) Only tithers are admitted into Mormon temples to be married for eternity, which is the prerequisite for entrance into the highest Mormon heaven to become gods and goddesses. No tithing—no heaven! (For more information on the early version of the temple ceremony, see Appendix A.)

I WANTED TO BE QUEEN OF HEAVEN

As all little Mormon girls do, early in life I began planning to be a faithful, obedient Latter-day Saint . . . someday. Then I could be married in the temple and be sealed for eternity to an upstanding elder—handsome and debonair, to be sure, with riches thrown in for good measure. That was what Mama had always urged upon me, as all good Mormon mothers should.

One bright Sunday morning my wishy-washy daydreams hardened into grim determination. My junior Sunday School teacher Miss Sadie May's pronouncement regarding servants in heaven really set me to serious planning for my future estate. "When this earth becomes heaven," she had begun, "the sealed-for-eternity Mormons will inherit vast farms and magnificent mansions. Those of us who die single and unclaimed must forever and ever be servants and nursemaids for the temple-sealed and married-for-eternity couples." I could tell that Sister Sadie did not intend to remain an "unclaimed blessing." Neither did I!

I would not be numbered among the vast crews of servants needed to staff the gods' mansions, work and manage their prodigious farms and vineyards, milk the cows, and produce the other necessary food and clothing for their ever-multiplying progeny. Other servants would be required to do the cooking, sewing and mending, care for the myriads of babies, wash the diapers (in my childhood days disposable diapers were unheard of) and all the other attendant chores of a large and prosperous household.

Miss Sadie May's assurance that even the servants would be happy in this celestialized Mormon earth-heaven did not impress me nor deter me from my set goal. I was determined to marry early and to marry well. My prospective bridegroom-God was already picked out. I would marry the Sunday School superintendent's son for time and for all eternity. Someone else could wash the dishes and the didies and tend to the runny-nosed heavenly kids. I intended to be a queen in heaven, not a servant.

As a heavenly queen I would have servants galore. More than plenty, for there would be a vast supply of "jack" Mormons to staff all of the gods' mansions and vast estates. "Jack" Mormons are borderline Saints—not too bad, not too good, just mediocre, so-so Mormons.

It was Brigham Young who first dubbed these fence-straddling, resistive Latter-day Saints jackass Mormons. He declared that they pull little of the load and kick a lot. They do not pay their tithes and assessments, support the bishopric, nor attend sacrament meetings regularly. They break the commandments by brazenly violating the Word of Wisdom. They publicly savor the church-forbidden coffee, tea, liquor and tobacco to their hearts' content and the church authorities' chagrin. And so, these tens of thousands of unworthy jack Mormons never receive their "temple recommends." They are never allowed to enter the temple to be married and sealed for eternity. They, along with all non-Mormons, except the vilest murderers, thieves and adulterers, must eternally be gardeners, milkmen, nursemaids, etc., in Mormonism's earthly styled heaven. Because of their vast number, they have assurance that they will not be overworked, especially since there will be no baby formula fixing when this earth becomes heaven.

The ability to breast feed and nourish all infants born to them here and in the hereafter is sealed upon the women by the power of the Mormon priesthood in the temple blessing service. This is an integral part of Mormonism's doctrine of progression to godhood—even though it and diaper washing may seem less than heavenly to you.

Lest you may suppose it to be a lying fabrication on my part, consider that God "... passed through the experiences of mortal life, including *death and resurrection* ..." and is an exalted man who "occupies space, has a body, parts and passions, can go from place to place, can eat, drink and talk as well as man; does not differ materially in size."[4] If God eats and drinks, then these purported heaven-born babies of the gods must also eat and drink. Following the ingestion of food and drink and the forces of nature, diapers must be furnished the babies; comfort stations and toilet tissues must be provided for the gods.

How very tragic it is that Mormonism has made the great Creator into a lowly creature who must eat, drink, and sleep. How gratifying and how much easier it would be if Mormons would denounce their God-man theory and in simple, childlike faith believe that "God is a Spirit," (John 4:24) then worship Him in spirit and in truth through faith in Christ's atoning, sacrificial blood. Because of their implicit trust in Joseph Smith and his teachings, the majority of Mormons have never thought through the mazes of Mormonism. They do not realize the complexity of the doctrines of Mormonism. Many of these doctrines eventually and inexorably lead to both the ridiculous and obscene. I know from my own experience that most Mormons certainly do not intentionally belittle God.

FOOTNOTES

1. Cowley, M.F., *Cowleys' Talks on Doctrine*, page 162.

2. McConkie, Bruce, *Mormon Doctrine*, page 674.

3. Taylor, John, *Journal of Discourses*, Volume 10, page 50.

4. *"Principles of the Gospel, High Priest's 3rd Year Course of Study for Quorums of the Priesthood,"* page 13.

JOSEPH SMITH.
(The Founder and First Prophet of the Mormon Church.)

Chapter Five

JOSEPH LIED, GOD NEVER DIED

Many do not know that Joseph Smith and succeeding prophets of Mormonism have taught that God the Father was once a son, that He had a father, a mother, a grandfather and grandmother, a great-grandfather and a great-grandmother, and so on and on way back into the wild blue yonder.

In his sermonizing that God Himself had once been a son in the family of the gods, Joseph Smith spelled it out thusly:

> I want to reason a little on this subject [of God's father] ... If Abraham reasoned thus—If Jesus Christ was the Son of God, and John [doubtless the apostle] discovered that God the Father of Jesus Christ had a father, you may suppose that He [God's father and Jesus' grandfather] had a father also. Where was there ever a son without a father? ... Paul says that which is earthly is in the likeness of that which is heavenly, hence if Jesus had a father, can we not believe that He [God] had a father also? I despise the idea of being scared to death at such a doctrine, for the Bible is full of it!

> Joseph Smith
> *History of The Church*
> Volume 6, Page 476

This sermon of Joseph Smith's was building upon the concepts of an earlier and much more important revelation where he told the people how God became God. In a Conference talk he gave in April, 1844, Joseph delivered what has become one of the classics of church literature.[1] Although a General Conference talk, it is commonly referred to as the "King Follett Funeral Discourse" because

Joseph made a reference to a Mormon elder named King
Follett who died about a month earlier when a tub of rocks
fell on his head while he was digging a well.

Because of the import of this sermon, laying as it does the
very foundation of the current Mormon doctrine of God,
here are major excerpts of what the prophet taught his
followers:

> My first object is to find out the character of the only
> wise and true, God, and what kind of a being He is . . .
>
> . . . I am going to inquire after God; for I want you all to
> know Him, and to be familiar with Him . . .
>
> I will go back to the beginning before the world was, to
> show what kind of a being God is.
>
> God himself was once as we are now, and is an exalted
> man, and sits enthroned in yonder heavens! That is the
> great secret. If the veil were rent today, and the great God
> who holds this world in its orbit, and who upholds all
> worlds and all things by His power, was to make himself
> visible,—I say, if you were to see him today, you would see
> him like a man in form—like yourselves in all the person,
> image, and very form as a man . . .
>
> . . . it is necessary we should understand the character
> and being of God and how He came to be so; for I am going
> to tell you how God came to be God. We have imagined and
> supposed that God was God from all eternity. I will refute
> that idea, and take away the veil, so that you may see.
>
> . . . It is the first principle of the gospel to know for a
> certainty the character of God, and to know that we may
> converse with him as one man converses with another,
> and that He was once a man like us; yea, that God himself,
> the Father of us all, dwelt on an earth, the same as Jesus
> Christ Himself did; and I will show it from the Bible.
>
> . . . Here, then, is eternal life—to know the only wise and
> true God; and you have got to learn how to be gods
> yourselves, and to be kings and priests to God, the same as
> all gods have done before you, namely, by going from one
> small degree to another, and from a small capacity to a
> great one; from grace to grace, from exaltation to
> exaltation, until you attain to the resurrection of the dead,
> and are able to dwell in everlasting burnings, and to sit in
> glory, as do those who sit enthroned in everlasting power.
>
> In the beginning, the head of the gods called a council of
> the gods; and they came together and concocted a plan to
> create the world and people it.

The mind or the intelligence which man possesses is co-equal [co-eternal] with God himself.

The first principles of man are self-existent with God. God himself, finding he was in the midst of spirits and glory, because he was more intelligent, saw proper to institute laws whereby the rest could have a privilege to advance like himself.

This is good doctine. It tastes good. I can taste the principles of eternal life, and so can you. They are given to me by the revelations of Jesus Christ.

. . . when I tell you of these things which were given me by inspiration of the Holy Spirit, you are bound to receive them as sweet, and rejoice more and more.

Joseph Smith
History of the Church
Volume 6, Page 304-312

It is this kind of doctrine concerning the nature of God the Father that separates Mormonism from Christianity forever. Though nobody can fully understand the nature of God, we can and must go on the basis of what He has revealed to us about Himself. We can know no more about His nature than what He reveals to us, but certainly we are in grave spiritual danger if we do not know that revelation about Himself.

Since Joseph Smith was revealing to his followers that God was once a man Himself, God ceased at that point to be the Self-existent One revealed in the Bible (and for that matter, in Joseph's own *Book of Mormon!*). Because God was not self-existent, and logic demands that something has to be self-existent, Joseph decided that man (as "intelligence") and matter are eternal.

He said that God said that:

Man was also in the beginning with God. Intelligence, or the light of truth, was not created or made, neither indeed can be . . .

For man is spirit. The elements are eternal, and spirit and element, inseparably connected, receive a fulness of joy.

Doctrine and Covenants
Section 93:29, 33

Continuing on with this Mormon theory, after God had instructed the self-existent intelligences, He then procreated spirit bodies for them to inhabit; they became spirits and God became a Father. But always and always my Mormon mind kept going back to the questions: How did the *first* God get His body? How and where did He get His first wife by which to beget His children and other wives? I didn't know. No one knew!

I did know that I must not question. I must live by faith, they said. Most Mormons believe what they are *told* to believe—nothing more, nothing less. I must simply believe in a God who is Himself progressive, whose glory is intelligence, who is Himself working toward a higher goal.

I must also believe that:

> Next to God, there may be, therefore, other intelligent beings so nearly approaching his power as to be co-equal with him in all things so far as our finite understanding can perceive... Such intelligent beings are as gods to us... there are many gods or beings so highly developed that they are as gods, in fact are gods... In short, *man is a god in embryo.*

John Widstoe
Rational Theology, Pages 24-25

In addition, I was also taught that God

> ... has had his [temple] endowments long ago; it is thousands and millions of years since He received His [temple] blessings, and if He had not received them, we could not give them to Him, for He is far in advance of us. I want you to understand this one thing, that our tithing, our labor, our works are not for the exaltation of the Almighty, but they are for us.

Wilford Woodruff
Journal of Discourses
Volume 4, Page 192

Thus Mormon leaders heap insult upon insult on God the Father as they seek to turn Him into just one of many self-exalted men. He supposedly has not only passed through all the experiences of mortal life *including death and resurrection,* but has had to pass through the Mormon temple endowment and marriage services just as all Mormon men do!

Some of this, I am aware, seems far-fetched to you but be reminded that this is deep-down Mormonism, not the surface fragments published for the world and spiritually immature Mormons. Remember, too, that these teachings were brought forth by Joseph Smith and his successors, and not by me. Bear in mind that no Mormon can really gainsay them, for if the first Mormon prophets did not know real Mormonism, then no one can.

On one point, though, we can all agree. Joseph Smith must have been swamped with difficulties as he attempted to keep all this rigmarole straight. He was, most likely, also swamped by derisive and chiding rebuttals which called for other revelations to doctor his doctrine now summarized by: *"As man is, God once was; as God is, man may become."*

Most assuredly such a sick doctrine needs immediate doctoring, or better still, sharp and sudden amputation to ward off the infection, pain and inflammation that must invariably attend such spiritual affliction. Complete and total severance of such a malignant appendage is surely just what the Doctor, God, the Great Physician, orders.

It is so much more childish and multiplied millions of times harder to worship a God who reputedly was once born a baby on an earth similar to this with parents, grandparents, great-grandparents, etc.—a baby who eventually grew to manhood, kept all the commandments of Mormonism, including marriage (quite probably to many wives), and then escorted them, one by one, through temple washings, anointings and endowment services to be blessed for all time and eternity. To believe all of this is much more difficult, I declare from personal experience, than to simply, in child-like faith, accept the Bible truth that "God is a Spirit," then "worship Him in spirit and in truth" by receiving Jesus Christ as Saviour and Lord.

I cannot fathom the minds of the men who first concocted and then kept adding to this loathsome doctrine that God Himself was once a man—just an ordinary man who had to first pass through all the experiences of an earth life, including birth and baptism, mirth and marriage, sex and sin, deterioration, death and resurrection.

It is a lie of the first order! The Bible says "The wages of *sin* is death," (Romans 6:23) but God the Father *never sinned,* nor did He have to die. *Joseph Smith lied, God never died!*

NO ONE CAN GO
TO HEAVEN SINGLE

With the revelation that God is a muchly-married (and thereby exalted) man, Joseph Smith had this time almost "revelated" himself into a corner. Those of his followers who dared to think for themselves denounced this new principle of their prophet when they realized the possible ulterior motivations and the ultimate complications to which such a belief would lead, and the ignominious violence it perpetrated against a Holy God. As happened several times before, many departed from Mormonism. Nevertheless, Joseph Smith kept pursuing his Latter-day doctrinal concept that: "As man is, God once was and as God is, man may become." He threw in a scripture verse now and then to attempt to prove his contentions.

To further his claim that the sexes must be coupled in heaven, Joseph the prophet cited I Corinthians 11:11: "Neither is the man without the woman, neither the woman without the man, in the Lord." This means to Mormons that no one can go the highest heaven *single.* A man must have a wife sealed to him by the Mormon priesthood so that he can earn an estate in the celestial kingdom, the highest of the three Mormon heavens. The woman must have a Mormon man who holds the Mormon priesthood to be her head. He is to resurrect her by calling her forth from the grave by the new name given her in the Mormon temple endowment and sealing ceremony.

However, the problem dealt with in the eleventh chapter of First Corinthians is that away back yonder in 50 A.D. God was opposing a "mod movement." He was trying to bring the female of the species back into line with His divine purpose for us. This scripture is dealing with the very earthly problem of how men and women would behave *in church,* not with heavenly mating such as this Mormon interpretation tries to promote. God, through Paul's writings, is reminding us that ever since the fall of Adam, the wife has been in subjection to her husband. He is her head, and so, in church the wife should cover or veil her head as a token of her respect and subjection to her husband. The man, too, has an order to follow. His head must not be covered; to preach or pray with his hat on dishonors Christ, who is the man's head. In verses 11, 12, Paul gives the other side of the truth. In the Lord's plan the man and the woman are necessary for each other. As the old song goes, "You can't have one without the other." From the very beginning, we have been irrevocably interdependent, for as the woman was made from man, even so man is born of woman.

If perchance Mormons were to read this whole passage and discover these truths for themselves, many would undoubtedly see this as just another of the many contextually false interpretations of Scripture.

Mormons are repeatedly warned to accept only those Bible passages which agree with Mormon beliefs and practices as found in their three standard works: *The Book of Mormon,* the *Doctrine and Covenants,* and *The Pearl of Great Price.* While still a Mormon, I found to my consternation and dismay that not one of these entirely agrees with itself, with the others, or with most Mormon doctrines. For instance, though I searched all through Mormon scriptures diligently, I could not find even the slightest mention of heavenly mothers, the birth of spirit babies, or even that God was once a man like us!

GOD IS MARRIED ... TO MARY

We now know that God is not single, and as we will see in detail in another chapter, He most certainly has to be a polygamist. To the uninitiated, all this talk about many gods, men can become gods, family and sex relations in the celestial spheres begins to sound somewhat like Greek or Roman mythology—certainly not the doctrines of Christianity for the last 2000 years! The parallel to Greek and Roman mythology becomes even more clear as we examine the Mormon doctrine concerning the relationship of God the Father to the birth of Jesus Christ. The great hero of Greek mythology, Hercules, was born after the head god, Zeus, came down and had sex relations with a mortal. There is nothing particularly supernatural in this mythological concept—in fact, it is all quite natural. So also is the "virgin" birth of the Jesus of Mormonism.

Please remember that the God of Mormonism is no more than an exalted man, and that He has a body of flesh and bones "as tangible as man's" *(Doctrine and Covenants, Section 130:22)*. Therefore, concerning the birth of Jesus Christ, Brigham Young said:

> When the time came that His first-born, the Saviour, should come into the world and take a tabernacle, the Father came Himself and favoured that spirit with a tabernacle instead of *letting any other man do it*. The Saviour was begotten by the Father of His spirit, by the same Being who is the Father of our spirits, and that is all the organic difference between Jesus Christ and you and me.

> Brigham Young
> *Journal of Discourses*
> Volume 4, Page 218

Also keep in mind at all times that to most Mormons the difference between Jesus Christ and ourselves is not one of nature, but only a difference in degree of progression, as Brigham Young made so clear in the above quote.

Orson Pratt was one of the top leaders of the early Mormon Church. He was one of the original 12 apostles chosen by Joseph Smith, and he was a leading spokesman for the church to the gentile world. In 1853 he was appointed by Brigham Young himself to ". . . write and publish periodicals, pamphlets, books, etc., illustrative of the principles and doctrines of the Church."[2] The major vehicle of this appointment was a periodical known as *The Seer,* which is still available in many Mormon bookstores as a reprint. Orson Pratt introduced *The Seer* by saying:

> The pages of *The Seer* will be mostly occupied with original matter, elucidating the doctrines of the Church of Jesus Christ of Latter Day Saints . . . we promise you a True and Faithful description of all the principal features, characterizing this great and last "dispensation of the fulness of time."

> Orson Pratt
> *The Seer,* Page 1

With the stage set concerning the teachings and authority of Apostle Orson Pratt, consider now his perspective on our topic:

If none but Gods will be permitted to multiply immortal children, it follows that each God must have one or more wives. God, the Father of our spirits, became the Father of our Lord Jesus Christ according to the flesh. Hence, the Father saith concerning him, "Thou art my Son, this day have I begotten thee." We are informed in the first chapter of Luke, that Mary was chosen by the Father as a choice virgin, through whom He begat Jesus. The angel said unto the Virgin Mary, "The Holy Ghost shall come upon thee, and the power of the Highest shall overshadow thee: therefore, also, that holy thing which shall be born of thee shall be called the Son of God." After the power of the Highest had overshadowed Mary, and she had by that means conceived, she related the circumstance to her cousin Elizabeth in the following words: "He that is Mighty hath done to me great things; and holy is His name." It seems from this relation that the Holy Ghost accompanied "the Highest" when He overshadowed the Virgin Mary and begat Jesus; and from this circumstance some have supposed that the body of Jesus was begotten of the Holy Ghost without the instrumentality of the immediate presence of the Father. There is no doubt that the Holy Ghost came upon Mary to sanctify her, and make her holy, and prepare her to endure the glorious presence of "the Highest," that when "He" should "overshadow" her she might conceive, being filled with the Holy Ghost; hence the angel said, as recorded in Matthew, "That which is conceived in her is of the Holy Ghost:" that is, the Holy Ghost gave her strength to abide the presence of the Father without being consumed: but *it was the personage of the Father who begat the body of Jesus: and for this reason Jesus is called "The only begotten of the Father"; that is, the only one in this world whose fleshly body was begotten by the Father.* There were millions of sons and daughters whom He begat before the foundation of this world, but they were spirits, and not bodies of flesh and bones; whereas, *both the spirit and body of Jesus were begotten by the Father*—the spirit having been begotten in heaven many ages before the tabernacle was begotten upon the earth.

The fleshly body of Jesus required a Mother as well as a Father. Therefore, *the Father and Mother of Jesus, according to the flesh, must have been associated together in the capacity of Husband and Wife; hence the Virgin Mary must have been, for the time being, the lawful wife of God the Father:* we use the term lawful wife, because it would be blasphemous in the highest degree to say that He overshadowed her or begat the Saviour unlawfully. It would have been unlawful for any man to have interfered with Mary, who was already espoused to Joseph; for such a heinous crime would have subjected both the guilty parties to death, according to the law of Moses. But God having created all men and women, had the most perfect right to do with His own creation, according to His holy will and pleasure: He had a lawful right to overshadow the Virgin Mary in the capacity of a husband, and beget a Son, although she was espoused to another; for the law which He gave to govern men and women was not intended to govern Himself, or to prescribe rules for his own conduct. It was also lawful in Him, after having thus dealt with Mary, to give her to Joseph her espoused husband. *Whether God the Father gave Mary to Joseph for time only, or for time and eternity, we are not informed.* Inasmuch as God was the first husband to her, it may be that He only gave her to be the wife of Joseph while in this mortal state, and that He intended after the resurrection to again take her as one of his own wives to raise up immortal spirits in eternity."

Orson Pratt
The Seer, page 158

From sad experience the Church of Jesus Christ of Latterday Saints, with her more than four million (1979) members, knows that these teachings *must not be made public,* for most persons would find them reprehensible. The Mormon church would be denounced rather than applauded, as she is now, under her false facade of Christian piety. Her 27,000 full-time missionaries would be universally turned away. The Mormon hierarchy, therefore, attempts to shield Mormonism's secret doctrines by merely denying their existence. By deceit and lies they camouflage their innermost tenents, accusing all "antiMormon" writers and lecturers of distortion, misrepresentation or worse. For these reasons I was *obliged* to include the major portion of this foul, sacrilegious discourse as it was once proudly published in *The Seer.* Can you imagine a *true* apostle of God preaching such doctrine? Surely not John, James, Peter or Paul!

Although the idea that Mary was married to God the Father may not be as widely believed as it was in the days of Orson Pratt, the fact remains *he did teach it as doctrine of the church* with the approval and sanction of the First

Presidency. The other aspect involving the "virgin" birth being nothing supernatural is still quite valid as far as Orson Pratt's successors are concerned. In fact, several times in recent years, current Mormon Apostle Bruce R. McConkie has made the position of the Mormon church on this point quite clear. In his widely acclaimed book, *Mormon Doctrine,* McConkie proclaims to the world that:

> Christ was begotten by an Immortal Father in the same way that mortal men are begotten by mortal fathers . . . God the Father is a perfected, glorified holy Man, an immortal Personage. And Christ was born into the world as the literal Son of this Holy being; he was born in the same personal, real, and literal sense that *any mortal son is born to a mortal father.* There is nothing figurative about his paternity; *he was begotten, conceived and born in the normal and natural course of events,* for he is the Son of God, and that designation means what it says.

> Bruce McConkie
> *Mormon Doctrine,* Pages 547, 742

If that were not clear enough for some people, Apostle McConkie "will remove all doubt" concerning his apostolic view of this matter; restating the same position in 1978 he said:

> Some words scarcely need definition. They are on every tongue and are spoken by every voice . . . Two such words are *Father* and *Son.* Their meaning is known to all, and to define them is but to repeat them. Mary provided the womb from which the spirit Jehovah *(Jesus is "Jehovah", while God the Father is "Elohim")* came forth, tabernacled in clay, as all men are to dwell among his fellow spirits whose births were brought to pass in like manner. There is no need to spiritualize away the plain meaning of the scriptures. There is nothing figurative or hidden or beyond comprehension in our Lord's coming into mortality. He is the Son of God in the *same sense and way* that we are the sons of mortal fathers. It is just that simple.

> Bruce McConkie
> *The Promised Messiah,* Page 468

Even the Mormon hierarchy's perfidy and turn-coat tactics toward my great-grandpa Lee, which were to send him to prison and to death, were nothing compared to this unholy perversion which Joseph Smith, Brigham Young, and successive Latter-day apostles have heaped upon a holy God and a tender young innocent virgin, a virgin so pure and spiritual that she was willing to bear the Child Jesus at such great personal sacrifice. She was quite probably branded a scarlet woman and forfeited her reputation, which must have been most dear to one so fine and pure. She placed her very life in double jeopardy; the danger to her life of giving birth to the baby Jesus in the lowly manger was nothing compared to the peril she faced at the hands of men, who could have, according to the law of Moses, stoned her to death for adultery.

Words are inadequate to describe the abomination of this vulgar corruption of God's Holy Word in making Mary's joyous recounting to Elizabeth: "He that is mighty hath done to me great things" (Luke 1:49) into a sexual act between Mary and God, turning it into a base, sexual encounter instead of the sacred supernatural, *spiritual* experience it was. May He that is merciful and mighty look down with compassion on those who still promote this ungodly doctrine. May He send missionaries to them to declare that Jesus verily was begotten by the *supernatural* act of the Holy Spirit as the Bible so beautifully states that He was.

GOD — A BEING OF BODY, PARTS AND PASSIONS

This monstrous distortion of the sacred doctrine of the virgin birth of Christ, so abhorrent and so contrary to true Christianity, is still earnestly defended and promoted by many of those Mormons who are acquainted with it.

One of my Mormon friends, the bishop of his Mormon ward, was amazed that I rebelled against his very frank version of the "virgin" birth. I challenged him: "Since Mormonism's God is a being of flesh and bones, a being of body, parts and passions, then Mormonism's doctrine that God overshadowed Mary in the capacity of a husband does away with the idea of a *virgin* birth. Do you believe in the virgin birth of Jesus or not?" I demanded.

"Sure I believe in the virgin birth. I believe also that God has a body just as I have. And that He uses His male parts for the same purposes that I use mine. I believe that Mary was a virgin when God came to earth to visit her and cause her to conceive. But she *was no longer a virgin* when God left her and went back to heaven."

Many other Mormons outwardly proclaim the virgin birth even though it clashes with their teachings that Jesus was not begotten by the Holy Ghost but was sexually sired by God the Father. Perhaps this, as is often the case, is a problem of Mormon redefinition of Christian terms.

These are frank facts, but no more plain-spoken than most of Mormonism's views on God and His wives. As a Mormon I had always taken it for granted that God has many wives amongst whom He regularly visits, showing no partiality. However, I had *never* been told that Mary was one of God's wives!

FOOTNOTES

1. This sermon has been published many times, beginning with the Mormon newspaper, *Times and Seasons,* for August 15, 1844, next in Volume 6 of the *Journal of Discourses,* then in the *Millenial Star, Teachings of the Prophet Joseph Smith* and quite probably at least a dozen other books, as well as a number of times in the official church magazines, the *Improvement Era* and its recent successor, the *Ensign.*

2. Pratt, Orson, (Quoting Brigham Young), *The Seer,* Page 2.

Brigham Young

Chapter Six

ADAM IS GOD?

As bad a doctrine as "God was once a man" may be, Brigham Young's public ministry extended that error into a dogma that even the Mormons *themselves* don't like to this very day! After Joseph Smith set the stage in the King Follett Discourse of the manhood of God, Brigham went him one better by identifying that man as no one else but the first of the human family — *Adam!* Even during his own lifetime, Brigham was fought against concerning his revelation about Adam. Now that he is safely dead, his doctrine has been all but buried with him. But the evidence concerning "Adam-God" has survived in abundance (thanks to the printed page, photocopy machines and, of course, the sovereignty of God).

As far as the public is concerned, the doctrine of Adam-God begins with a General Conference sermon of Brigham Young given on April 9th, 1852. Please remember that the sessions of General Conference are the appointed time and place for the Mormon people to receive the will of the Lord, for beyond any other instance, that is the time when the elders of the church can be expected to be "moved upon by the Holy Ghost," and what they say "shall be scripture." *(Doctrine and Covenants, 68:4)*

So much has been said and written about this particular sermon, both pro and con, that I even hesitate to quote from it, lest I just be warming over 100-year-old leftovers. But for the sake of completeness, I have to present to you major excerpts of this sermon. The prophet proudly proclaimed:

> The question has been, and is often, asked, who it was
> that begat the Son of the Virgin Mary ... I will tell you

how it is. Our Father in Heaven begat all the spirits that ever were, or ever will be, upon this earth; and they were born spirits in the eternal world.

Now here it, O inhabitants of the earth, Jew and Gentile, Saint and sinner! When our father Adam came into the garden of Eden, he came into it with a *celestial body*, and brought Eve, *one of his wives*, with him. He helped to make and organize this world. He is Michael, *the archangel*, the Ancient of Days! about whom holy men have written and spoken—He *is* our Father *and our God, and the only god with whom we have to do.* Every man upon the earth, professing Christians or nonprofessing, must hear it, and *will know it sooner or later* . . . . When Adam and Eve had eaten of the forbidden fruit, their bodies became mortal from *its effects,* and therefore their offspring were mortal. When the Virgin Mary conceived the child Jesus, the Father had begotten him in his own likeness. He was *not* begotten by the Holy Ghost. And who is the Father? He is the first of the human family; . . .

What a learned idea! Jesus, our elder brother, was begotten in the flesh by the same character that was in the garden of Eden, and who is our Father in Heaven. Now, let all who may hear these doctrines pause before they make light of them or treat them with indifference, for they will prove their salvation or damnation.

I have given you a few leading items upon this subject, but a great deal more remains to be told. Now, remember from this time forth, and for ever, that Jesus Christ was not begotten by the Holy Ghost.

Brigham Young
Journal of Discourses
Volume 1, Pages 50-51

That is certainly a revealing sermon, and as I said, one that the successive generations of Mormons have done their best to bury and forget. I would be one of the very first to forget that Brigham Young ever preached such doctrine, if that were the *only* evidence concerning this subject. However, there is much, much more! The mass of evidence that is available from original sources completely negates the prime Mormon argument that Brigham was misquoted. Closely tied to the misquotation argument is the idea that we are misunderstanding what Brigham meant by that sermon. Again, if that were the only information available, I could grant them that.

MUCH MORE WAS TOLD

Brigham promised his people that "a great deal more remains to be told," *and tell them he did.* To again confirm that to become a god, one would become an Adam, he said:

> If you look at things spiritually, and then naturally, and see how they appear together, you will understand that when you have the privilege of commencing the work that Adam commenced on this earth, you will have all your children come and report to you of their sayings and acts; and you will hold every son and daughtes [sic] of yours responsible *when you get the privilege of being an Adam on earth.*

Brigham Young
Journal of Discourses
Volume 4, Page 271

Brigham, who apparently was not one to discriminate, also reassured the womenfolk that they too, were to be involved directly in the role of "Eve-goddess" when he said:

> After men have got their exaltations and their crowns— have become Gods, . . . they have the power then of propagating their species in spirit; and that is the first of their operations with regard to organizing a world. Power is then given to them to organize the elements, and then commence the organization of tabernacles. How can they do it? Have they to go to that earth? *Yes, an Adam will have to go there, and he cannot do without Eve.* He must have Eve to commence the work of generation, and they will go into the garden, and continue to eat and drink of the fruits of the corporeal world, until this grosser matter is diffused sufficiently through their celestial bodies to enable them according to the established laws, to produce mortal tabernacles for their spiritual children.

Brigham Young
Journal of Discourses
Volume 6, Page 275

Adam and Eve were also occupied before they came here to their earth—busy producing billions of spirit babies in heaven. I'm sure that Eve had a lot of help in that area from her many sister-wives; after all, Brigham did say that Adam "...brought Eve, *one* of his wives, with him." But nonetheless, Eve (as the senior wife) would get the credit as the mother of the spirit children, such as Brigham hinted at when he said, "Adam and Eve are the parents of all pertaining to the flesh, and I would not say that they are not also the parents of our spirits."[1] The reason he could not say they weren't the parents of our spirits is because he did believe that they were!

ADAM CAME FROM ANOTHER PLANET

Another major aspect of the Adam-God doctrine is the idea that Adam came to this planet from another world after his resurrection to begin the life cycle here by "generation." Today, this concept is most certainly denied by the Mormon leadership. In a chapter of one of his books which is devoted to Adam, Joseph Fielding Smith, the 10th prophet of the church, stated categorically that, " . . . Adam's body was created from the dust of the ground, that is, from the dust of *this ground, this earth.* "[2] With that, the 10th Mormon prophet completely contradicted the 2nd Mormon prophet, who said:

> Though we have it in history that our father Adam was made of the dust of this earth . . . yet it is not so . . .
>
> He was the person who brought the animals and the seeds from other planets to this world, and brought a wife with him and stayed here. You may read and believe what you please as to what is found written in the Bible. Adam was made from the dust of an earth, but *not from the dust of this earth.*

Brigham Young
Journal of Discourses
Volume 3, Page 319

Brigham said this more than once. He also said, "Mankind are here because they are the offspring of parents who were first brought here from another planet . . . ."[3]

NOT WITHOUT A FIGHT

Brigham had difficulties with his doctrine. Most never did accept it—and some of those were excommunicated for *not* accepting it. In 1857 Brigham stated, "Some have grumbled because I believe our God to be so near to us as Father Adam. There are many who know that doctrine to be true."[4] He may have been thinking of the trouble in the English Mission just a few years before. In the meeting of the General Council in London, there were several objections raised and answered concerning Adam-God:

> ... some of the officers [of the church] have not met in council for three years. They are lacking faith on one principle—the last "cat that was let out of the bag." Polygamy has been got over pretty well, that cloud has vanished away, but they are troubled about Adam being our Father and God ...

> Concerning the item of doctrine alluded to by Elder Caffal and others viz., that Adam is our Father and God, I have to say do not trouble yourselves, neither let the Saints be troubled about that matter ... If, as Elder Caffal remarked, there are those who are waiting at the door of the Church for this objection to be removed, tell such, *the Prophet and Apostle Brigham has declared it, and that is the Word of the Lord.*

> *Millennial Star*
> Volume 15, Pages 482, 534

Even as late as 1873, just a handful of years before he died, Brigham was still hammering home the point about his god—Adam. After twenty-one years of hard preaching on his part, apparently it was *still* a struggle to get his people in line. In a discourse published in the *Deseret News* (the Mormon newspaper), Brigham said:

> ... I have been found fault with a great many times for casting reflections upon men of science, and especially upon theologians, because of the little knowledge they possess about man being on the earth, about the earth itself, about our Father in heaven, his Son Jesus Christ, the order of heavenly things, the laws by which angels exist, by which the worlds were created and are held in existence, &c. How pleased we would be to place these things before the people if they would receive them! *How much unbelief exists in the minds of the Latter-day Saints in regard to one particular doctrine which I revealed to them, and which God revealed to me — namely that Adam is our Father and God* ... Our Father Adam is the man who stands at the gate and holds the keys of everlasting life and salvation to all his children who have or who ever will come upon the earth ...

> ... "Why was Adam called Adam?" He was the first man on the earth, and its framer and maker ... Then he [Adam] said, "I want my children who are in the spirit world to come and live here. I once dwelt upon an earth something like this, in a mortal state, I was faithful, I received my crown and exaltation. I have the privilege of extending my

work, and to its increase there will be no end. I want my children *that were born to me* in the spirit world to come here and take tabernacles of flesh."

Brigham Young
Deseret Weekly News
June 18, 1873, Page 308

I hope that by now it is *becoming crystal clear* that Brigham Young *did believe and teach that:*

- Adam is the God of this planet.
- Adam is the father of our spirits, as well as our flesh.
- Adam was the one who "begat" Jesus in the flesh.
- After we become a god, we get to be "an Adam."
- It is Adam we are to worship, not Adam's God or that God's God.
- God Himself revealed this to Brigham.

There are quite literally hundreds of pages of documentation available about Brigham's doctrine of Adam-God. Another of Brigham's many sermons on this subject was delivered at General Conference in October 1854. In his personal diary for that period, Wilford Woodruff made the following entry:

Oct. 8, President Young preached to a congregation of several thousand, out of doors and I believe that he preached the greatest sermon that ever was delivered to the Latter Day Saints since they have been a people. Elder Watt reported. I also took minutes.

"Journal of Wilford Woodruff"
Entry for Oct. 6-8, 1854

Just exactly what was the subject of the "greatest sermon" that ever was delivered? *Adam-God, of course!* The following excerpts of that sermon are taken from a typed copy of the manuscript in the Brigham Young papers collection in the LDS Church Archives. As such, spelling, punctuation, crossed-out words and similar errors are included exactly as in the original. Words that were added in the manuscript are shown in parentheses:

Every world has had an Adam, and an Eve: named so,

simply because the first man is always called Adam, and the first woman, Eve: and the oldest son has always had the privilege of being ordained, appointed and called to be heir of the family, ...

But let us turn our attention to the God with which we have to do. I tell you simply, he is our father; the God and father of our Lord Jesus Christ, and the father of our spirits. Can that be possable? Yes, it is possable, he is the father of all the spirits of the human family.

I tell you more, Adam ~~was~~ is the father of our spirits. He live upon an earth; he did abide his creation, and did honor to his calling and preisthood, and obeyed his master or Lord, and probably many of his wives did ~~also~~ (the same) and they lived, and died upon an earth, and (then) were resurrected again to immortality and eternal life.

Our spirits and the spirits of all the human family were begotten by Adam, and born of Eve.

I tell you, when you see your father ~~Adam~~ in the heavens, you will see Adam; When you see your Mother that bear your spirit, you will see mother Eve.

I wish you to understand well the position I have taken, and the nature of the remarkes I have made. Profit by them, both saints and sinners. You have had things laid before you that does not ~~particularly~~ belong to ~~you~~ the world, nor to men and women, who callculate to apostatise. They belong to the wise; to those who are serving God with all their hearts.

Brigham Young Papers
Addresses, 1854 July — October
Manuscript for 8 October
Pages 11, 12, 16, 18, 21, and 26

The fact that things "belong to the wise" may have been the reason that Brigham didn't have this sermon published. Perhaps he knew the reaction it would bring outside of the Utah Territory!

ADAM—GOD TODAY

In fairness to my Mormon people, I must make it clear that the vast majority of them *do not believe such doctrine,* nor have most of them even heard of it! In fact, the current Mormon prophet, Spencer W. Kimball, denounced the Adam-God doctrine as *false* as recently as the October General Conference for 1976. President Kimball said:

We warn you against the dissemination of doctrines

which are not according to the scriptures and which are *alleged to have been taught* by some of the General Authorities of past generations. Such, for instance is the Adam-god theory.

We denounce that theory and hope that everyone will be cautioned against this and other kinds of *false doctrine.*

Spencer W. Kimball
Church News
October 9, 1976

Notice how carefully he worded this denunciation. He warned against teaching doctrines not according to the Scriptures "which are alleged to have been taught by some of the General Authorities." We are far beyond the point of mere allegation—*Brigham Young did teach Adam-God!* When Mr. Kimball declared Adam-God to be false doctrine without identifying its source (Brigham), perhaps he was attempting to leave Brigham's station and reputation as a prophet of God intact. Mr. Kimball would have to try this because his own line of authority goes *directly* back to Brigham. In fact, all of the successive prophets after Brigham Young (except one) were either ordained by Brigham personally or by someone that Brigham ordained.

I can whole-heartedly agree with Spencer Kimball that Adam-God is false doctrine. What I would call to his attention (and to yours) is that Deuteronomy 13:1-5 clearly tells us that if a man claims to be a prophet of God and tries to teach about another God "which thou hast not known," *that man is a false prophet!* Brigham did teach "another god" and is a false prophet. All those who derive their "authority" from him have little chance of being true prophets, for a *corrupt tree cannot bring forth good fruit.* (Matthew 7:18)

A final word on this subject. Even though the vast majority of the Mormon people do not believe this doctrine (or even know about it), there are those who know about it and believe it to this very day. They are commonly called "Fundamentalist Mormons" and are the same ones who believe in and practice polygamy, and to a much lesser extent, even Blood Atonement.[5] Though the fundamentalists may be relatively few in number (it is estimated by some to be about 30,000 in all), they are not without influence in the Rocky Mountain area. Many "regular" Mormons, when confronted with the real teachings of Joseph and Brigham, will join (secretly in many cases) with the fundamentalists rather than recognize the error of their former prophets and come to Jesus instead. It saddens my heart to think that they would rather choose darker doctrines of Joseph that the freedom of the light of Christ.

Even my mama's own brother, my Uncle Pete, was affected by fundamentalism. I glory at Mama's spunk in her reaction to Uncle Pete's attempt to convince her that Adam was God. With indignation she sternly ordered Uncle Pete, "You stop talking such rot or else get out of my kitchen!" Good for you, Mama.

FOOTNOTES

1. Young, Brigham, *Journal of Discourses*, Volume 7, page 290.

2. Smith, Joseph Fielding, *Doctrines of Salvation*, Volume 1, page 90.

3. Young, Brigham, *Journal of Discourses*, Volume 7, page 285.

4. *Ibid.*, Volume 5, page 331.

5. The gangland style murder of a fundamentalist leader by the name of Allred in 1978 is a good example of Blood Atonement in modern times. This murder was quite probably a "hit" by a rival fundamentalist group.

Chapter Seven

GRANDPA
WAS A POLYGAMIST

My maternal grandfather, ever a staunch believer in Mormon "sealing and loosening" powers, advancement to godhood, and all other claims of Joseph Smith and the Mormon priesthood, remarried soon after the death of his first wife. He planned all the while to be married and sealed for eternity to both his second wife and his deceased first wife, my grandmother.

This wonderful grandmother of mine, whom I do not remember, had had the blessed privilege of being born the daughter of a godly mother and stalwart Christian father in West Virginia. She made the mistake of marrying a man who did not believe in the saving blood of Jesus Christ, and migrated west with him. There, believing the promises of the Mormon missionaries that their powers of the Mormon priesthood, coupled with her faith, would heal her tiny sickly baby boy, she had allowed them to baptize her.

Even though her baby remained ill with convulsions, she continued on with her husband in the Church of Jesus Christ of Latter-day Saints, though never fully accepting its doctrines. Mama Coddy, as we lovingly called her, never again got to see her beloved parents and other loved ones back home in the hills of West Virginia. Never again was she privileged to stand and sing "Amazing Grace" with fellow-believers in the blood that cleanses from all sin. Death must have brought a sweet release and repose for her wearied lonely soul. For Grandpa it brought free license to marry another wife and become a polygamist in heaven.

And so, Grandpa Coddy with his new wife journeyed to

the Mesa, Arizona, Mormon temple, where he was married and sealed for eternity to *both* wives. These wives along with their children were supposedly sealed to him by the Mormon priesthood for his "eternal weight in glory." (Weight or wait? As a Mormon I never really was sure. We heard much of Mormons' "eternal weight in glory" but never of the "weight of sin which doth so easily beset us." Heb. 12:1) To the day of his death and ever after, Grandpa religiously wore the holy temple undergarments he had donned on his double wedding day.

This idea of sealing for eternity was something about life after death that baffled me as a child, so I asked Mama about it. "How could I be sealed to you and Papa for eternity to live in your heavenly world and also be sealed to a Mormon husband to live with him in *his* own world? Just how could I possibly belong to and be with you both?"

Mama did not know either. Neither would she discuss it. This, I discovered, was something else we Mormons were not to conjecture about. It seems that every puzzling problem that perplexed me about Mormonism's plan for my future estate was just one more of the duplicities of Mormonism we Mormons did not talk about. What we did not know we were not to even think about. By the holy Mormon priesthood authority we were sealed for eternity with an endless increase of mansions, children, worlds and gods stretching out before us. With this we were to be content.

In life and in death Grandpa Coddy had expected through his priesthood, his two wives, good works, tithing and strict obedience to Mormon edicts, to eventually attain to the exaltation of godhood in the highest Mormon heaven. Both of these wives, he believed, were essential to his progress to godhood, for according to (early) Mormonism a "one-woman man" could not become a god. President Brigham Young vigorously and clearly proclaimed that "The only men who become gods, even the sons of God, *are those who enter into polygamy.*"[1]

In another volume of the *Journal of Discourses,* we find still another of Mormonism's most highly prized polygamy sermons. Under the heading "Plural Marriage—for the Righteous only—Obedience Imperative—Blessings

Resulting" is reported the fiery sermon of the man who became Mormonism's sixth president, Joseph F. Smith. President Smith therein charged all Mormons that they were obligated to engage in plural marriages for time and eternity when he said:

> The principle [of polygamy] is correct, great, ennobling and calculated to bring joy, satisfaction, and peace . . . some of the Saints have said and believe that a man with one wife, sealed to him by the authority of the Priesthood for time and eternity, will receive exaltation as great and glorious, if he is faithful as he possibly could with more than one [wife]. *I want here to enter my solemn protest against this idea, for I know it is false . . . this is only the beginning of the law, not the whole of it.*
>
> Joseph F. Smith
> Journal of Discourses
> Volume 20, Page 28

JOSEPH SMITH RULES
IN THE SPIRIT WORLD

Along with most other Mormon men, Grandpa Coddy heartily endorsed and expected to enjoy a plurality of wives in the hereafter. These expectations, he believed, depended on the sealing power of the Mormon priesthood and on his own continuing subservience to his superiors' edicts, especially those commands of Joseph Smith. Even now, no Mormon dares defy or deny Joseph Smith, for he alone "holds the keys of this last dispensation."

Some Latter-day Saints still fear damnation and exclusion from the highest celestial kingdom of God for neglecting or refusing to conform to Joseph Smith's "revelation" on polygamous marriages. Many have been stampeded into plural marriages, forced to side with Joseph Smith, who according to various Mormon historians, had between twenty-seven and eighty-four wives. No one can know for sure, for most of his marriages were secret. But it was not secret that the Mormon gentry were expected to stand by their prophet and follow his leading. None dared refuse.

According to Mama's Mormon Sunday School lesson book, "The Vision:"

If we ask who will stand at the head of the resurrection in this last dispensation, the answer is—Joseph Smith, Jr. the prophet of God . . . No man or woman in this dispensation will ever enter into the Celestial Kingdom of God without the consent of Joseph Smith. From the day that the priesthood was taken from the earth to the winding-up scene of all things every man and woman must have the certificate of Joseph Smith, Jr., as a passport into the mansions where God and Christ are—I with you and you with me. *I cannot go there without his consent. He holds the keys of that kingdom for the last dispensation—the keys to rule in the spirit world: as supreme a being in his sphere, capacity and calling as God does in heaven.*"

> N. B. Lundwall
> "The Vision," Pages 59-60
> (Quoting Brigham Young
> *Journal of Discourses*
> Volume 7, Page 289)

I say again that repetitions of this (and other Mormon doctrines) are preplanned and purposed to impress upon you the little-known Mormon teaching that *"no man or woman in this dispensation will ever enter in the celestial kingdom of God without the consent of Joseph Smith."* Mark it well. Ask your Mormon friends if they are aware of this current Mormon teaching that *NO ONE* can go to heaven without the consent of Joseph Smith.

Thus, according to Mormonism, every person, Mormon or non-Mormon, born since the time of the demise of Christ's first apostles, must obey Joseph Smith and his teachings. Even though dead the last dozen decades, he assertedly still possesses the power to bind and loose, to bless or to curse.

This important Mormon tenet hinges on Joseph's polygamous eternal marriage "revelation." Therein he has caused God to declare:

> . . . that whatsoever you [Joseph Smith] seal on earth shall be sealed in heaven, and whatsoever you shall bind on earth, in my name and by my word, saith the Lord, it shall be eternally bound in the heavens; and whatsoever sins you remit on earth shall be remitted eternally in the heavens; and whatsoever sins you retain on earth shall be retained in heaven. And again, verily I say, whosoever

you bless I will bless and whomsoever you curse I will curse, saith the Lord.

Doctrine and Covenants
Section 132:46-47

Grandpa Coddy had been obedient to the voice of the prophet. He had faithfully followed Joseph Smith's visions, commandments, revelations, whims and examples except in one circumstance—he had come far short of the glory of Joseph Smith, who had married for time and eternity dozens of wives, while my poor grandfather had only two. Nevertheless, Grandpa had looked forward to the singular joy of plurality of wives *in heaven.* He fully believed that by this connubial conniving he would ultimately become a god.

But alas, several years after Grandpa's demise, his eternal celestial happiness and welfare, his status and standing suffered a severe setback: his station in heaven was jeopardized when his second wife (recently remarried), sued him for a divorce! His widow, now the wife of another Mormon elder, desired to be the celestial bride of her latest husband rather than her late husband. And so she sued Grandpa for a temple divorce on the grounds of infidelity to both her and the Mormon church, bootlegging moonshine whiskey (which she, by the way, had helped him make, bottle and sell) and sundry other practices unbecoming of a Mormon elder.

Along with her documented affidavits, she charged that she and her children would be better off and happier in heaven without Grandpa. I guess since they had not been able to get along with him on earth, they surely would continue scrapping and quarreling in heaven.

Other pleas made to the Mormon temple divorce court included:

• She and her children would not be happy in heaven under the dominion of Grandpa's first wife who, because of her seniority as wife number one on earth, would be the ruling queen of Grandpa's dynasty in heaven.

• That she would be hindered in her advancement to queendom not only by wife number one's prior claim but by

Grandpa's numerous earthly backslidings. His earthly wrongdoings undoubtledly had made his advancement to godhood and his standing in heaven slippery and uncertain, thus inhibiting her own heavenly progress, for, according to Mormonism, a man's wives and children cannot rise beyond his station in heaven. Since, as Joseph Smith had said, "No man is saved any faster than he saves himself," Grandpa most certainly could not be counted on to save his wives either surely or speedily, for he may not have saved himself!

• Moreover, she alleged, her last husband would surely become a god sooner than Grandpa. According to her, he was a much nobler, kinder, more obedient and diligent Mormon elder. Also, since he had been privileged to live longer on earth than Grandpa, he had gotten more work done and thereby had earned a higher exaltation.

• And finally, if she perchance should be her last husband's first wife in heaven, she then would be the ruling queen instead of a subservient one.

Therefore, for these reasons and various others, she pled that the Mormon priesthood powers of binding and sealing be loosed and she be greatly blessed and eternally benefited by a switch in heavenly husbands.

We understand that after lengthy investigation and due deliberation, the temple authorities denied his widow's plea for divorce. They reasoned that: "It is unlawful and wrong to rob the dead." The case was dismissed by the Mormon hierarchy, but it was never dismissed by Mama and her brothers and sisters.[1]

POLYGAMISTS ARE VIRILE

In addition to material and spiritual blessings and eventual exaltation to godhood, Mormon men were promised that polygamous temple marriages would also bring physical rejuvenation and youthful vigor. Apostle Heber C. Kimball, on the very auspicious occasion of the twenty-seventh anniversary of the founding of the Mormon Church, made these astounding declarations. From the

Mormon pulpit in the Bowery, Great Salt Lake City, Utah, on April 6, 1857, he preached that plurality of wives would prevent Mormon men "from getting into dotage."

He prophesied:

> I would not be afraid to promise a man who is sixty years of age, if he will take the counsel of brother Brigham and his brethren [to embrace polygamy], that he will renew his age. I have noticed that a man who has but one wife, and is inclined to that doctrine, soon begins to wither and dry up, while a man who goes into plurality [of wives] looks *fresh, young and sprightly.* Why is this? Because God loves that man, and because he honours His work and word. Some of you may not believe this; but I not only believe it—I also know it. For a man of God to be confined to one woman is small business; for it is as much as we can do now to keep under the burdens we have to carry, and I do not know what we should do if we had only one wife apiece.

Heber C. Kimball
Journal of Discourses
Volume 5, Page 22

Surely his polygamous peers who also had to "keep up" under the same "burdens" must have sympathized with and succored this surfeited saint. For he (counting some of Joseph and Hyrum Smith's widows) headed a harem of thirty-seven wives. And, moreover, he anticipated that Joseph Smith would offer him "thousands more in the spirit world."[2]   Whether Brother Heber C. himself held up "fresh, young and sprightly" under his burgeoning burdens and polygamous pleasures as he had promised that all Mormon polygamy practicers would do, I must leave to your conjecture. However, in 1945, little more than a century after his demise, his offspring were estimated to be in excess of 2,500 souls. Of this multitudinous progeny, Spencer W. Kimball, current prophet, president, seer and revelator of the Church of Jesus Christ of Latter-day Saints, is perhaps the most renowned.

NO FEMALES IN HELL

Perhaps Heber Kimball's predictions as to the availability of many wives in heaven for the devout

Mormon elder was due to the speculation that God is reserving *all* females as wives for Mormons and that no woman would go to hell. For example, Brigham propounded:

> Man is the Lord of this earth, not woman. It is frequently told you that all creatures of God, except man, will abide and honour the law under which they are placed. The vegetable, mineral and animal kingdoms, except man, will abide the law by which they were made, and will be prepared to dwell on the new earth, in the midst of the new heavens . . .
>
> I doubt whether it can be found, from the revelations that are given and the facts as they exist, *that there is a female in all the regions of hell.* We are not complained of not having more wives than one. I don't begin to have as many as I shall have by and by, nor you either, if you are faithful."

Brigham Young
Journal of Discourses
Volume 8, Page 222

No official "gueṣstimate" has ever been made as to the number of God's wives. But if it is as Mormons assert, that it takes nine months in heaven for each of God's wives to bear a spirit-child, and if over three thousand babies are born on this earth every minute, the number of God's wives would not only be an astronomical figure, but I venture to say a ludicrous one. Remember, Solomon had 700 wives and surely The God of Mormonism would have to have more!

Once again the prophets of Mormonism "revelated" Mormonism into a corner with their injudicious invention that for every child born on this earth God has had to have a physical sexual relationship with one of his goddesses. In deifying man and humanizing God, Mormon leaders have tragically misled their followers.

They have also humiliated them. A fine young Mormon woman in a neighboring state, who had heard me testify of how Jesus had delivered me from sin and from Mormonism, called to ask that I please not divulge any more Mormon secrets. She said, "For, I am ashamed to go back to work and face my fellow employees and their questions."

I replied, "But you should not believe anything of which you are ashamed. God does not have many wives. He does

THE CRISIS OF A LIFE—ENTERING INTO POLYGAMY.

not have nor need even one wife."

"Oh, but He does," she exclaimed. "God has many wives. For in heaven, God is ruled by all the same laws that we are, natural, physical and spiritual, and therefore in heaven it takes nine months to have a baby. It is necessary for God to have many, many wives. But, I do wish that you would go on back to Arizona and not be telling our Mormon secrets. These people around here have need of the milk of the word, and you are giving them the strong meat of the gospel."

I explained, "My aim is not to be entertaining, facetious, vulgar or uncharitable, but to do my duty as a Christian. It is high time someone had the courage to speak forthrightly in order to bring to light the secrets of Mormonism. To divulge basic, glossed-over doctrines for the sake of my Mormon people, that they might face facts and think through Mormonism's ungodly doctrines." I then asked, "Have you heard your local Stake President Peter Smith's discourse on how God made Adam and Eve?"

"Yes," she said.

"Do you agree with Elder Smith's bluntly put assertion that when God said 'Let us make man' he was talking to one of his wives?"

"I'd rather not say," she then hedged.

"Not only did your missionary say that God was talking to one of his wives, he said also that 'God and one of his wives lay down together in the Garden of Eden on one of the other planets and made Adam after God's own image. When it came time to make Eve, God and wife again lay down together in the Garden and created Eve. Adam was made in God's image and Eve was made in the image of God's wife.' Is that what you believe?"

"That's what I believe," she said, "but it's none of your business or anyone else's!"

These teachings were heartily endorsed by that Mormon lady and perhaps by many others who publicly deny their *existence*. They are in strict accordance with Mormon doctrines, the enactment of the creation story in the secret temple rituals and Mormonism's doctrine of Adam's "sin," which to Mormons is no sin but a blessing. More than ample proof for these contentions may be found in many Mormon books currently in use.

ABRAHAM'S RIGHTEOUSNESS

The Church of Jesus Christ of Latter-day Saints openly promoted plurality of wives until the United States Government sent federal troops and civil authorities into Utah to enforce the federal law prohibiting polygamy. After being forced at that time to publicly disclaim polygamy and sign oaths never again to practice it, Mormon officials and their followers secretly continued to live with their many wives.

However, the commandment on polygamy, an integral part of the Mormon religion, is still printed in every edition of their *Doctrine and Covenants*. Therein Mormons are given the essentials for the attainment of the status of godhood which Joseph Smith and his followers are to enter into:

> ...And if ye abide not that covenant [polygamous temple marriages], then are ye damned; for no one can reject this covenant and be permitted to enter into my glory...and I have appointed unto my servant Joseph Smith to hold this power in the last days...*Abraham received concubines and they bore him children; and it was accounted unto him for righteousness*...as Isaac also and Jacob...they have entered into their exaltation, according to the promises, and sit upon thrones, and are not angels but are gods."
>
> *Doctrine and Covenants*
Section 132:4,7,37

Even a casual, once-over-lightly reading of pertinent Bible passages would have informed Joseph Smith, Brigham Young, my great-grandfather Lee and all Mormons that Abraham's *faith* was accounted unto him for righteousness, and *not* Abraham's having received concubines who bore him children. The Bible says:

> Abraham believed God and it was counted unto him for righteousness .... To him that worketh not but believeth on him that justifieth the ungodly, his *faith* is counted for righteousness.
>
> Romans 4:3,5

In the third chapter of Galatians, Paul asks who had put an evil spell on the foolish Galatians to turn them from their faith in Christ back to the law of works. He therein again vows that "Abraham believed God, and it was accounted to him for righteousness...no man is justified by the law in the sight of God." Most especially not by any "law" of polygamy, which Abraham foolishly and sinfully entered into at *Sarah's* insistence, not at the command of God, as Mormonism would have us believe. Polygamy, then and now, brings sorrow and tragedy, not happiness and exaltation. The Mormons of today do not understand that only one—the Seed or Child of Abraham's lineage, Jesus Christ—could fulfill God's everlasting covenant that: "In thee [Abraham] shall all the nations be blessed." (Galatians 3:8) This true, everlasting covenant was promised on faith and not on law and works, nor on plurality of wives as found in Joseph Smith's eternal marriage covenant. God's covenant was made to Abraham and to his one descendant. The Bible does not say his *descendants*—meaning many people. It says "And to thy seed, which is Christ." (Galatians 3:16)

Over and over Paul and all true prophets have reiterated that the birth of the one Seed, Christ Jesus (and not "seeds, as of many"), was the fulfillment of God's covenant or promise. By grace (God's free, unmerited favor) through faith in Christ's precious blood any person can receive full and complete pardon for all his sins, past, present and future—even the vile sin of supplanting the holy gospel truth of the blood of the Lamb with Joseph Smith's repetitious polygamous teachings that:

> He that abideth not this law [of polygamy] can in no wise enter into my glory, but shall be damned saith the Lord ...Go ye, therefore and do the works of Abraham, enter ye into my law [of polygamy] and ye shall be saved...Abraham received concubines and they bore him children; and it was accounted unto him for righteousness.
>
> *Doctrine and Covenants*
> Section 132:27,32,37

JESUS CHRIST A POLYGAMIST

A natural outgrowth of Joseph Smith's so-called

revelation that Abraham, Moses, David, Solomon and others had become gods because they received many wives and concubines was the teaching that Jesus Christ had to be a polygamist to become a god.

Apostle Orson Hyde made it plain when he said:

> It is true that the people of Utah believe in and practice polygamy. Not because our natural desires lead us into that condition and state of life but because our God hath commanded it. Even the wisest and best men—men after God's own heart, entered the most deeply into this practice. Nor was this practice limited to the days of the Old Testament.

> It will be borne in mind that once on a time, there was a marriage in Cana of Galilee; and on a careful reading of that transaction, it will be discovered that *no less a person than Jesus Christ* was married on that occasion. If He was never married, his intimacy with Mary and Martha and the other Mary also whom Jesus loved, must have been highly unbecoming and improper to say the best of it.

> I will venture to say that if Jesus Christ were now to pass through the most pious countries in Christendom, with a train of women such as used to follow him, fondling about him, combing his hair, anointing him with precious ointment, washing his feet with tears, and wiping them with the hair of their heads and unmarried or even married, he would have been mobbed, tarred and feathered and rode out of town, not on an ass, but on a rail.

> What did the old prophet mean when he said (speaking of Christ) "He shall see his seed, prolong his days, etc."? Did Jesus consider it necessary to fulfill every righteous command or requirement of his Father? He most certainly did . . . Did he multiply, and did he see his seed? Did he honor his Father's law by complying with it, or did he not? Others may do as they like, but I will not charge our Saviour with neglect or transgression in this or any other duty . . .

> How much so-ever of holy horror this doctrine may excite in a person not impregnated with the blood of Christ, and whose minds are consequently dark and benighted, it may excite still more when they are told that *if none of the natural blood of Christ flows in their veins, they are not the chosen or elect of God.* Object not, therefore too strongly against the marriage of Christ but remember that in the last days, secret and hidden things must come to light, and that your life also (which is in the

blood) is hid with Christ in God.

Orson Hyde
Journal of Discourses
Volume 4, Page 259-260

The primacy of polygamy in the minds of Mormonism's leadership is evidenced by the fact that the doctrine of polygamy found its way into nearly every Mormon message. Even when speaking on "Uniformity" Elder Jedediah M. Grant attempted to prove that Christ and His apostles were united by the practice of polygamy. In so doing he stooped so low as to quote Celsus, a bitter first century enemy of the Lord Jesus and of Christianity, who derided the blessed story of the virgin birth, the blood and the resurrection. Elder Grant concurred with Celsus in saying:

> ... The grand reason why the Gentiles and philosophers of his school persecuted Jesus Christ was, because he had so many wives. There were Elizabeth, and Mary, and a host of others that followed him. After Jesus went from the stage of action, the apostles followed the example of their master. For instance, John the beloved disciple, writes in his second Epistle, "Unto the elect lady and her children, whom I love in the truth." Again he says, "Having many things to write unto you [or communicate] I would not write with paper and ink; but I trust to come unto you, and speak face to face, that our joy may be full." Again "The children of thy elect sister greet thee." This ancient philosopher [Celsus] says they were both John's wives. Paul says, "Mine answer to them that do examine me is this:— Have we not power to lead about a sister, a wife, as well as other apostles, and as the brethren of the Lord, and Cephas?" He, according to Celsus, had a numerous train of wives.

> The grand reason of the burst of public sentiment in ananthemas upon Christ and his disciples, casuing his cruxifiction, *was evidently based upon polygamy,* according to the testimony of the philosophers who rose in that age. A belief in the doctrine of a plurality of wives caused the persecution of Jesus and his followers. We might almost think that they (Jesus and His followers) were Mormons.

Jedediah M. Grant
Journal of Discourses
Volume 1, Pages 345-346

In promoting polygamy Mormon parents not only heap

disgrace and degradation on Jesus, his disciples and even God himself, but bring shame, embarrassment and grief to their children as well. One of the saddest, most crestfallen young men I have ever known was the son of the local Mormon bishop in a southern city where I, in giving my testimony, had stated that Mormonism teaches that the Bible is not a safe guide and that Jesus had many wives. After the service this young high school lad, an earnest, well-mannered, stalwart specimen of American youth, in a troubled voice said to me, "But Mrs. Geer, we Mormons do believe the Bible to be true."

"Son, all that I have told you about Mormon beliefs is true," I said to him as gently and persuasively as I could. I knew from experience the troubled awakening of his heart as he, perhaps for the first time in his life, had heard that Jesus alone can save. I know that he, as I had once done, was attempting to quell rising doubts and substantiate his faith in Mormonism. Gently I pressed upon his heart his need to implicitly trust God's Word.

"To really believe the Bible to be true is to accept every word of it, not callously believing that it is partly true and partly false. You must believe with all your heart that it is God's entire word—entirely true. Just this morning God led me to underline in red these verses of the Book of Mormon that destroy faith in the Holy Bible. Here, read them with me:

> They have taken away from the gospel of the Lamb many parts which are plain and most precious; and also many covenants of the Lord have they taken away... because of the many plain and precious things which have been taken out of the book [Bible], an exceeding great many do stumble, yea insomuch that Satan hath great power over them.
>
> *Book of Mormon*
> I Nephi 13:26,29

"Maybe you do not know," I continued, "that it is the Book of Mormon, and not the Bible, that has been changed. Mormon church authorities have added and deleted thousands of words in the Book of Mormon. Some of them completely reverse the meaning of the original 1830 version. Futhermore, when Joseph Smith attempted to correct the King James version, which he claimed to be untrue because of alleged mistranslations, he added over 12,000 words which are not in the King James version or supported by any ancient manuscripts. These additions, which reverse the meaning and change the message of the Bible, are dangerous and damning. Even though the Mormon Church has Joseph Smith's "corrected" Bible known as the *Inspired Version* of the Bible, you Mormons still use the King James version. Why, I wonder, do Mormons not use their prophet-corrected Bible?"

Since my new-found, questioning Mormon friend had never even heard of Joseph Smith's *Inspired Version* of the Holy Scriptures, he changed the subject.

"But Mrs. Geer," he pathetically, almost pleadingly, said, "we don't believe that Jesus was married."

"I know how bewildered you feel," I said, "for I spent thirty years in the Church of Jesus Christ of Latter-day Saints and was never allowed to know of the Mormon belief that Jesus was married to many wives. Your daddy believes that Jesus was a polygamist. He and the Mormon church have dealt treacherously with you in making you a Mormon while withholding from you this and many other secret doctrines. You have a right to know all of Mormonism. You go home and ask your daddy forthrightly about Mormonism's teachings about Jesus and His wives."

That very night that sad, misled lad came again to hear me sing and testify of Jesus' power to save and set free. I both felt and saw the earnestness mirrored in his eyes as he listened again to my testimony of what Jesus means to me and what He wants to mean to my Mormon people.

After the service he said to me, very gently and oh, so sadly, "Mrs. Geer, my dad said that we do believe that Jesus was a married man with many wives but that Jesus could not have said 'It is finished' until he had seen his own natural born children or seed."

May God bless that young Mormon lad and all Mormons everywhere with the heartfelt knowledge and peace that Jesus gives when he comes into the heart to whisper, "It is finished."

POLYGAMY IN LOW LIFE:—THE POOR MAN'S FAMILY.

POLYGAMY IN HIGH LIFE:—THE "PROPHET'S" MANSION.

May He make me ever more grateful that Christ has finished the work begun by the Holy Spirit's convicting power in my heart. How thankful I am that my salvation is completed and securely sealed for eternity by He who died that I might live.

POLYGAMY IS STILL VALID

Polygamy and Mormonism can *never* be divorced. Polygamy cannot be forsaken, for it is the chief cornerstone, the very foundation of the Latter-day Saint's eternal progression. "Without it [polygamy] man would come to a complete stop," declared President Joseph F. Smith, in his funeral eulogy for Elder William Clayton. Mr. Clayton was highly extolled for having... been, as Joseph Smith's scribe, the first to write the prophet's 1843 revelation on polygamy. Being of such prime importance, the revelation on polygamy and marriage for eternity received greater laudation than did the deceased amanuensis. "Without the knowledge contained in that revelation," Joseph F. Smith said:

> ... we never could consummate the object of our mission to this earth, we never could fulfill the purposes of God in this estate ... this doctrine *of the eternal union of husband and wife and of plural marriage, is one of the most important doctrines ever revealed to man in any age of the world.* Without it man would come to a full stop; without it we never could be exalted to associate with and BECOME GODS neither could we attain to the power of eternal increase or the blessings pronounced upon Abraham, Isaac and Jacob, the fathers of the faithful.
>
> Joseph F. Smith
> *Journal of Discourses*
> Volume 21, Pages 9-10

Noteworthy of our interest and concern is this Mormon leader's assertion that *without* eternal and plural marriage Mormon men could not procreate children in heaven and thereby become gods nor associate with other gods. However, our major concern should be that in this distortion of gospel truth Mormonism bypasses the atoning blood of Jesus Christ, without which man will not only "come to a full stop," as President Joseph F. Smith suggested, but will be plunged into hell! Without His precious blood's atoning we could never be saved from sin, never associate with God nor have the privilege of exalting and honoring Him. Ever and ever I will be humbly grateful "just" to be an *adopted child* of God by His grace through faith in Jesus Christ. This is the consummation, the object of our "mission" on this earth, the fulfillment of God's purpose for our lives, the highest and holiest calling of all men—just to be a lowly sinner saved by grace.

It is the Mormon *men* who rejoice that:

> Each God through his wife or wives raises up a numerous family of sons and daughters; indeed, there will be no end to the increase of his own children: for each father and mother will be in condition to multiply forever and ever.

Orson Pratt
The Seer, Page 37

However, some Mormon *women* prefer to renege on the celestial baby business of multiplying forever and ever. They do not look forward to being big as a barrel bearing and tending babies eternally. Even though childbirth up there is supposed to be painless and pleasurable, I can't help thinking that the gestation period would still play havoc with a heavenly girlish figure!

Whereas the Mormon female's future lot in heaven seems somewhat dreary, her polygamist partner looks forward to heavenly pleasures and blessings. For him polygamy promises plural pleasures—not ponderous perpetual pregnancies.

Latter-day Saints still hope, and intend to openly practice polygamy even though the Church of Jesus Christ of Latter-day Saints was forced to outwardly abandon this tenet. The belief still persists that God will soon re-institute polygamy by forcing the United States Government to endorse Mormonism's plurality of wives and to allow its practice. Until this prophesied time, God supposedly will continue to severely chastise America for forcing the Mormon church and her authorities to forsake this "holy principle of the gospel."

In the meantime, some Mormon elders, knowing they will

be excommunicated if caught by the civil authorities and exposed, marry numerous wives and "live their religion" on the sly. Others are married and sealed in Mormon temples for eternity to many women, both living and dead, expecting to claim their numerous brides on the resurrection morning.

FOOTNOTES

1. Young, Brigham, *Journal of Discourses,* Vol. 11, page 269.
2. Kimball, Heber. C., *Journal of Discourses,* Vol. 4, page 209.
3. From new information, I now understand that Grandpa's widow eventually was granted the petitioned divorce. But only after she had researched geneology records and discovered the name of a female who had not already been claimed by, married and sealed for eternity to another Mormon elder. Grandpa's widow, Sarah, then was baptized and received the gift of the Holy Ghost by the laying on of hands of the temple priesthood authorities in behalf of the deceased Hagar (not their real names). And thus even though Hagar may have been dead thousands of years, she was assertedly born again—born of the water, born of the Spirit—and became a Mormon.

   Determinedly, my step-grandmother, Sarah, underwent the required temple ordinances and endowments in the stead of the dead, which included the washing, anointing and blessing of her own body in behalf of Hagar's body; the donning of holy temple (under)garments and bridal gown, wedding veil and fig leaf apron; the repeating and the giving of various oaths, covenants and the penalties if these vows were broken; plus the handclasps and tokens everyone (including the deceased Hagar) must be able to give to Joseph Smith when they, according to Brigham Young, seek Joseph Smith's "certificate...as a passport into the mansions where God and Christ are...". (See this book, page 80.)

   Then Sarah, on behalf of Hagar, the soon-to-be replacement in my grandpa's heavenly harem, was invited by the temple veil worker to "enter through the veil" into the celestial room of the temple, which betokens the highest of the three Mormon kingdoms of heaven where God the Father and His thousands of wives assertedly cohabit.

   Grandpa's now temple-divorced widow and her current Mormon husband then reportedly "acted as proxies" for Hagar and Grandpa and were vicariously married and sealed for eternity in behalf of and in the stead of the deceased couple. Thus the living became "saviours of our dear departed dead" and Sarah was freed from Grandpa so she could "marry for eternity" another eternal husband.

   The brand-new divorcee and her civilly married husband then went through the same temple marriage ceremonies on their own behalf to be "married and sealed for eternity" to each other. Thus, my erstwhile eternal step-grandmother became the "eternal bride" of another "eternal bridegroom," thereby becoming someone else's eternal step-grandmother. I trust her new step-grandchildren loved and honored her as I still do.

MOUNTAIN MEADOW MASSACRE—EMIGRANTS KILLED BY MORMONS AND INDIANS.

Chapter Eight

HOLY MURDER

Unless you have just returned from an extended trip to the moon, you must be well aware of the horrible events that took place in Jonestown, Guyana. In that place, in the fall of 1978, the world saw the dramatic results of the cultic mentality—almost a thousand men, women and children lay dead at the command of their leader. The American people and the world at large were shocked; how could such a thing happen? How could such a *seemingly* upright organization (the People's Temple) with all of its "godly" rhetoric, high moral standards, as well as social action, anti-crime, drug abuse counseling and similar programs be responsible for such a heinous crime against God and man? Second Corinthians, Chapter 11 gives an answer:

> For such are false apostles, deceitful workers, transforming themselves into the apostles of Christ. And no marvel; for Satan himself is transformed into an angel of light. Therefore it is no great thing if his ministers also be transformed as the ministers of righteousness; whose end shall be according to their works.
>
> II Corinthians 11:13-15

We have further guidance from Jesus Himself in Matthew 7:15-20, where He warns us about false prophets and tells us clearly to "know them by their fruits." But the People's Temple did have "good fruits," with all their godly talk and good living, didn't they? It is obvious that that was not the fruit to check!! Remember that Paul told us that these "deceitful workers" *transform themselves into ministers of righteousness for the very purpose of deception.*

The important fruit to examine is the fruit of the prophet himself—what does he say about God, Jesus Christ, salvation, etc? It is the *fruit of doctrine* that will most clearly identify the false prophets from the true prophets, not the seemingly "good" appearances of lifestyles and rhetoric.

Jim Jones was a false prophet who led his people down to their destruction, physically, and more importantly, spiritually. We are now finding out that there were many practice runs for the mass suicide, couched in terms like "loyalty" and "righteousness." This event did not happen overnight; the groundwork was very carefully laid beforehand. The doctrine was preached by the prophet and received by the people.

As you have already guessed, I see a parallel between what happened at Jonestown and some of the doctrine espoused by the early leadership of Mormonism, or I wouldn't have even mentioned it. There is such a parallel in the Mormon doctrine commonly known as individual "Blood Atonement." On one hand, I truly thank God that it is not nearly as well known as it was in the days of Brigham Young, but I also pray to God that more and more of my deceived Mormon people will discover that it was actively promoted and practiced and that they will see for themselves that Brigham Young and his successors are false prophets and will withdraw from the soul-destroying system of false doctrine.

Just as we all know for a certainty that Jim Jones was and is forever a false prophet for preaching his doctrine, so also are Joseph Smith and Brigham Young false prophets because of their doctrines. Could we who know firsthand the horrors of Jonestown imagine that Jim Jones could ever be considered a true prophet by anyone other than the most horribly deceived of his remaining followers? But what if the People's Temple survived another hundred years, and his successors were successful in a cover-up of the events surrounding Jim Jones and of watering down some of his more horrible teachings? Is it believable that the world of a hundred years from now could extol Jim Jones as a great leader, pioneer and prophet of God? You better believe that it could happen—for that is the very case with Joseph Smith and Brigham Young.

The doctrine known as individual Blood Atonement can

be simply summarized as the idea that there are some sins that the shed blood of Jesus Christ *cannot atone for*, but rather the blood of the person committing the sin must be shed to atone for that sin. Beyond the horror of killing people for their alleged sins, the really *satanic* aspect of this doctrine is that it is saying that the blood of Jesus Christ is not good enough to do the job, and that *your own blood* is in fact more important. That is an attack on my Saviour's lordship which comes right out of the pit of hell itself.

I can honestly say that I really abhor this doctrine of Blood Atonement and don't even like to talk about it, but I am obligated to you to do so—that you may examine it and judge for yourself. I want to let the leadership speak for itself, for it does nobody any good merely to lay out unsubstantiated charges concerning such things. Please keep in mind that throughout most of this book those whom I quote concerning the doctrinal issues are for the most part "General Authorities" of the Mormon church. These are the men sustained twice a year by the membership at large as being the official, authoritative representatives of God Himself.

LOVE THY NEIGHBOR TO DEATH

Let's begin with an examination of a sermon by Brigham Young where he described a rather vivid dream he had had the night before:

> Then I saw two ruffians . . . and they crept into a bed, where one of my wives and children were . . . I took my large bowie knife, that I used to wear as a bosom pin in Nauvoo, and cut one of their throats from ear to ear, saying, "Go to hell across lots." The other one said, "You dare not serve me so." I instantly sprang at him, seized him by the hair of the head, and bringing him down, cut his throat, and sent him after his comrade; then told them both, if they would behave themselves they would yet live, but if they did not, I would unjoint their necks. At this I awoke.
>
> *I say, rather than that apostates should flourish here, I will unsheath my bowie knife and conquer or die.* (Great commotion in the Congregation, and a simultaneous burst of feeling, assenting to the declaration.) Now you, nasty

apostates, clear out, or judgment will be laid to the line and righteousness to the plummet. (Voices, generally, "go it, go it.") *If you say it is right, raise your hands. (All hands up.)* Let us call upon the Lord to assist us in this, and every good work.

Brigham Young
Journal of Discourses
Volume 1, Page 83

In another of his sermons in the *Journal of Discourses,* we discover Brigham Young's "love thy neighbor" sentiments: "When will we love our neighbors as ourselves?" the prophet Brigham demanded of his Latter-day Saint congregation.

. . . Suppose that he [our neighbor] is overtaken in a gross fault, that he has committed a sin that he knows will deprive him of that exaltation which he desires, and that he cannot attain to it without the shedding of his blood, and also knows that by having his blood shed he will atone for that sin, and be saved and exalted with the Gods, is there a man or woman in this house [Salt Lake City Tabernacle] but what would say, "shed my blood that I may be saved and exalted with the gods."

All mankind love themselves, and let these principles be known by an individual, and he would be glad to have his blood shed. That would be loving themselves, even unto an eternal exaltation. Will you love your brothers or sisters likewise, when they have committed a sin that cannot be atoned for without the shedding of their blood? *Will you love that man or woman well enough to shed their blood? . . .*

I could refer you to plenty of instances where men have been righteously slain in order to atone for their sins. I have seen scores and hundreds of people for whom there would have been a chance . . . if their lives had been taken and their blood spilled on the ground as a smoking incense to the Almighty, but who are now angels to the devil . . . I have known a great many men who have left this Church for whom there is no chance whatever for exaltation, but if their blood had been spilled, it would have been better for them. The wickedness and ignorance of the nations forbid this principle being in full force, but the time will come when the law of God will be in full force.

This is loving our neighbor as ourselves; if he needs help, help him and if he wants salvation and it is necessary to spill his blood on the earth in order that he may be saved, spill it. Any of you who understand the

principles of eternity, if you have sinned a sin requiring
the shedding of blood, except the sin unto death, would not
be satisfied nor rest until your blood should be spilled,
that you might gain that salvation you desire. That is the
way to love mankind.

Now, brethern and sisters, will you live your religion?
How many hundreds of times have I asked you that
question? Will the Latter-day Saints live their religion?...
I am happy to think that the people called Latter-day
Saints are striving now to obtain the spirit of their calling
and religion ... Now let us begin, like children, and walk in
the straight and narrow path, *live our religion, and honor
our God.*

Brigham Young
Journal of Discourses
Volume 4, Pages 219-220

Such a sermon promoting human sacrifice for the sin of
failing to "live your religion" leaves me cold and
frightened. But not so the majority of Brigham Young's
attentive followers for they, incensed to feverish zeal by
this and countless other Mormon Blood Atonement
sermons, straightway, according to Grandpa John D. Lee,
increased in these Mormon graces of "loving your neighbor
to death" as Brigham Young preached that they should do.
Fanatically they cold-bloodedly practiced the sacrifice of
human life as an "atonement" for the person's sins of
apostasy from the Mormon church, forsaking or revealing
temple oaths and secrets, marrying a Negro, committing
adultery, etc.

Heretofore Blood Atonement had been *secretly* promoted
and practiced in Mormon communities in Missouri and
Illinois. Now, isolated in the wide open spaces of the
Territory of Utah, the leading Mormons dared to publicly
preach such inflammatory Blood Atonement sermons as
this one by Jedediah M. Grant, Brigham Young's Second
Counselor in the church presidency. In rebuking the Latter-
day Saints for iniquity on September 21, 1856, Grant
advised the Latter-day Saints to have their blood shed to
atone for their sins.

Some have received the priesthood and a knowledge of
the things of God [an obvious reference to the temple
endowment], and still they dishonor the cause of truth,
commit adultery, and every other abomination beneath
the heavens.

The same characters will get drunk and wallow in the mire and filth, and yet call themselves Saints and seem to glory in their conduct.

... my prayer is that God's indignation may rest upon them, and that He will curse them from the crown of their head to the soles of their feet.

I say there are men and women that I would advise to go to the President [Brigham Young] immediately and ask him to appoint a committee to attend to their case; and then let a place be selected, and *let that committee shed their blood.*

We have those amongst us that are full of all manner of abominations, those who need to have their blood shed, for water [a reference to baptism] will not do, their sins are too deep a dye.

You may think that I am not teaching you Bible doctrine, but what says the Apostle Paul? I would ask how many [temple] covenant breakers there are in the city and in this kingdom. I believe that there are a great many; and if they are [temple] covenant breakers we need a place *where we can shed their blood.*

We have been trying long enough with this people, and I go in for letting the sword of the Almighty be unsheathed not only in word, but in deed.

Brethren and sisters, we want you to repent and forsake your sins. And you who have committed sins that cannot be forgiven through baptism, *let your blood be shed,* and let the smoke ascend, that the incense thereof may come up before God as an atonement for your sins, and that the sinners in Zion may be afraid.

Jedediah Grant
Journal of Discourses
Volume 4, pages 49-51

Such preaching provoked "covenant breakers" to fanatical frenzies, primed and anxiously ready to fulfill their vows, so zealously and fervently contracted in Mormon temple rites. In the early versions of the ceremonies, they raised their hands "to the square" and solemnly vowed to have their throats slit from ear to ear, their tongues drawn out by the roots, their hearts and lungs pierced through, their stomachs ripped open, their entrails fed to the beasts of the field and their bones broken if they revealed the temple secrets or were untrue to their temple covenants. As a constant reminder of these vows they wore the holy temple garments with the sacred "marks" over the breast, the stomach and the knee.

Such far out, wild excesses as these are difficult to harmonize with the seeming sedateness of today's Mormonism. That the Church of Jesus Christ of Latter-day Saints once believed in and participated in such extremes is little known—even by Mormons themselves.

Do some Mormons still believe in having their blood shed to atone for their sins? Yes, whenever possible. The recent execution of a Mormon man named Gilmore by a Utah firing squad bears this out. He chose the firing squad rather than hanging so that his blood could be shed.

I do know that many early Mormons did live their religion to the full extent—*they literally died for it!* Many times I have heard my grandmother and her sister Nellie (daughters of John D. Lee) recount the horrors of seeing five men "atoned" one Sunday afternoon in the public square. These "covenant breakers," Grandma said, had requested the Mormon priesthood to "attend to their case" as Elder Jedediah Grant had advised. Calmly and deliberately they had, according to Grandma and Nellie, laid their necks across a long cottonwood log. Then the "Avenging Angels" or "Danites" had dutifully cut their throats to shed their blood and help save their souls. My own great-grandfather Lee may have been one of these Angels or Danites. The five men were then unceremoniously dumped in one long grave, which the victims themselves had dug. I well understood Grandma's and Nellie's avowal that those deaths had for years served as warnings of the fate of "covenant breakers." Even now, long, icy fingers of horror grip my soul as they first did when I heard the story so long ago.

Whether the story is true in all its details, I cannot prove. I do know that Grandma and Nellie told it for the truth. In addition, their report is in full accord with the Mormon doctrine of Blood Atonement, the Latter-day Saint history and the temperament of those times. Many historians, both Mormon and non-Mormon, have attested to this. For instance, Brigham Young stated: "I could refer you to plenty of instances where men have been righteously slain, in order to atone for their sins."[1] Mormon historian Juanita Brooks cites great-grandfather John D. Lee's statement that a man's "life was endangered by a public announcement that he had been cut off from the Church."[2] She tells of a Mormon couple of Grandpa's acquaintance who, because they had engaged in pre-marital sex, ". . . offered their lives to pay the debt . . . wanted to go to Brigham, confess and *have their heads taken off.*"[3]

Those were the days of the fanatical, so-called Mormon "reformation," days in which Mormon authorities deliberately and continuously fanned to a white-hot inferno the sentiments of the "Saints." Torrents of bloodshedding sermons spewed forth from Mormon pulpits until Blood Atonement possessed the minds and wills of Brigham Young's devoted followers. Whatever their Mormon prophet spoke must be believed and obeyed "as though God Himself spoke." (See *Doctrines & Covenants* 1:38) Thus, on the same day that Jedediah Grant preached his blood-curdling sermon that I quoted earlier in this chapter, the prophet Brigham said:

> There are sins that men commit for which they cannot receive forgiveness in this world, or in that which is to come, and if they had their eyes open to see their true condition, they would be perfectly willing to *have their blood spilt* upon the ground, that the smoke thereof might ascend to heaven as an offering for their sins; and the smoking incense would atone for their sins, whereas, if such is not the case, they will stick to them and remain upon them in the spirit world.
>
> I know, when you hear my brethren telling about cutting people off from the earth [this means to kill them] that you consider it is strong doctrine, but it is to save them, not to destroy them.
>
> . . . And furthermore, I know that there are transgressors, who, if they knew themselves, and the only condition upon which they can obtain forgiveness, *would beg of their brethren to shed their blood,* that the smoke thereof might ascend to God as an offering to appease the wrath that is kindled against them, and that the law might have its course. I will say further: *I have had men come to me and offer their lives to atone for their sins.*
>
> It is true that the blood of the Son of God was shed for sins through the fall and those committed by men. *Yet men can commit sins which it can never remit . . . they must be atoned for by the blood of the man.* That is the reason why men talk to you as they do from this stand; they

understand the doctrine and throw out a *few words* about
it. You have been taught that doctrine, but you do not
_ understand it.

Brigham Young
Journal of Discourses
Volume 4, Pages 53-54.

Won't you, Mormon reader, as Brother Brigham was wont
to say so often, "Pause before you make light of these
sayings or treat them with indifference"? *Stop, look and
listen!* Think for yourselves. Do not follow the leading of
this 19th century Jim Jones, who under the guise of
Christianity was so callous as to lead his followers into
human sacrifice! This is a doctrine far more savage and
ungodly than that of the misled heathen head-hunters.
Whereas their victims were sacrificed in ignorance and
superstition, Brigham Young's priestly puppets died as
pawns of their prophet's despotic arrogance and greed for
power.

A FIRSTHAND EXAMPLE

In describing the power of the Mormon priesthood
Grandpa John D. Lee tells of a case he was involved in:

> At Parowan, in 1855 or 1856, there was a case that for
> awhile shook my faith in the Church, but I soon got over it
> and was like the others, satisfied that all was done for the
> glory of God, but that I was so sinful that I could not
> understand it.
>
> There was a man living there by the name of Robert
> Gillespie. He was a member of the Church, had one wife,
> and owned a fine property. Gillespie wanted to be sealed to
> his sister-in-law, but for some reason his request was
> denied. He had known of others obtaining wives by
> committing adultery first and then being sealed to avoid a
> scandal. So he tried it, and then went to apostle George A.
> Smith, and again asked to be sealed to the woman; but
> George A. [Smith] had a religious fit on him, or something
> else, so he refused to seal him or let him be sealed, giving
> as his reason for refusing that Gillespie had exercised the
> rights of sealing without first obtaining orders to do so. A
> warrant was issued and Gillespie arrested and placed
> under guard, he was also sued in the Probate Court, before
> James Lewis, Probate Judge, and a heavy judgment was
> rendered against him and all his property was sold to pay

the fine and costs. The money was put into the Church fund and Gillespie was broken up entirely and forced to leave the Territory in a destitute condition.

Many such cases came under my observation. I have known the Church to act in this way and break up and destroy many, very many men. The Church was then, and in that locality, supreme. None could safely defy or disobey it. The Church authorities used the laws of the land, the laws of the Church, and Danites and Angels *(terms for the Mormon secret police)* to enforce their orders, and rid the country of those who were distasteful to the leaders. And I say as a fact that there was no escape for any one that the leaders of the Church in Southern Utah selected as a victim.

In 1854 (I think that was the year) there was a young man, a Gentile, working in Parowan. He was quiet and orderly, but was courting some of the girls. He was notified to quit, and let the girls alone, but he kept going to see some of them. This was contrary to orders. No Gentile was at that time allowed to keep company with or visit any Mormon girl or woman. The authorities decided to have the young man killed, so they called two of Bishop Dames' Destroying Angels, Barney Carter and old man Gould, and told them to take that cursed young Gentile "over the rim of the basin." That was a term used by the people when they killed a person.

The Destroying Angels made some excuse to induce the young man to go with them on an excursion, and when they got close to Shirts' Mill, near Harmony, they killed him and left his body in the brush.

The Indians found the body, and reported the facts to me afterwards. I was not at home that night, but Carter and Gould went to my house and stayed all night. Rachel asked them where they had been. They told her they had been on a mission to take a young man, a Gentile, over the rim of the basin, and Carter showed her his sword, which was all bloody, and said he used that to help the Gentile over the edge. Rachel knew what they meant when they spoke of sending him over the rim of the basin. It was at that time a common thing to see parties going out of Cedar City and Harmony with suspected Gentiles to send them over the rim of the basin, and the Gentiles were always killed.

This practice was supported by all the people, and everything of that kind was done by orders from the Council or by orders from some of the Priesthood. When a Danite or a Destroying Angel was placed on a man's track, that man died, certain, unless some providential act saved him, as in Tobin's case; he was saved because the Angels believed he was dead.

The Mormons nearly all, and I think every one of them in Utah, previous to the massacre at Mountain Meadows, believed in blood atonement. It was taught by the leaders and believed by the people that the Priesthood was inspired and could not give a wrong order. It was the belief of all that I ever heard talk of these things—and I have been with the Church since the dark days in Jackson County Missouri—that the authority that ordered a murder committed, was the only responsible party, that the man who did the killing was only an instrument, working by command of a superior, and hence could have no ill will against the person killed, but was only acting by authority and committed no wrong. In other words, if Brigham Young or any of his apostles, or any Priesthood, gave an order to a man, the act was the act of the one giving the order, and the man doing the act was only an instrument of the person commanding—just as much of an instrument as the knife that was used to cut the throat of the victim. This being the belief of all good Mormons, it is easily understood why the orders of the Priesthood were so blindly obeyed by the people."

> John D. Lee
> *Mormonism Unveiled*
> Pages 274-75, 278-80

Grandpa Lee related how another Mormon, William Laney, had befriended and aided a member of the ill-fated Fancher wagon train prior to its being destroyed at Mountain Meadows. He was therefore charged by the leading Mormon men:

... with being unfaithful to his obligations. They said he had supported the enemies of the Mormon Church and given aid and comfort to one whose hands were still red with the blood of the Prophets. A few nights after that the Destroying Angels, who were doing the bidding of Bishop Dame,[4] were ordered to kill William Laney *to save him from his sins* he having violated his endowment oath and furnished food to a man who had been declared an outlaw by the Mormon Church. The Angels were commanded by Barney Carter, a son-in-law of William H. Dame, who now lives in Los Angeles County, California. The Angels called Laney out of the house, saying that Bishop Dame wished to see him. As Laney passed through the gate into the street, he was struck across the back of the head with a large club by Barney Carter. His skull was fractured somewhat and for many months Laney lay at the point of death, and his mind still shows the effect of the injury he then received, for his brain has never quite settled since. I have frequently talked with Laney about this matter, but as he was fully initiated into the mysteries of the Church, he knows that he will yet be killed if his life can be taken with safety, if he makes public the facts connected with the conspiracy to take his life. He is still strong in the Mormon faith, and almost believes that Dame had the right to have him killed. At the time Carter attempted to take the life of Laney, the Mormon Church was *under the blaze of the reformation, and punishment by death was the penalty for refusing to obey the orders of the priesthood.*

John D. Lee
Mormonism Unveiled
Page 281

At that time Brigham Young wielded absolute control over every living soul in the Utah Territory. His word was law. He issued his orders under the pretext that they emanated from God. Infractions of his commands constituted treason against the controlled state, the Church, and assertedly against God. Every disobedience called for a severe penalty—even the "atoning" death of the transgressor.

You might question that such despotic rule and murderous tyrannies could exist in the United States of America. Please bear in mind that in 1847 the Mormons had deliberately secluded themselves in the wilds of the Great Salt Lake basin—then owned by Mexico. In this foreign land they hoped to "live their religion" uninhibited by United States' laws, which prohibited their polygamous marriages and church/state dictatorship.

To their chagrin, the United States soon acquired these Mexican holdings, and the Latter-day Saints were *again* under the hated rule of the United States of America. But even so, there in the isolated western wilds of Utah Indian country, the Mormon hierarchy still held absolute control over every area of life.

Until about 1858 there were *no courts of law* in the entire Utah Territory other than those controlled and manipulated by the High Councils of the Mormon Church. The only state, county and city peace officers were Mormon priesthood holders, obligated to carry out without question their superior's orders.

This had been the case, also, in the Mormon city of

Nauvoo, Illinois, where Grandpa Lee, as a member of the Nauvoo police force and one of the church's Destroying Angels, helped to "atone" apostates and snooping strangers. Brigham Young's Destroying Angels were diligently

> ... on the watch, and every suspicious man was closely tracked up and no strategy neglected to find out his business. If they [the destroying angels who were also the Nauvoo police] were suspicious that any man wanted to serve a writ on His Honor, Brigham Young, they were careful never to let that man escape. Sometimes they would treat them with great kindness, and in that way decoy them to some out-of-the-way place and "save" them, as they called it. They were not only on the track of officers [Illinois state and county law officials] but all suspected characters who might come on to spy out what was going on; for instance, the consecrating of the stock of their enemies, by the Saints, and driving it in at night and butchering it, and distributing it among their friends ... If any of them was caught in a scrape, it was the duty of the rest to unite and swear him out ... Whatever the police were ordered to do they were to do and ask no questions. Whether it was right or wrong mattered not to them, they were responsible only to their leaders and they [the leaders] were amenable only to God.

> John D. Lee
Mormonism Unveiled
Pages 158-159

Grandpa Lee also relates that he knew "of several men who were put out of the way" by blood atoning them—"apostates and enemies of the Church at Nauvoo alike." He confesses that he had "been deeply steeped in fanaticism, even more than I was aware of until I felt the bitter pangs of the direful influence on me."[5]

Other "direful influences" inflicted even more "bitter pangs" when Grandpa, with thousands of other exiled Latter-day Saints, fled Nauvoo in the dead of winter (February 2, 1846). He and his company crossed the ice-covered Mississippi River bound for a "new Zion in the West." The struggles, the heartbreak, the hungers of their bleak existence is written in every line as Grandpa shares with his readers the sufferings of his numerous dependent children born to him by his first wife Agatha Ann, and the nine new wives given to him by Brigham Young during the previous year of 1845.

Grandpa's family burdens seemed almost greater than he could bear until he considered those of his Mormon leaders: Brigham Young had his seventeen wives; Heber C. Kimball had taken "many wives (thirty-two, according to some sources) and his family at this time numbered over one hundred souls."[6]

As their wives had multiplied so had their troubles. In the main, it had been the practice of plurality of wives that had caused the death of Joseph Smith. It had made outcasts of his followers who had chosen to forfeit houses and lands in the Mormon Mecca of Nauvoo that they might "live their religion" of plurality of wives in the West.

Now, as vagabonds and outcasts, some 12,000 of them were scattered across the plains of Iowa and Nebraska in makeshift tents, dug-outs and lean-tos. In frugality and leanness of body and soul they awaited the coming of spring that they might press on westward to establish another "New Zion." At the main camp, known as Winter Quarters or Misery Bottoms (where today stands the city of Florence, Nebraska), Great-grandpa Lee and his families— along with nearly one-third of the refugees—spent the remainder of the winter of 1846. Here, in spite of his multitudinous other troubles and trials, he received from Brigham on the same day three more wives.

It was here, also, that President Young had become indebted $285 to Grandpa for the presidential carriage and teams. Grandpa Lee wrote:

> I presented Brigham Young with seventeen ox teams, fully equipped, when he started out with the people from Winter Quarters to cross the plains to the new resting place of the Saints. He accepted them and said, "God bless you John." But I never received a cent for them . . . for in giving property to Brigham Young, I thought I was loaning it to the Lord.
>
> I believe that Brigham Young spoke by direction of the God of Heaven. *I would have suffered death rather than have disobeyed any command of his.* I had this feeling until he betrayed and deserted me.

John D. Lee
Mormonism Unveiled
Page 216

FIGHT FOR WIFE AND LIFE

Grandpa was not too fortunate in his affairs with other fellow "Saints." They were, he said, "constantly raising the fuss and finding fault." Grandpa soon tired of the oppressions of his Mormon brethren, most especially those of one Charles Kennedy and his attentions to Grandpa's lovely young wife, Emeline, the youngest daughter of his fifth wife, Abigail Woolsey, and sister of his first, sixth and seventh wives, Agatha Ann, Rachel A. and Andora Woolsey. Grandpa eventually soundly thrashed this romancing adversary for his interference in Grandpa's marital affairs, which were, as you can guess, already *more* than complicated. One wonders why Grandpa did not author the song "I'm My Own Grandpa." Surely he had ample inspiration and agitation.[7]

Neither his aggravations nor his victory over Emeline's suitor claimed much of Grandpa's time and energies. He had none to spare. Because he had fought for his wife he had to fight for his life. Grandpa Lee reported:

> I was at once cited to appear before the High Council, and be dealt with according to the rules of the Church for a breach of the peace and unchristian conduct . . . They [fellow Mormons] then began consecrating my property to their own use; killed my cattle, and ate them and stole nearly everything that was loose. They stole wheat from my granaries, had it ground and eat [sic] it, and bragged about it. Kennedy, by the evil influences he commanded, induced my young wife, Emeline, to leave me and go to his house, and she went with his family to Winter Quarters. That was the reason that I turned her away and refused to take her back again. She repented and wished to come back, but I would not take her again. Similar influences were brought to bear on all of my family, but without much success. Such horrid treatment was not calculated to bond me to such a people. . . . I was in great trouble, in place of friends I had found enemies. There was a great struggle in my mind to decide what I should do. I looked upon those of my family that remained true and shared my persecutions and knew that if I left the Church I could not keep and live with them; that if I left I must part with all but my first wife and children — to do so was worse than death.
>
> I finally appeared before the High Council to meet my accusers, who had formed a combination to destroy me . . . The result of that trial was that I was ordered to confess

that I had been in fault, and that I alone was to blame, and must ask the people to forgive me. If I refused, I was to be cut off from the Church. To a man in my situation it was equivalent to death to be cut off from the Church; my wives would be taken from me, my property consecrated to the Church, and I turned adrift, broken and disgraced, and *liable to suffer death at the hand of any brother of the Church who wished to take my life, either to save my soul, or for purposes of revenge.*

John D. Lee
Mormonism Unveiled
Pages 208-209

JUDAS — "KICKED UNTIL HIS GUTS GUSHED OUT"

This Mormon doctrine of Blood Atonement is still upheld by Mormon elders of my own acquaintance. They cite Old Testament practices as proof that God not only condones human sacrifice, but also commands it. On many occasions I have heard Mormon elders quote Apostle Heber C. Kimball (grandfather of current Mormon prophet, Spencer W. Kimball) that:

Judas lost that saving principle [the priesthood] and they took him and killed him. It is said in the Bible that his bowels gushed out; but *they actually kicked him until his bowels came out.*

I know the day is right at hand when men will forfeit their Priesthood and turn against us and the [Mormon Temple] covenants they have made and they will be destroyed as Judas was."

Heber C. Kimball
Journal of Discourses
Volume 6, Pages 125-126

Mormonism's Blood Atonement kept Grandpa Lee from attempting to escape from prison while awaiting trial for his part in the massacre at Mountain Meadows. He preferred to face the United States firing squad rather than to suffer death at the hands of — or perhaps rather, the feet of — his zealous Mormon brethren. Perhaps they would have dutifully dealt with him according to Apostle Kimball's sermon and "kicked him until his guts gushed out," as recently one of Grandpa Lee's elderly grandsons so graphically phrased it.

FOOTNOTES

1. Young, Brigham, *Journal of Discourses,* Vol. 4, page 220.

2. Brooks, Juanita, *John D. Lee,* page 293.

3. *Ibid.,* page 189.

4. Grandpa's superior officer in the Iron County, Utah, militia and the Mormon priesthood. It was under his orders that the Mormon elders attacked and murdered the immigrants at Mountain Meadows. See Chapter 10.

5. Lee, John D., *Mormonism Unveiled,* page 161.

6. Whitney, Orson F., *Life of Heber C. Kimball,* page 386.

7. In his book Grandpa Lee expresses his regret for not allowing Emeline to return to the only home she had ever known. Grandpa's widowed mother-in-law, Abigail Woolsey, and her tiny daughters had made their home with Grandpa ever since Rachel was five years old. As each little step-daughter reached puberty, they were given to Grandpa in marriage by the Mormon authorities. Since every woman must have a Mormon elder to claim and resurrect her, Grandpa felt obligated to marry his mother-in-law "for her soul's sake, for her salvation in the eternal state." And so, Agatha Ann, his first wife, gave her mother and sister Rachel to Grandpa in the same temple sealing services. Within the next year and a half, Grandpa married his two youngest step-daughters, Andora and her baby sister, Emeline. This made him husband to the mother and her four daughters!

Chapter Nine

THE BLOOD FLOWS IN UTAH

Great-grandfather Lee details in his book that just before the Mountain Meadows Massacre one "sinful member" was blood atoned by order of Cedar City, Utah, Bishop's Council.

... The sinful member was to be slain for the remission of his sins, it being taught by the leaders and believed by the people that the right thing to do with a sinner who did not repent and obey the [Church] Council, was to take the life of the offending party and thus save his everlasting soul. This was called "Blood Atonement."

The most deadly sin among the people was adultery, and many men were killed in Utah for that crime.

Rosmos Anderson was a Danish man who had come to Utah with his family to receive the benefits arising from an association with the Latter-day Saints. He had married a widow lady somewhat older than himself, and she had a daughter that was fully grown at the time of the [Mormon] reformation. The girl was very anxious to be sealed to her stepfather, and Anderson was equally anxious to take her for a second wife, but as she was a fine looking girl, Klingensmith [the Mormon Bishop of Cedar City] desired her to marry him, and she refused. At one of the meetings during the reformation, Anderson and his step-daughter confessed that they had committed adultery, believing when they did so that Brigham Young would allow them to marry when he learned the facts. Their confession being full, they were rebaptized and received into full membership. They were then placed under covenant that if they again committed adultery, Anderson should suffer death. Soon after this a charge was laid against Anderson before the Council, accusing him of adultery with his step-daughter. This Council was composed of Klingensmith and his two counselors; it was the Bishop's Council. Without giving Anderson any chance to defend himself or make a statement, *the Council voted that Anderson must die for violating his covenants.* Klingensmith went to Anderson and notified him that the orders were that he must die by having his throat cut, so that the running of his blood would atone for his sins. Anderson, being a firm believer in the doctrines and teachings of the Mormon Church, made no objections, but asked for half a day to prepare for death. His request was granted. His wife was ordered to prepare a suit of clean clothing in which to have her husband buried, and was informed that he was to be killed for his sins, she being directed to tell those who should enquire after her husband that he had gone to California.

Klingensmith, James Haslem, Daniel McFarland and John M. Higbee dug a grave in the field near Cedar City, and that night, about 12 o'clock, went to Anderson's house and ordered him to make ready to obey the Council. Anderson got up, dressed himself, bid his family good-bye, and without a word of remonstrance accompanied those that he believed were carrying out the will of the "Almighty God." They went to the place where the grave was prepared. Anderson knelt upon the side of the grave and prayed. Klingensmith and his company then *cut Anderson's throat from ear to ear* and held him so that his blood ran into the grave.

As soon as he was dead they dressed him in his clean clothes, threw him into the grave and buried him. Then they carried his bloody clothing back to his family, and gave them to his wife to wash, when she was again instructed to say that her husband was in California. She obeyed their orders.

No move of that kind was made at Cedar City unless it was done by order of the Council or of the High Council. I was at once informed of Anderson's death because at that time I possessed the confidence of all the people who would talk to me confidentially, and give me the particulars of all crimes committed by order of the Church. Anderson was killed just before the Mountain Meadows Massacre. The killing of Anderson was considered a *religious duty and a just act.* It was justified by all the people, for they were bound by the same [temple] covenants, and the least word of objection to thus treating the man who had broken his covenant would have brought the same fate upon the person who was so foolish as to raise his voice against any act committed by order of the Church authorities."

John D. Lee
Mormonism Unveiled
Pages 282-283

In 1958 Gustin O. Larson, Professor of Church History at Brigham Young University, related yet another incident very similar to this one of Grandpa Lee's and states that such a case is "understandable."

> To whatever extent the preaching of Blood Atonement may have influenced action, it would have been in relation to Mormon disciplinary action among its own members. In point would be the verbally reported case of a Mr. Johnson in Cedar City who was found guilty of adultery with his stepdaughter by a Bishop's Court and *sentenced to death* for atonement of his sin. According to the report of reputable eye witnesses, judgment was executed with consent of the offender who went to his unconsecrated grave in full confidence of salvation through the shedding of his blood. Such a case, however primitive, is understandable within the meaning of the doctrine and emotional extremes of the Reformation."
>
> Gustin Larson
> *Utah Historical Quarterly*
> Jan. 1958, Page 62, Footnote 39

Proof that Blood Atonement had been preached in Mormon meetings as early as 1845 is afforded by the Prophet Joseph Smith's brother, William Smith, who testified in court: "I left Nauvoo, Illinois in 1845 because *my life was in danger* if I remained there because of my objections and protests against the doctrine of Blood Atonement and other new doctrines brought into the Church."[1]

SINS REQUIRING BLOOD ATONEMENT

In this century-and-a-third (since 1845), scores of sermons promoting Blood Atonement have been preached in Mormon pulpits and dutifully recorded in Mormon publications for the indoctrination of ensuing generations. To deny that the practice of Blood Atonement has been promoted and preached by the Church of Jesus Christ of Latter-day Saints is a deliberate evasion of the truth, a ruse to shield this secret doctrine of Mormonism — such a strong one that most of today's converts would never knowingly accept it.

Nevertheless, many do *unknowingly* subscribe to it in Mormon temple services. Therein they don the holy temple garments and vow to allow their lives to be taken if they reveal any part of the temple rites or are unchaste and untrue to their temple covenants.

Proof that the twin evils of Mormonism, Blood Atonement and polygamy, are necessary pinionings for each other is found in every edition of Mormonism's special Scripture, the *Doctrine and Covenants.* Therein a purported "revelation" given through Joseph Smith the prophet at Nauvoo, Illinois, recorded July 12, 1843, commands both Blood Atonement and polygamy. Verse 26 of Section 132 states:

> Verily, verily I say unto you, if a man marry a wife according to my word, and they are sealed by the Holy Spirit of promise, according to mine appointment and he or she shall commit *any sin or transgression of the new and everlasting covenant whatever . . . they shall be destroyed in the flesh . . .*

Verses 41, 52, 54, 63 and 64 demand that for adultery, lying and impurity the temple-sealed Mormon *female* "shall be destroyed."

During the Mormon Reformation (up to 1857) both Blood Atonement and polygamy were most emphatically, distinctly and mutually taught. They are laid down in older Mormon publications as specifically as any other Latter-day Saints' doctrine. Dozens of sermons by Mormon prophets and apostles, recorded in the *Journal of Discourses,* declare that any person guilty of the sins of stealing, murder, not receiving the Mormon Gospel, marriage to an African, and apostasy should be slain. The following are some of the various categories of sins worthy of Blood Atonement and some representative supporting documentation.

Murder:

Joseph Smith himself insisted upon Blood Atonement for the sin of murder. He stated:

> I replied, I was opposed to hanging, even if a man kill another. I will shoot him or cut off his head, *spill his blood on the ground,* and let the smoke thereof ascend up to God.

Joseph Smith
History of the Church
Volume 5, page 296

Adultery and Immorality:

Orson Pratt, one of the original twelve apostles, bragged that:

> The people of Utah are the only ones in this nation who have taken effectual measure ... to *prevent* adulteries and criminal connection between sexes. The punishment in that territory [Utah] for these crimes is *death to both male and female*. And this law is written on the hearts and printed in the thoughts of the whole people.

Orson Pratt
The Seer, Page 223

He had earlier avowed that the citizens of Utah territory "know that if they have any connections out of the marriage covenant, they not only *forfeit their lives by the Law of God*, but they forfeit their salvation also."[2] Apostle George A. Smith asserted: *"The man who seduces his neighbor's wife must die, and her nearest relative must kill him."*[3]

The residuals of this doctrine survive to the present era in this attitude expressed by Apostle Bruce R. McConkie who, in his book *Mormon Doctrine,* states:

> Modern governments do not take the life of adulterers, and some of them have done away with the supreme penalty where murder is involved — *all of which is further evidence of the direful apostasy that prevails among the people who call themselves Christians.*

Bruce McConkie
Mormon Doctrine
1958 Edition, Page 104

Stealing:

Brigham Young advised his fellow Mormons:

> If you want to know what to do with a thief, that you may find stealing, *I say kill him on the spot* and never suffer him to commit another iniquity.

> If you will cause all those whom you know to be thieves, to be placed in a line before the mouth of one of our largest cannon, well loaded with chain shot, I will prove by my works whether I can mete out justice to such persons, or not. I would consider it just as much my duty to do that [kill a thief] as to baptize a man for the remission of his sins.

Brigham Young
Journal of Discourses
Volume 1, Pages 108-109

Apostasy:

Apostle Orson Hyde agreed that:

> It would have a tendency to place a terror on those [apostates] who leave these parts, that may prove their salvation when they see the heads of those thieves taken off, or shot down before the public . . . I believe it to be pleasing in the sight of heaven to sanctify ourselves and put these things [apostasy and thievery] away from our midst.

Orson Hyde
Journal of Discourses
Volume 1, Page 73

Not Receiving the "Gospel:"

Brigham Young preached that:

> The time is coming when justice will be laid to the line and righteousness to the plummet; when we shall ask "Are you for God?" and if you are not heartily on the Lord's side, *you will be hewn down.*

Brigham Young
Journal of Discourses
Volume 3, Page 226

Marriage to an African:

Brigham also said:

> Shall I tell you the Law of God in regard to the African race? If the white man who belongs to the chosen seed [Mormons] mixes his blood with the seed of Cain [Negroes] the penalty, under the Law of God is *death on the spot. This will always be so.*

Brigham Young
Journal of Discourses
Volume 10, Page 110

Covenant Breaking:

Jedediah Grant, second counselor to Brigham Young, preached:

> I would ask how many covenant breakers there are in this city and in this kingdom. I believe there are a great many, and if they are covenant breakers we need a place designated *where we can shed their blood.*

Jedediah Grant
Journal of Discourses
Volume 4, Page 50

Heber C. Kimball, first counselor to Brigham Young, preached that "if men turn traitors to God and His servants *their blood will surely be shed,* or else they will be damned, and that too according to their covenants."[4]

During that stormy decade of the rabid Mormon Reformation, and even before, Mormons fanatically reported all transgressions — their own, their families', and their neighbors'. Every transgressor must, willingly or unwillingly, submit to the "Elders of Israel" or "Danites" to be blood atoned for the above-mentioned offenses. To this day the *Journal of Discourses* containing these Blood Atonement sermons may be readily purchased from Mormon sources. In fact, the *Journal of Discourses,* is currently for sale in our local Mormon bookstore! All twenty-six volumes of it. (See Appendix C, page 179.)

BLOOD ATONEMENT STILL VALID

In another highly prized publication, the 1970 edition of *Doctrines of Salvation,* we are informed that there are "certain sins that the *blood of Jesus will not remit.*"

The preface of this popular compilation of President Joseph Fielding Smith's sermons cites him as the "leading gospel scholar and greatest doctrinal teacher of this generation . . ." who has answered gospel questions "with authoritative *finality* of the oracles of God."[5]

In his *Doctrines of Salvation* the 10th Latter-day Saint prophet vainly attempted to explain away the Blood Atonement doctrine, preaching and practices of his Latter-day Saint predecessors who in *their* day were the "leading gospel scholars, greatest doctrinal teachers and authoritative oracles of God." Valiantly he plugged away at the insurmountable task of plugging up the flagrant faults and oozing leakage of doctrines which when first uttered were meant to remain sequestered. Determinedly he mopped and scrubbed away at the religious quagmire inherited from his Latter-day prophet predecessors. And then President Joseph Fielding Smith finally states that under "certain circumstances" *Blood Atonement is necessary.*

PORTRAITS OF LEADING MORMONS.

Are you aware that there are certain sins that man may commit for which the atoning blood of Christ does not avail? Do you not know, too, that this doctrine is taught in the Book of Mormon?

Just a word or two now, on the subject of Blood Atonement. What is that doctrine? . . . it is simply this: through the atonement of Christ all mankind may be saved, by obedience to the laws and ordinances of the gospel.

But man may commit grievous sins — according to his light and knowledge — that will place him beyond the reach of the atoning blood of Christ. If then he would be saved he must make sacrifice of his own life to atone — so far as in his power lies — for that sin, for the blood of Christ alone under certain circumstances will not avail.

Do you believe this doctrine? If not, then I do say you do not believe in the true doctrine of the atonement of Christ!

Do you want a few references where men were righteously slain to atone for their sins?

After listing *Book of Mormon* characters, Nehor and Zemnarihah, and Biblical ones Er and Onan, Nadab, Abihu and Achan, President Smith concludes with:

Joseph Smith taught that there were certain sins so grievous that man may commit, that they will place the transgressors beyond the power of the atonement of Christ. If these offenses are committed, then the blood of Christ will not cleanse them from their sins even though they repent. Therefore, their only hope is to have their own blood shed to atone, as far as possible in their behalf.

This is scriptural doctrine, and is taught in all the standard works of the Church [Mormon Scriptures].

> Joseph Fielding Smith
> *Doctrines of Salvation*
> Volume 1, Page 133

Please ever remember that these are present, up-to-the-minute doctrines of the Church of Jesus Christ of Latter-day Saints. Be warned that this, the 10th Mormon prophet, who "spoke in God's stead," is still greatly honored and his utterances are held sacred and authoritative.

Herein both the first Mormon prophet, Joseph Smith, Jr., and his grand-nephew, the late Joseph Fielding Smith, have tragically expounded and exposed their ignorance of

Christ's atonement and their lack of faith in, and submission to, the blood "that cleanses from all sin." Any true prophet knows that there are *NO* certain sins so grievous that man may commit, that they will place the transgressors beyond the power of the atonement of Christ, as Joseph Fielding Smith would have us believe. God's unfailing word declares that "the blood of Jesus Christ, His Son cleanseth from *all* sin. If we say we have no sin, we deceive ourselves, and the truth is not in us. If we confess our sins, He is faithful and just to forgive us our sins, and to cleanse us from *ALL* unrighteousness." (I John 1:7-9).

Every person who in his heart truly repents and confesses his sin of unbelief and receives salvation from sin by God's grace through faith in Jesus' blood will ever afterward know that the blood of Jesus Christ cleanses from *all* sin —past, present, and future. Moreover he will never, never be guilty of promoting some other means of salvation from sin such as Mormon baptism, Mormon church membership, temple marriage, etc., and least of all the shedding of their blood to atone, "as far as possible," for their sins.

The only sin which Christ's blood will not remit is the sin of continuing unbelief, such as demonstrated by the Jewish scribes when they ascribed to the devil the miraculous works of the Holy Spirit. Be it ever remembered that as soon as an individual trusts in the blood of Jesus to cleanse him from all sin, that individual is *SAVED* and *SAFE*. He, then and there, becomes an adopted child of God, an heir with Christ of all the heavenly bliss of worshipping God in spirit and in truth, here and hereafter.

Whoever coined the maxim "what tangled webs we mortals weave" must have had in mind just such a snare as Mormonism has turned out to be. Each additional teaching of Mormonism has plunged each succeeding Latter-day prophet into ever deepening hot water. Present-day Mormon leaders just barely keep their heads above water long enough to explain away or deny early-day favorite teachings, once publicly and earnestly propounded from Mormon pulpits. As an example consider Joseph Smith's supposed revelation from God stating: "He that kills shall not have forgiveness in this world nor in the world to come.

And again I say, thou shalt not kill: but he that killeth shall die." *(Doctrine and Covenants,* Section 42:18-19)

As a professed prophet, Joseph Smith should have been able to foresee the difficulties his great-nephew, Joseph Fielding Smith, would face trying to explain how "he that killeth shall die." Since the utmost consideration, according to this Blood Atonement doctrine, is that the *offender's* blood be shed, what about suicides, so-called "mercy killings" (where consent is granted) or abortion? Who then would "blood atone" the abortionists to save *their* souls? Further, who would "atone" the "blood atoner"? And on it goes!

Since such weighty problems are hard to handle, some modern Mormon apologists have attempted to deny Blood Atonement by first saying that they never even preached it much less practiced it, and then admit that although they believe it even now, they cannot practice it. Such a one is current Apostle Bruce McConkie. The denial of the doctrine of Blood Atonement goes like this:

> . . . wickedly and evilly-disposed persons have fabricated false and slanderous stories to the effect that the Church, in the early days of this dispensation, engaged in a practice of blood atonement whereunder the blood of apostates and others was shed by the Church as an atonement for their sins. These claims are false and were known by their originators to be false. There is not one historical instance of so-called blood atonement in this dispensation, nor has there been one event or occurrence whatever, of any nature, from which the slightest inference arises that *any such practice either existed or was taught.*

> Bruce McConkie
> *Mormon Doctrine,* Page 92

Apostle McConkie then asserts that these wicked persons lie about the church by taking one sentence from one page and another from a succeeding page or even tying together parts of sentences which are several pages apart. All of this is an attempt to prove that Brigham and the others taught something ". . . just the opposite of what they really believed and taught."[6]

Finally, he clears the matter up by explaining the *true* doctrine of Blood Atonement by saying:

But under certain circumstances there are some serious sins for which the cleansing of Christ does not operate, and the law of God is that *men must then have their own blood shed to atone for their sins.*

Bruce McConkie
Mormon Doctrine, Page 92

Here we see first the denial that "... such a practice either existed or was taught," and then an immediate reversal stating as true, *the very doctrine just denied!* He attempts then to remove the practice from the modern era by saying that the early leaders were merely expounding on doctrines pertaining to the law of Moses, and as proof of that he states:

This doctrine can only be practiced in its fulness in a day when the civil and ecclesiastical laws are administered in the same hands.

Bruce McConkie
Mormon Doctrine, Page 93

But the ecclesiastical and civil laws *were* administered by the same hands during this period. Brigham Young was the Territorial Governor and under him the Mormon priesthood ruled totally unchallenged until the end of the 1850's, when the federal government finally sent in new administrators and judges in an attempt to break up the Mormon empire that was being established. Brigham Young, Jedediah Grant, Heber Kimball, Orson Pratt and the others who were so strongly expounding this doctrine *had the power in their hands* to do just what they said should be done.

During this period the leading Mormons were frankly outspoken in their sanction of the union of the Church and State. In Utah, John Taylor asked: "Was the kingdom that the prophets talked about, that should be set up in the latter times, going to be a Church? Yes, it was going to be both Church and State, to rule temporally and spiritually."[7]

He recalled that before their migration to Utah, "We used to have a difference between Church and State, but it is all one now. Thank God, we have no more temporal and spiritual! *We have got Church and State together.* . . ."[8]

Mormon Apostle Orson Pratt remarked that "ours is an ecclesiastical Church and an ecclesiastical state [Utah]."[9]

The legacy of this doctrine remains on the law books of the State of Utah to this day because:

> . . . Utah incorporated in the laws of the Territory provisions for the capital punishment of those who willfully shed the blood of their fellow men. This law, which is now the law of the State, granted unto the condemned murderer the privilege of choosing for himself whether he die by hanging, or whether he be shot, and thus *have his blood shed in harmony with the law of God;* and thus atone, so far as it is in his power to atone, for the death of his victim. Almost without exception the condemned party chooses the latter death.
>
> Joseph Fielding Smith
> *Doctrines of Salvation*
> Volume 1, Pages 135-136

Because of this Mormon doctrine of Blood Atonement, the fifty-four Mormon men were easily led by their priesthood superiors to cold-bloodedly murder the emigrants at Mountain Meadows. Because Grandpa Lee believed that the blood of the trangressor must be shed as an atonement for his sins, he elected to be put to death by the federal firing squad rather than the hangman's noose. Even though Grandpa had renounced Brigham Young, his tactics and his tenets, he could not put aside this dreadful doctrine that had been drummed into his ears for more than a quarter of a century. He therefore chose one of the cruelest, most ignominious of all modern executions — death by the firing squad — so that his blood would be shed and his soul "atoned." In earlier days of Mormonism the slitting of the throat from ear to ear of the condemned person was the most common and acceptable method of civil execution, thus shedding his blood and atoning for his sins. However, this mode of execution could no longer be *publicly* practiced after federal authorities and other gentiles moved in among the "Saints."

Let me reiterate and again impress upon your mind that these Mormon Blood Atonement doctrines *are not obsolete.* They are still current; every one of these cited Mormon sermons was preached and is still stressed by Mormon authorities. They are still printed on Mormon-owned presses, still published far and wide by the Church of Jesus Christ of Latter-day Saints, still sold around the world in Mormon bookstores.

The *Journal of Discourses*, from which I quoted but a few of the sermons proclaiming Blood Atonement, plurality of wives, Adam is the God of this world, no man can go to heaven without the consent of Joseph Smith, etc., were ordered from a leading Mormon elder in Salt Lake City. He wrote glowingly of the great worth of the Latter-day apostles' sermons, which comprise the *Journal of Discourses*. He highly recommended the reading of them, saying, "they are equal in value with those of the Bible." Another Mormon leader, Preston Nibley, stated in an address delivered at Salt Lake City, May 31, 1925:

> One may go through volume after volume of the *Journal of Discourses* without finding sermons equal to his [Brigham Young's]. There are interesting, instructive, and learned discourses in those volumes but I would say that Brigham's sermons stand out pre-eminent as faith-promoting . . . To young Latter-day Saints, fruitful and faith-inspiring hours may be enjoyed by reading with studious care the sermons of Brigham Young.
>
> Preston Nibley
> "Brigham Young the Man and Leader"
> Pamphlet, Page 15

How ironic it is that even though Mormons endorse these *Journal of Discourses* sermons, they are to be *repudiated* if found in something other than Mormon literature. Most Mormons will refuse to read this written testimony of mine — they are to count me an accursed apostate. In reality, though, many are just afraid to face the truth, for Mormonism *cannot stand investigation*. And so Latter-day Saints are counseled by Mormon authorities to shun all anti-Mormon literature.

Again I declare that I have not had to lie in order to expose Mormonism. Neither should Mormons lie to shield it. Leading Mormon elders, bishops, missionaries, seventies, apostles, counselors to the presidency, and the President-Prophet have at their disposal every one of the sermons I have here quoted, and more. The top leadership know full well that the Blood Atonement doctrine was preached and *practiced*. Some still secretly uphold these doctrines. Others deny their existence. Surely God is highly displeased that these gullible people believe a lie, then lie to shield these blasphemous Mormon doctrines.

Perhaps the most visible and undeniable result of all this blood atoning talk was the Mormon version of what happened in Jonestown, Guyana—the Mountain Meadows Massacre. I sorrow to say that my own great-grandpa, John D. Lee, was a major figure in that episode, and his story is told in detail in the next chapter.

FOOTNOTES

1. Smith's, William, testimony of, *Temple Lot Case,* page 98.

2. Pratt, Orson, *The Seer,* page 42.

3. Smith, George A., *Journal of Discourses,* Vol. 1, page 97.

4. Kimball, Heber C., *Journal of Discourses,* Vol. 4, page 375.

5. Smith, Joseph Fielding, *Doctrines of Salvation,* Vol. 1 preface (written by Apostle B. R. McConkie, the compiler of Smith's writings).

6. McConkie, Bruce, *Mormon Doctrine,* page 92.

7. Taylor, John, *Journal of Discourses,* Vol. 6, page 24.

8. *Ibid.,* Vol. 5, page 266.

9. Pratt, O., *Ibid.,* Vol. 8, page 105.

Chapter Ten

GRANDPA PAYS FOR MOUNTAIN MEADOWS

Once again orders from Mormon headquarters in Cedar City in southern Utah were issued to Grandpa Lee calling him away from his familiar and pleasant family duties. His priesthood and military superior, Elder Isaac Haight, who was both president of the local Stake and Lieutenant Colonel of the Iron County Mormon Battalion, ordered Grandpa Lee to lead in the pillage and attack of a wagon train of families headed for California from Arkansas and Missouri. Grandpa Lee wrote:

> About the 7th of September, 1857, I went to Cedar City from my home at Harmony, by order of President Haight...
>
> He wanted to have a long talk with me on private and particular business. We took some blankets and went over to the old Iron Works, and lay there that night so that we could talk in private and safety.
>
> John D. Lee
> *Mormonism Unveiled*
> Page 218

There that Sunday night it was agreed that those in authority in the church would approve of the destruction of the emigrant wagon train, if it could be done by the Indians. They also agreed that they would stir up the Indians further and encourage them to attack the wagon train compound and rob the cattle and goods.

Grandpa Lee went on to say:

> Haight said he had sent Klingensmith and others over

[133]

towards Pinto, and around there, to stir up the Indians and force them to attack the emigrants.

On my way from Cedar City to my home at Harmony, I came up with a large band of Indians under Moquetas and Big Bill, two Cedar City chiefs; they were in their war paint, and fully equipped for battle. They halted when I came up and said they had had a big talk with Haight, Higby and Klingensmith and had got orders from them to follow up the emigrants and kill them all, and take their property as the spoil of their enemies.

These Indians wanted me to go with them and command their forces. I told them I could not go with them that evening, that I had orders from Haight, the big Captain, to send other Indians on the war-path to help kill the emigrants, and that I must attend to that first; that I wanted them to go on near where the emigrants were and camp until the other Indians joined them; that I would meet them the next day and lead them.

John D. Lee
Mormonism Unveiled
Page 226

Meanwhile, high-up Mormon officials busied themselves stirring up the Indians and the Mormons as well. Great-grandmother Rachel Lee noted in her diary that on the night of August 16, 1857 Apostle George A. Smith and company arrived in Harmony. On the following morning, he and his company paraded into battle formation in order to show the officers of the Harmony militia "how to discipline their men aright. Martineau of Parowan commanded the movements. At seven o'clock they met at the meeting house. President G. A. Smith delivered a discourse on the spirit that actuated the United States towards this people — full of hostility and virulence, and all felt to rejoice in the Lord God of our Fathers."[1]

In addition to the military orders and war-mongering sentiments he conveyed to the Latter-day Saints, Apostle Smith also had a most significant epistle for Jacob Hamblin, one of Grandpa Lee's many brothers-in-law.

This letter from Brigham Young dated August 4, 1857, appointed Jacob Hamblin as President of the Santa Clara Indian Mission of the Church. He was adjured:

... to enter upon the duties of your calling immediately.

Continue the conciliatory policy towards the Indians,

which I have ever recommended, and seek by works of righteousness to obtain their love and confidence, for they must learn that they have either got to help us or the United States will kill us both ... Seek to unite the hearts of the brethren on that mission, and let all under your direction be knit together in the holy bonds of love and unity.

Then followed a paragraph of an "abundance of news" regarding the appointment of

... an entire set of [*Federal*] officials for the Territory. These gentry are to have a bodyguard of 2500 of Uncle's Regulars ... to start from Ft. Leavenworth July 15th ... the current report is that they somewhat query whether they will hang me with or without trial. There are about 30 others they intend to deal with.[2]

Jacob Hamblin, who was concerned about his new responsibilities to enlist the Indians to do their part in the approaching war, escorted leading Indian chiefs of his district to confer with Brigham Young in Salt Lake City. Under the date of September 1, 1857, the *Journal History of the Church* recounts: "Bro. Jacob Hamilton arrived in G.S.L. City from Santa Clara Mission with 12 Indian chiefs who had come to see Pres. Young . . . Pres. Young had an interview for about one hour with the Indians."

Brigham Young evidently persuaded the Indians that "they must either help us or the United States will kill us both." Seven days later, these Indian chiefs and about 400 of their braves joined my great-grandfather John D. Lee and 53 other Mormon leaders and attacked the wagon train of settlers at Mountain Meadows.

In the ensuing hard-fought and bloody gun battle the emigrants had, to the surprise of the marauding Mormons and Indians, put up a valiant counter-offensive. Desperately and bravely they defended themselves and families for five long, fearful days and horrifying nights. The Mormon elders, tiring of the long, drawn-out struggle, which they had confidently expected to win in a matter of hours, withdrew and formed a church Council of War. They laid plans to bring the battle to a speedy finish. They then, as a pre-planned ruse to draw the resisting emigrants from their entrenchments, promised to conduct the embattled travelers safely back to Cedar City, Utah if they would give

THE MOUNTAIN MEADOWS MASSACRE.

up their guns and surrender. This they did believing the Mormon men to be friendly benefactors who were defending them against the Indians. Trustingly they marched up the valley, each one side by side with an accompanying Mormon elder. At the pre-arranged signal, "Boys, do your duty," each Mormon elder turned on the defenseless, unarmed emigrant man at his side and ruthlessly shot him down in cold blood. On up the valley a short way the helpless, wounded emigrants, being transported in one of their own wagons, were likewise murdered by the Mormon leaders, leaving the now wildly fleeing, terrified women and children to be savagely slaughtered and scalped by the Indians so that the Mormon elders would not be guilty of the shedding of "innocent blood."

All together 127 men, women and children were ruthlessly murdered by these fanatical Mormon elders — every one of them leading elders and bishops — and by the band of Indians incited to robbery and murder by the Latter-day Saints. This dastardly priesthood-prompted, wholesale slaughter, known as the Mountain Meadows Massacre, has gone down in the annals of American history as one of the bloodiest, cruelest acts ever perpetrated in the name of religion, and has only recently been "outdone" by the bloodbath in Guyana.

Directly after the brutal murders, part of the Mormon men began butchering the emigrants' cattle for the Indians' suppers, thus enticing them away from their fiendish ransacking of the emigrant camp. In whooping jubilation they were tossing pots and pans, dishes and clothing helterskelter, while on down the canyon others of their tribe and some of the white men were stripping clothing, shoes, money, watches, knives and other valuables from the mangled, bloody bodies of the slain. The sumptuous repast of all the beef they could gorge and a minor portion of the other booty of the monstrous carnage was allowed the exultant braves for aiding their Mormon friends in the slaughter.

It must indeed have been a somber, sorry sight as the blood-spattered, weary Mormon men on the following day transported to Cedar City, Utah, the major portion of the spoils of war—the emigrants' cattle, wagons and teams, household goods, jewelry and trinkets, along with the seventeen wailing emigrant children huddled together in the creaking, swaying wagon bed, so terror stricken, so sad, so recently orphaned, their lives spared only because they were deemed to be too young to tell the story of the massacre and incriminate murderers of their parents. These defenseless little ones were given into the concerned care of the conscience-stricken Mormon elders with the injunction: "Show them what love and affection you can. They are orphan children and deserve all the care and kindness we can give them."

It may have been this haunting guilt that caused these same elders to consign to the Cedar City Mormon tithing office the plunder taken from their murdered victims. Juanita Brooks, noted Mormon historian and author of several well-documented books on early day Mormon history, details how "profoundly affected" the people of Cedar City were because of the massacre.

> The extra wagons in the tithing office yard and the orphaned children in so many homes made them all acutely conscious of the tragedy at the Meadows . . .
>
> There were now on the tithing office shelves many pairs of shoes, tied together and arranged by size, there were quilts and blankets, cooking utensils and dishes, and some clothing. There were muted whisperings of bloody shirts and dresses that were soaked in so many waters, washed in suds, and ironed ready to wear, and of women who became nauseated or turned faint over the task but remained tight-lipped and stoic."
>
> Juanita Brooks
> *John D. Lee,* Page 225

MORMONISM'S SCAPEGOAT
FOR MOUNTAIN MEADOWS

For Grandpa Lee, along with his portion of the booty of this priest-led bloody battle, there were soon to be other spoils of war, intangible rather than material: the heartbreaking, faith-shattering fruits of his misguided obedience to his church leaders and Brigham Young. It fell Grandpa's lot to be made the victim for the Mormon church—to bear the shame and blame for the whole foul, priesthood-plotted and directed massacre, to be the scapegoat to bear the sins and disgrace of the sordid affair for the Mormon church and to suffer, as all scapegoats have, the loss of family, friends, farm and fireside. He was to spend the rest of his life wandering, cold, hungry, sick and forsaken, in hiding for nineteen long, troublous years until finally arrested and tried by a United States Court, and sentenced to death.

He was taken back for his execution to Mountain Meadows, where he had helped to murder in the name of God and the Church of Jesus Christ of Latter-day Saints more than 127 men, women and children. There on March 23, 1877, where most of the slaughtered strangers had been interred in one long shallow grave that they themselves had dug as the battle trench in which they had so resolutely defended themselves against their Mormon marauders, Grandpa Lee faced calmly the United States firing squad and death.

Among the last requests (allowed every condemned man), my grandfather Lee requested that three pictures of himself seated on his coffin box be made for his remaining three loyal wives. The others had forsaken him when Brigham Young, thirteen years after the massacre, had excommunicated Grandpa Lee, all because he had followed his superiors' ecclesiastical edicts and had helped rob and annihilate the wagon train.

Just before the handkerchief was to be placed over his eyes, Grandpa motioned to the photographer, James Fennimore, who was adjusting his camera nearby. "Come over here," he said, beckoning with his hand. "I want to ask a favor of you; I want you to furnish my three wives each a copy of the picture. Send them to Rachel A., Sarah C., and Emma B." Grandpa repeated carefully the names of these three faithful companions who had borne such hardships and revilings with him and for him, saying to this special young friend of his, who had lived with Grandpa and his family at Lonely Dell, "Please forward them. You will do this?"

Mr. Fennimore responded affirmatively. Grandpa then posed himself on the edge of the coffin and the picture was taken. He then arose from his coffin, where he had been seated, and looking calmly around at the soldiers and spectators, made his farewell speech and bore his testimony in an even and unexcited tone of voice:

I have but little to say this morning.

I feel resigned to my fate . . . I am ready to meet my Redeemer and those that have gone before me, behind the veil. I am not an infidel. I have not denied God and His mercies.

I am a strong believer in these things. Most I regret is parting with my family; many of them are unprotected and will be left fatherless . . .

I am a true believer in the gospel of Jesus Christ. I do not believe everything that is now being taught and practiced by Brigham Young. I do not care who hears it. It is my last word — it is so. I believe he is leading the people astray, downward to destruction. But I believe in the gospel that was taught in its purity by Joseph Smith, in former days.

I studied to make this man's [Brigham Young] will my pleasure for thirty years. See now, what I have come to this day!

I have been sacrificed in a cowardly manner . . .

Evidence has been brought against me which is as false as the hinges of hell, and this evidence was wanted to sacrifice me. Sacrifice a man that has waited upon them [*the Mormon hierarchy*], that has wandered and endured with them in the days of adversity, true from the beginning of the Church! And I am now singled out and am sacrificed in this manner! What confidence can I have in such a man! I have none, and I don't think my Father in heaven has any.

Still, there are thousands of people in this Church that are honorable and good-hearted friends, and some of whom are near to my heart. There is a kind of living, magnetic influence which has come over the people, and I cannot compare it to anything else than the reptile that enamors his prey, till it captivates it, paralyzes it, and it rushes into the jaws of death.

I regret leaving my family; they are near and dear to me. These are things which touch my sympathy, even when I think of those poor orphaned children.

I declare I did nothing designedly wrong in this unfortunate affair. I did everything in my power to save that people, but I am the one that must suffer.

Having said this I feel resigned, I ask the Lord, my God,
if my labors are done, to receive my spirit.

John D. Lee
Mormonism Unveiled
Pages 387-389

After a short prayer delivered by the prison chaplain, a
Methodist minister named George Stokes (for whom the
older members of our family still express their high regard
and deep appreciation), Grandpa made one final request: "I
ask one favor of the guards — spare my limbs and center my
heart ... Let them shoot the balls through my heart! Don't let
them mangle my body!"[3]

As the fatal word *"Fire!"* rang out clear and strong on the
chill morning air on that 23rd day of March, 1877, a sharp
report was heard and Grandpa fell back into his coffin, dead
and motionless, and his spirit crossed over the dark river of
death, to stand before the Judge of the quick and the dead.

Some have said that through the prison chaplain's
ministry and benevolences toward Grandpa as he awaited
trial and execution, that Grandpa received Jesus as his
personal Saviour and made his peace with God. I wish I
knew.

But *this* I do know: that at the time when Grandpa's own
church brethren had flagrantly betrayed and utterly
forsaken him, this Methodist minister's friendship and
compassion meant much to my forlorn and forsaken
forebear. This clergyman must have been a providential
blessing, especially sent by a merciful and sympathizing
God to accompany and strengthen Great-grandfather Lee
as he had returned, for the first time since its perpetration,
to the scene of the horrendous crime and its haunting,
brutal memories. This Christian minister had pityingly
and prayerfully sought every means to assuage the grief
and despair of the doomed man, undergirding him every
tortuous step of the way to the ever hungry, gaping and
grasping, merciless jaws of death and its unrelenting
finality, beyond which no human power, care nor prayer
can avail. Grandpa's fate and his final destination were
sealed; for in spite of all the preaching and prophesying to
the contrary by Joseph Smith, Brigham Young or any other
false proclaimer of salvation after death, there is,

EXECUTION OF JOHN D. LEE.

according to the Bible, no redemption of the soul beyond the grave. The cleansing from sin through faith in the blood of "the Lamb," who was slain for our sins, must be accomplished here on earth for "where the tree [man] falleth there it shall be." (Ecc. 11:3) No changing of directions or stations, for after death comes the judgment, where we must face up to whether we rejected or accepted Christ's atoning blood for our sins.

"It is appointed unto man once to die, but after this the judgment." (Hebrews 9:27) Not a one of the Mormon "scriptures" or any version of the Bible even mentions an intermediate place for departed spirits. There is no purgatory, no temporary prison place. For the believer in the blood of Jesus there is heaven and paradise which are the same place. Paul states in II Cor. 12:2 & 4 that he, "a man in Christ...was caught up to the third heaven...caught up into *paradise.* The *Living New Testament* states it thus: "Fourteen years ago I was taken up to heaven [literally the third heaven] for a visit. Don't ask me whether my body was there or just my spirit, for I don't know; only God can answer that. But anyway, there I was in paradise."

Paul, in writing to fellow believers in the cleansing blood of Jesus, declares, "that whilest we are at home in the body, [*on earth*] we are absent from the Lord," but that when we are "absent from the body" we are "present with the Lord." (II Cor. 5:6, 8). Very plainly God had it written for just such a time and circumstance as ours today, that we are either "in the body" or "present with the Lord" in the third heaven, which is paradise.

MORMON SADIE HAWKINS DAY

Even before Grandfather Lee's fate was sealed, most of his wives were becoming *unsealed.* This was in accord with Mormon theology and church policy that Brigham Young, who had sealed these many wives to Grandpa in the first place, should feel obligated at Grandpa's excommunication to advise his nineteen wives of their solemn and religious duties. They were being loosed from Grandpa in order that they could be sealed for eternity to other more worthy Mormon elders. For when Grandpa was cut off from *The*

True Church, his presumptive powers of the priesthood were also forfeited. No longer did he have the power and authority to call forth his wives from their graves and stand as their head in the Mormon celestial kingdom.

Every woman is supposed to have a man to call her forth from the grave, and Grandpa Lee, for the lack of the priesthood power, could no longer do so. It was more expedient for those nineteen Mrs. John D. Lees to be loosed from Grandpa Lee. Brigham Young, therefore, according to my paternal grandmother (who thoroughly disliked "Brigham, the old Boss," as he was commonly called) sent "bills of divorcement" to all of Grandpa's wives, stating that they were no longer legally nor spiritually married and sealed to Grandpa. Brigham the prophet had arbitrarily cut them free. They were to seek without delay other Mormon men who, if and when proposed to, were obligated to marry the woman to help save her soul by fulfilling the law of celestial marriage. For Grandpa Lee's wives, every day was "Sadie Hawkins Day." Every year was leap year for the unattached Mormon female.

On every side the church authorities kept "counseling" them to hastily be loosed from their disgraced excommunicated husband. They then should speedily be sealed to other Mormon elders so that they could diligently be about their new master's business: that of "raising up seed" to enlarge his exaltation and kingdom, as well as the fold and the power of Mormonism.

All of Great-grandfather Lee's wives except my own paternal great-grandmother and two others eventually were turned against Grandpa Lee and accepted Brigham Young's proffered civil and temple divorces. Most of them and their children were sealed to other Mormon elders expecting, and expected, to speedily bear their new husbands many more children here on earth and in heaven. Thus they would hasten their new "heads" and resurrectors on to godhood, instead of Grandpa.

But wait! All is not lost! The Mormon authorities have recently reversed the fortunes of Grandpa Lee's widows and their second husbands.

GRANDPA LEE IS REINSTATED
83 YEARS LATER!

Once again the Mormon Church has reversed not only itself but Grandpa Lee's fate and destiny. On April 20, 1961, eighty-three years after Grandpa's execution and almost one hundred years since the massacre for which he was excommunicated, the ruling body of the Mormon church has stated "that authorization be given for the reinstatement to membership and former blessings to John D. Lee."

In the following month, on May 8th and 9th, male descendants of Grandpa Lee stood proxy for "vicarious temple works" and rituals performed in Grandpa's behalf. These temple rituals included: rebaptism by immersion for the reremission of Grandpa's sins, reimposition of hands for the rebestowal of the Holy Ghost, reordination by the laying on of hands for the degrees of the Mormon priesthood which Grandpa had held more than one hundred years earlier.

Then came the redonning in Grandpa's behalf of the holy underwear, and the priesthood wedding garments. By his request, his special temple garments had been buried with him; hurriedly thrown on top of his bullet-riddled body before it was lowered into the grave at Panguitch, Utah. This his grieving sons had done even though, according to Mormonism, he was no longer worthy of them. But now because of his pardon and reinstatement he presumably would be allowed to wear them.

Finally, and it was to be hoped *permanently* this time, came the vicarious marriage and "sealing for eternity" ordinances. If, as the Latter-day Saints authorities had promised, all his "former blessings" were restored to Grandpa, then he must have been vicariously re-married to all his nineteen former wives, long mouldering in their graves, dressed as the brides of their later late husbands.

However, if Grandpa's former nineteen wives were restored to his bosom and harem in heaven, how were these twice sealed, once loosed and now retrieved wives to be replaced in their second husband's kingdom? One is made to wonder if, even yet, other sealings and loosenings are in the offing—for surely this knotty, naughty dilemma is still unresolved.

All of these restorative rituals in Grandpa's behalf must have been rather exhausting, and time-consuming since it required two days and several participants to reaccomplish these "vicarious works for the dead" for our progenitor. Even though these "saviours of their dear departed dead," in full faith expectantly and earnestly sought to rescue Grandfather Lee, he may still be "dead in trespass and sin." That is unless, of course, prior to his execution he actually *did* repent of his sin of unbelief and trust the real Jesus as his personal Saviour.

Moreover, true salvation is not time-consuming. In the twinkling of an eye, in just a flash of heart-felt contrition toward God and loving gratitude to Christ, one can most securely and permanently be born again, rescued from sin and spiritual death, to be alive with Him forevermore. All of this could have happened to Great-grandfather Lee as it did to me. I hope that it did. Only God knows.

I want to impart to you, as my grandmother did to me, my Great-grandfather Lee's grieving despair over the impious cruelty that Mormon neighbors and erstwhile friends heaped upon him and his wives and children. Compelled, with his three loyal wives and their children, to flee for his life, this once well-to-do, respected Mormon bishop became a poverty stricken fugitive, forced into heartaching homesickness and loneliness. Destitution, danger and disease, empty bloated bellies and broken spirits became their lot. All of these horrors, and more, haunted their desolate hiding places at Lonely Dell and Lee's Ferry (their hiding places in later years). But most haunting of all, I'm sure, was the perfidy of his Mormon priesthood superiors.

As their scapegoat, Grandpa had been consigned to hell. There he supposedly had waited until his progeny, after a century of importuning and perhaps a great deal of pressuring and politicking, had finally secured a reversal of his excommunication, not just for Grandpa's glory and exaltation but for their own, as well.

In most Mormon minds no man can be by-passed or superseded by his progeny (unless adopted to another man, as Grandpa had been to Brigham Young). Therefore Grandpa Lee's prodigious posterity had been in a precarious predicament. Even the most sanctified saint among them reportedly might wait around in the intermediate Prison Place (Paradise) until Grandpa Lee had progressed onward and upward. Then they, in turn, could occupy his vacated place. And so perhaps the Lee grandsons' concern for their own heavenly status is what prompted the diligence with which they labored for Grandpa's reinstatement in the Church of Jesus Christ of Latter-day Saints and "former blessings," his priesthood powers thus clearing the way for their own eventual exaltation to godhood.

Though it may appear that only selfishness and an arrogant seeking for self-glory motivates Mormon man to so faithfully perform his family genealogy and temple works, to force his father, grandfather and great-grandfather, *ad infinitum* on ahead in order that the Mormon man can occupy the vacated station, such is not the case.

A great deal of the Mormon parents' concern is anxiety for their children's eternal welfare, that they be not hindered in their progression to exaltation, glory and godhood. Herein lies part of the answer for the Mormon's diligence in good works, tithing, church activities, missionary endeavors, and subservience to those in authority of the Mormon priesthood and its sealing powers. May God bless all Mormons everywhere with the heartfelt knowledge and peace that Jesus gives when He comes into the heart to whisper "It is finished." May He make me ever more grateful that Christ has finished the work begun by the Holy Spirit's convicting power in my heart. How thankful I am that my salvation is completed and securely sealed for eternity in Him who died that I might live.

The works of righteousness I now feebly, and to my shame, so poorly and erratically do, were begun in my heart that glorious day I fully trusted in Jesus. Among these good works is the writing of this book to the glory of God and in honor of His dear Son that others, Mormons especially, might be saved and bring honor and glory to Him the Lamb of God whose "blood cleanseth us from all sin."

May God use me and this written testimony to bring
many to Jesus even though it will, I fear, again sever
longed-for relationships of Mormon loved ones and friends,
bringing again festering insults and recriminations
against me; some of which, I am aware, are my just dues.

But to Him who "is able also to save them to the uttermost
that come unto God by Him," I commit all things, my very
life itself; confident that He who hath begun this good work
in me is able to perform it and to bring me again to Mama's
House, up there where there will be no wall of partition and
Mama can again be proud of me. But most of all we will
forever sing:

Our New Song
Mama's and Mine

You are worthy to take the scroll
And to break open its seals.
For you were killed, and by your death
You bought men for God,
From every tribe, and language and people, and nation.

The Lamb who was killed is worthy
To receive power, wealth, wisdom and strength
Honor, glory and praise!

To Him, who sits on the throne, and to the Lamb,
Be praise and honor, glory and might,
Forever and ever! Amen!

Revelation 5:9, 12, 13
Today's English Version

FOOTNOTES

1. The original journal is owned by the Henry Huntington
   Library in California.

2. This letter is found in the *Church Letter Book No. 3,* pages
   737-38. The original is owned by the Jacob Hamblin
   family and quoted in Juanita Brooks' *Mountain Meadow
   Massacre,* page 389.

3. Lee, John D., *Mormonism Unveiled,* page 389.

Epilogue

As I write this epilogue it is the first Sunday of another new year in Jesus. On this day, I celebrated my thirty-second *new* birthday. Again I awoke to the joy of Jesus in my heart, wanting to praise and thank Him just as I have every morning since the moment of my being born again. Once again, I prayed the prayer that God the Holy Spirit taught me thirty-two years ago:

> Thank God for Jesus. Thank you Jesus for caring so much that you willingly laid aside your heavenly glory and pre-eminence and came to earth to be made sin for me. Jesus, I'm sorry that I kept you waiting so long. Help me this day to die to self and live for Thee that I might bring others to Thee — that together we will give Thee pre-eminence.

If ever I begin my devotions any other way, I have to "crawdad" back up and say, "Let me begin again, dear Father, and thank Thee first of all for Jesus."

And so, first of all it seems proper that I again remind you that the things written in this book were written in order

> . . . that you may believe that Jesus is the Christ, the Anointed One, the Son of God, and that through believing and cleaving to and trusting in and relying upon Him, you may have life through *(in)* His name *(that is, through what He is)*.

> John 20:31
> *Amplified Bible*

Mormonism taught me to bear my testimony, but it was Jesus that gave me a testimony worth bearing! My testimony of Jesus is that He shed His blood for *all who would receive Him* as their atonement for sin. But as I began to publicly bear this testimony years ago, Mama (bless her precious memory) cried and said, "Oh Honey, be a good girl. Don't go talking about the Mormons again!"

I tried to comfort her as I said, "But Mama, I don't go to talk *about* Mormons, I go to talk *for* them. I am obligated to God and His dear Son to tell everyone, *especially Mormons,* how thankful I am to finally realize that Jesus loved us — you, me and all other Mormons — enough to die for *our* sins. Please believe me when I say how sorry I am to see you grieve so." And again, Mama and I would part in tears.

My heart rejoices today that there will be no more parting in heaven — no more tears and heartaches!

In the past eight years since Mama went home to be with Jesus, I've tried to love her brothers and sisters in Mama's place and for Jesus' sake. Some have already turned to Jesus for their salvation. For those who have not yet done so, deep sorrow and concern engulfs me. All of the old aching loneliness I had for Mama's salvation returns. But through it all Jesus bids me to lean on Him for comfort and direction.

My remembrance of the loneliness for Mama stirs anew my love and longing for Papa. Grief and pain tear my soul as I recall his gentle love, care and concern for me. Tears flow as I remember his commitment to family, friends, and neighbors — *but not to Jesus.* He died fully committed to a system that promised him a temporary stay in hell to pay for his personal "transgressions." How horrible it is that the stay is not temporary — but eternal!

"Would to God," I cry, "that some stalwart Christian had pressed upon Papa the need for his commitment to Jesus!" Friends often ask, "Has God erased your pain and sorrow of knowing that your father has to stay in hell?"

I reply, "I haven't even asked God to take away that pain. I ask God to *intensify* it so that I'll always remember that there are over 4,000,000 more Mormons out yonder who are still steeped in this Mormon fallacy." There are millions of precious souls needing to be rescued and brought to harbor in Jesus — as Mama and I were.

Through it all Jesus has been my mentor, my strength, my resting place. As He promised, He is my all-in-all — my father, my mother, my brother. He fills every need, supplies every comfort and cheers my sorrows. His promises continue to sustain me for my two closest remaining beloveds: my older sister and brother.

I long for the coming of our Lord Jesus, and until then I'll still be bearing my testimony and giving Jesus the pre-eminence, saying, *"Come and hear, all ye that fear God, and I will declare what He hath done for my soul!" (Ps. 66:16)*

My dear Mormon friend and all who read these pages,

Would *you* be released from your prisonhouse of sin? Oh that you would come to know that same Jesus who said "Come unto me, all ye that labor and are heavy laden, and I will give you rest. Take my yoke upon you, and learn of me; for I am meek and lowly in heart, and ye shall find rest unto your souls."

1. YOU NEED TO BE SAVED. God has declared "There is not a just man upon earth, that doeth good, and sinneth not." (Eccl. 7:20) "For *all* have sinned and come short of the glory of God." (Rom. 3:23) "For the wages of sin is death, but the gift of God is eternal life *through Jesus Christ,* our Lord."(Rom. 6:23)

2. JESUS HAS ALREADY PROVIDED FOR YOUR SALVATION. "For Christ also hath once suffered for sins, the just for the unjust, that He might bring us to God." (I Pet. 3:18) "God hath made Him to be sin for us, who knew no sin; that we might be made the righteousness of God in Him." (II Cor. 5:21) "God so loved the world, that He gave His *only* begotten Son, that whosoever believeth in Him should not perish, but have everlasting life." (John 3:16)

3. YOU CANNOT SAVE YOURSELF, NOR CAN ANY CHURCH SAVE YOU. "Not by works of righteousness which we have done, but according to His mercy He saved us." (Tit. 3:5) "There is a way which seemeth right unto a man, but the end thereof are the ways of death." (Prov. 14:12) "Jesus saith unto him, I am the way, the truth, and the life: no man cometh unto the Father, but by me." (John 14:6)

4. YOU MUST RECEIVE CHRIST TO BE SAVED. "But as many as received Him, to them gave He power to

become the sons of God, even to them that believe on His name; which were born not of blood, nor of the will of the flesh, nor of the will of man, but of God. And the Word (Jesus) was made flesh, and dwelt among us, and we beheld His glory, the glory as of the only begotten of the Father, full of grace and truth." (John 1:12-14)

YOU CAN RECEIVE CHRIST RIGHT NOW BY FAITH THROUGH PRAYER:

"Lord Jesus, I need you. Being convinced that I am a sinner, and believing that Christ died for me, I now put my trust entirely in Jesus Christ as my Saviour and Lord. Thank you for forgiving my sins and giving me eternal life."

_____

Write your name here as a testimony of your decision.

Begin reading your Bible daily. Start with the Gospel of John. Pray daily for wisdom and guidance. Let others know of your new relationship to God through the Lord Jesus Christ. Write to me at Rt. 2 Box 723, Safford, Arizona 85546, and I will send you some helpful material and will faithfully pray for you.

APPENDIX A
CIRCA 1870 MORMON TEMPLE CEREMONY

Quite often throughout this book I have made reference to the Mormon temple ceremony (or "endowments"). The endowment ceremony is drawn directly from some of the ceremonies originated by Masonry. It was adopted into Mormonism by Joseph Smith shortly after he himself became a Mason. To this very day, the temple ceremony retains its basic similarity to Masonry, but the ceremony itself has undergone much revision in dialogue.

To understand Mormonism one must become familiar with the temple endowment ceremony and realize its significance to the Mormon. Because the center of my focus in this book has been in the last century — the beginnings of Mormonism — I felt it most fitting and appropriate for me to reproduce for you an early expose of the temple ceremony during the heyday of Brigham Young. The one I chose came from J. H. Beadle's *Life in Utah, Or The Mysteries And Crimes Of Mormonism*, which you can tell from the title was not an official publication of the Mormon church. Nonetheless it is an accurate account of the temple endowment ceremony circa 1870 ... experienced by my Mormon forebears.

Both Mormon and non-Mormon will be enlightened by the current, exact and entire temple ceremony contained in *What's Going On In There?* by Chuck Sackett, former Mormon temple "veil worker" and by Tanner's *Mormonism: Shadow or Reality?* 600 pages of photocopy proofs of thousands of changes in LDS scriptures, doctrines, history and temple rituals. Order these books for $3.00 and $11.95, respectively, plus 15% postage from: Calvary Missionary Press, P.O. Box 13532, Tucson, Arizona 85732.

[155]

MORMON TEMPLE IN SALT LAKE CITY.

CHAPTER XX

MORMON MYSTERIES—THEIR ORIGIN.

The Endowment—Actors—Scenery and dress—Pre-requisites—
Adam and Eve, the Devil and Michael, Jehovah and Eloheim—A new
version—Blasphemous assumptions—Terrible Oaths—Barbarous
penalties—Origin—Scriptures and Paradise Lost—Eleusinian
mysteries—"Morgan's Free-masonry"—The witnesses—
Probabilities—Their reasons—Changes.

THE ENDOWMENT.
Dramatis Personae.

ELOHEIM, or *Head God* .... Brigham Young,
JEHOVAH .... George A. Smith,
JESUS ....Daniel H. Wells,
MICHAEL .... George Q. Cannon,
SATAN .... W. W. Phelps,
APOSTLE PETER .... Joseph F. Smith,
APOSTLE JAMES .... John Taylor,
APOSTLE JOHN .... Erastus Snow,
EVE ....Miss Eliza R. Snow.
*Clerk, Washers, Attendants, Sectarians, Chorus and
Endowees.*

I.

THE FIRST (PRE-EXISTENT) ESTATE.

The candidates present themselves at the Endowment
House, provided with clean clothes and a lunch; they are
admitted to the outer office, and their accounts with the
Church verified by a clerk. Their names, ages and the dates
of their conversion and baptism are entered in the register;
receipts are carefully inspected, and if found correct an
entry thereof is made. This last is indispensable before
initiation. Evidence is also presented of faithful attendance
at public service and at the "School of the Prophets." If any
husband and wife appear who have not been sealed for
eternity, a note is made of the fact, the ceremony to be
performed in the initiation. They then remove their shoes
and, preceded by the attendants, who wear slippers, with
measured and noiseless step enter the central ante-room, a

narrow hall separated by white screens from two other rooms to the right and left; the right one is for men, and the left for women.

Deep silence prevails, the attendants communicating by mysterious signs or very low whispers; a dim light pervades the room, mellowed by heavy shades; the faint plash of pouring water behind the screens alone is heard, and the whole scene is calculated to cast a solemn awe over the ignorant candidates, waiting with subdued but nervous expectancy for some mysterious event. After a few moments of solemn waiting, the men are led to their washing-room on the right, and the women to the left. The female candidate is stripped, placed in the bath and washed from head to foot by a woman set apart for the purpose. Every member is mentioned, with a special blessing.

Washer:—Sister, I wash you clean from the blood of this generation, and prepare your members for lively service in the way of all true Saints. I wash your head that it may be prepared for that crown of glory awaiting you as a faithful Saint, and the fruitful wife of a priest of the Lord; that your brain may be quick in discernment, and your eyes able to perceive the truth and avoid the snares of the enemy; your mouth to show forth the praise of the immortal *gods,* and your tongue to pronounce the true name which will admit you hereafter behind the veil, and by which you will be known in the celestial kingdom. I wash your arms to labor in the cause of righteousness, and your hands to be strong in building up the kingdom of God by all manner of profitable works. I wash your breasts that you may prove a fruitful vine, to nourish a strong race of swift witnesses, earnest in defence of Zion; your body, to present it an acceptable tabernacle when you come to pass behind the veil; your loins that you may bring forth a numerous race, to crown you with eternal glory and strengthen the heavenly kingdom of your husband, your master and crown in the Lord. I wash your knees, on which to prostrate yourself and humbly receive the truth from God's holy priesthood; your feet to run swiftly in the ways of righteousness and stand firm upon the appointed places; and now, I pronounce you clean from the blood of this generation, and your body an acceptable temple for the indwelling of the Holy Spirit."

A similar washing is performed upon the male candidate in his own room, and a blessing pronounced upon his body in like manner.

He is then passed through a slit in the curtain to the next compartment forward; as he passes, an apostle whispers in his ear "a new name, by which he will be known in the celestial kingdom of God."

Reaching the second room, the candidate is anointed with oil, which has been previously blessed and consecrated by two priests, poured upon his head from a horn, or from a mahogany vessel shaped to resemble one. The oil is rubbed into his hair and beard, and upon each of his limbs, which are again blessed in order. At the same time the women are anointed in their own washing room. The candidate is then dressed in a sort of tunic, or close-fitting garment, reaching from the neck to the heels. This, or a similar one, blessed for the purpose, is always to be worn next to the body, to protect the wearer from harm and from the assaults of the devil. Many Mormons are so strenuous on this point, they remove the garment but a portion at a time when changing, partly slipping on the new before the old is entirely off. It is generally believed that Joe Smith took off his tunic the morning he went to Carthage, to avoid the charge of being in a secret society; and that he would not have been killed, if he had retained it. Over the tunic comes the ordinary underclothing, and above a robe used only for this purpose; it is made of fine linen, plaited on the shoulders, gathered around the waist with a band, and falling to the floor behind and before. On the head is placed a cap of fine linen, and on the feet light cotton slippers.

At this point begins, in the adjoining room, the preparatory debate in the grand council of the gods, as to whether they shall make man. Eloheim, Jehovah, Jesus and Michael intone a drama in blank verse, representing the successive steps in the creation of the world. Eloheim enumerates the works of each day, and commends them all; at the close of each, all the others unite in a responsive chorus of surprise and praise at the glory and beauty of the work, concluding:

Eloheim. "Now all is done, and earth with animate life is glad. The stately elephant to browse the forest, the ramping lion in the mountain caves, gazelles, horned cattle and the fleecy flocks spread o'er the grassy vales; behemoth rolls his bulk in shady fens by river banks, among the ooze, and the great whale beneath the waters, and fowl to fly above in the open firmament of heaven. Upon the earth behold bears, ounces, tigers, pards, and every creeping thing that moves upon the ground. Each after his kind shall bring forth and multiply upon the earth; and yet there lacks the master work, the being in the form and likeness of the gods, erect to stand, his Maker praise, and over all the rest dominion hold."

Jehovah, Jesus, Michael and Eloheim. "Let us make man, in image, form and likeness as our own; and as becomes our sole complete representative on earth, to him upright, dominion give and power over all that flies, swims, creeps or walks upon the earth."

The attendants have meanwhile placed the candidates on the floor and closed their eyes, when the gods enter and manipulate them limb by limb, specifying the office of each member, and pretending to create and mould. They then slap upon them to vivify and represent the creative power, breathe into their nostrils "the breath of life," and raise them to their feet. They are then supposed to be "as Adam, newly made, completely ductile, mobile in the maker's hand."

II.

SECOND ESTATE.

Men file into the next room, with paintings and scenery to represent the Garden of Eden. There are gorgeous curtains and carpets, trees and shrubs in boxes, paintings of mountains, flowers, and fountains, all shown in soft light and delicate tints, together presenting a beautiful and impressive scene. While they move around the garden to measured music, another discussion ensues between the gods; Michael proposes various animals, in turn, to be the intimates of man, which are successively rejected by Jehovah, Jesus and Eloheim. The men are then laid recumbent, with closed eyes, in pantomime a rib is extracted from each, out of which, in the adjoining room, their wives are supposed to be formed; the men are then commanded to awake, and see their wives for the first time since parting in the entry, dressed nearly like themselves.

They walk around the garden by couples, led by the officiating Adam and Eve, when Satan enters. He is dressed in a very tight-fitting suit of black velvet, consisting of short jacket and knee-breeches, with black stockings and slippers, the last with double points; he also wears a hideous mask and pointed helmet. He approaches Eve, who is separated from Adam, and begins to praise her beauty; after which he proffers the "temptation." (Here there is a difference in the testimony. John Hyde says, the "fruit offered consisted of some raisins hanging on a shrub;" one lady states that the temptation consists of gestures and hints "not to be described;" while another young lady, after implying that Adam and Eve were nearly naked, merely adds: "I cannot mention the nature of the fruit, but have left more unsaid that the imagination held with the loosest possible rein would be likely to picture. . . the reality is too monstrous for human belief, and the moral and object of the whole is socially to unsex the sexes." A third lady states that the fruit consisted merely of a bunch of grapes, and adds:

"Those conducting the ceremonies explained to us beforehand that this portion of the affair should be conducted with the men and women entirely naked; but that, in consequence of the prejudice existing in the minds of individuals against that method of proceeding, coupled with the fact that we were not sufficiently perfect and pure-minded, and that our enemies would use it as a weapon against us, it was considered necessary that we should be clothed." (It is quite probable the ceremony is frequently changed.)

Eve yields and partakes of the "fruit"; soon after she is joined by Adam, to whom she offers the same; he first hesitates, but overcome by her reproaches, also eats. They grow delirious from its effects, join hands, embrace, and dance around the room till they sink exhausted.

A loud chorus of groans and lamentations is heard behind the curtain, followed by a sudden crash as of heavy thunder; a rift opens in a curtain painted to represent a dense wood, and in the opening appears Eloheim, behind him a brilliant light; he is clothed with a gorgeous dress, bespangled with brilliant and bright stripes to dazzle the eyes.

Eloheim. "Where art thou, Adam,
Erst Created first of all earth's tribes,
and wont to meet with joy thy coming Lord?"

Adam. "Afar I heard Thy coming,
In the thunder's awful voice,
Thy footsteps shook the earth,
And dread seized all my frame,
I saw myself in naked shame,
Unfit to face Thy Majesty."

Eloheim. "How knew'st thou of thy shame?
My voice thou oft has heard,
And feared it not. What has thou done?
Hast eaten of that tree
To thee forbid?"

Adam. "Shall I accuse the partner of my life
Or on myself the total crime avow?
But what avails concealment with earth's Lord?
His thoughts discern my inmost hidden sense.
The woman Thou gav'st to be my help
Beguiled me with her perfect charms,
By Thee endowed, acceptable, divine,
She gave me of the fruit, and I did eat."

Eloheim. "Say, woman, what is this that thou has done?"

Eve. "The serpent me beguiled and I did eat."

Eloheim then pronounces a curse—literally copied from
the Scripture—upon the serpent, or rather Satan, who fell
upon the ground, and with many contortions wriggles out
of the room. A curse is next pronounced upon Eve, and then
upon Adam, paraphrased from the Scripture. They fall
upon the ground, beat their breasts, rend their clothes, and
bewail their lost and sinful condition.

Eloheim. "Now is man fallen indeed. The accursed
power which first made war in heaven, hath practiced
fraud on earth. By Adam's transgression should be under
sin; the moral nature darkened, and none could know the
truth. But cries of penitence have reached my ears, and
Higher Power shall redeem. Upon this earth I place My
holy priesthood. To them as unto Me in humble reverence
bow. Man, fallen by Satan's wiles, shall by obedience rise.
Behold, the Woman's Seed shall bruise the Serpent's head;
from her a race proceed endowed on earth with power
divine. To them shall man submit, and regain the paradise
now lost through disobedience. With power divine the
priesthood is endowed, but not in fullness now. Obey them
as the Incarnate Voice of God, and in time's fullness
Woman's Seed shall all that's lost restore to man. By

woman, first fallen, Adam fell; from Woman's Seed the priesthood shall arise, redeeming man; and man in turn shall Eve exalt, restoring her to the paradise by her first lost. Meanwhile go forth, ye fallen ones, with only nature's light, and seek for truth."

The attendants now place upon each of the initiates a small square apron, of white linen or silk, with certain emblematical marks and green pieces resembling fig leaves, worked in and handsomely embroidered.

The candidates then kneel and join in a solemn oath, repeating slowly after Adam: that they will preserve the secret inviolably, under the penalty of being brought to the block, and having their blood spilt upon the ground in atonement for their sin; that they will obey and submit themselves to the priesthood in all things, and the men in addition, that they will take no woman unless given them by the Presidency of the Church. A grip and a key-word are then communicated, and the *First Degree* of the *Aaronic Priesthood* is conferred. Man is now supposed to have entered into life, where the light has become as darkness. They pass through a narrow opening into the next room, which is almost dark, heavy curtains shutting out all but a few rays of light. Here they stumble about, fall against blocks and furniture; persons are heard calling, "here is light," "there is light," etc., and a contest goes on among those who call themselves Methodist, Baptist, Presbyterian, Catholic, etc. The curtains are constantly agitated, and being darkly painted with hideous figures, discover a thousand chimerical shapes. The sectarians seize hold of the initiates and pull them violently about, till the latter are quite exhausted. Satan now enters, commends the sectarians, laughs, chuckles and is quite delighted; the latter recommence their struggle for the initiates, when a sudden fall of curtains throws in a full blaze of light, and Peter, James and John descend into the room. They order the devil to withdraw; he falls upon the ground, foams, hisses and wriggles out, chased and kicked by the Apostle Peter.

The initiates are then ranged in order to listen to a lecture—

> *Peter.* "Brethren and Sisters, light is now come into the world, and the way is opened unto men; Satan hath desired

to sift you as wheat, and great shall be his condemnation who rejects this light.—(The ceremony is explained up to this point.)—The holy priesthood is once more established upon earth, in the person of Joseph Smith and his successors. They alone have the power to seal. To this priesthood as unto Christ, all respect is due; obedience implicit, and yielded without a murmur. He who gave life has the right to take it. His representatives the same. You are then to obey all orders of the priesthood, temporal and spiritual, in matters of life or death. Submit yourselves to the higher powers, as a tallowed rag in the hands of God's priesthood. You are now ready to enter the kingdom of God. Look forth upon the void and tell me what ye see." (Curtain is raised.)

Adam and *Eve.* "A human skeleton."

Peter. "Rightly have ye spoken. Behold all that remains of one unfaithful to these holy vows. The earth had no habitation for one so vile. The fowls of the air fed upon his accursed flesh, and the fierce elements consumed the joints and the marrow. Do ye still desire to go forward?"

Adam. "We do."

The initiates then join hands and kneel in a circle, slowly repeating an oath after Peter. The penalty is to have the throat cut from ear to ear, with many agonizing details. The *Second Degree* of the *Aaronic Priesthood* is then conferred, and the initiates pass into the third room in the middle of which is an altar.

III.

THIRD ESTATE.

Emblematic of celestialized men.

Michael. "Here all hearts are laid open, all desires revealed, and all traitors are made known. In council of the gods it hath been decreed that here the faithless shall die. Some enter here with evil intent; but none with evil intent go beyond this veil or return alive, if here they practice deceit. If one among you knows aught of treachery in his heart, we charge him now to speak, while yet he may and live. Brethren, an ordeal awaits you. Let the pure have no fear; the false-hearted quake. Each shall pass under the Searching Hand, and the Spirit of the Lord decide for his own."

The initiates are placed one by one upon the altar, stretched at full length upon the back, and the officiating

SCENES IN THE ENDOWMENT CEREMONIES.

1. Preparation—Washing and Anointing.   2. Eloheim Cursing Adam and Eve—Satan Driven Out.   3. Trial of Faith—The "Searching Hand."   4. Oath to Avenge the Death of Joseph Smith.   5. The "Blood Atonement."

priest passes an immense knife or keen-edged razor across their throats. It is understood that if any are false at heart, the Spirit will reveal it, to their instant death. Of course, all pass. They again clasp hands, kneel and slowly repeat after Jehovah, another oath. The penalty for its violation is to have the bowels slit across and the entrails fed to swine — with many horrifying and disgusting details. Another sign, grip and key word are given, and the *First Degree* of the *Melchizedek Priesthood* is conferred, being the third degree of the Endowment. Copies of the Bible, *Book of Mormon* and *Doctrine and Covenants* are placed upon the altar, and another lecture delivered. The initiates are now instructed that they are in a saved condition, and are to go steadily on in the way of salvation; but that temporal duties demand their first care, chief among which is a positive, immediate duty to avenge the death of the prophet and martyr, Joseph Smith. The account of his martyrdom is circumstantially related, after which the initiates take a solemn oath to avenge his death; that they will bear eternal hostility to the Government of the United States for the murder of the prophet; that they renounce all allegiance they may have held to the government and hold themselves absolved from all oaths of fealty, past or future; that they will do all in their power towards the overthrow of that government, and in event of failure teach their children to pursue that purpose after them. Another oath of fidelity and secrecy is administered, of which the penalty is to have the heart torn out and fed to the fowls of the air. The initiates are now declared acceptable to God, taught a new form of prayer, "in an unknown tongue," and the *Second Degree* of the *Melchizedek Priesthood* is conferred. They are then passed "behind the veil," a linen curtain, to the last room.

IV.

FOURTH ESTATE.

The kingdom of the gods.

The men enter first, and the officiating priest cuts certain marks on their garments and a slight gash just above the right knee. Then, at the command of Eloheim, they one by one introduce their women to the room. Very few instances have occurred of women being admitted to these rites

before marriage. "Sealing for eternity" is then performed
for all who have previously been only "married for time."

The initiated then retire, resume their regular dress, get a
lunch and return to hear a lengthy address, explaining the
entire allegory, and their future duties consequent on the
vows they have taken. The entire ceremony and address
occupy about ten hours.

Such is the Endowment, as reported by many who have
passed through it. The general reader will readily recognize
that portion which is paraphrased from the Scriptures and
Milton's *Paradise Lost.* The general outline is evidently
modeled upon the *Mysteries* or *Holy Dramas* of the Middle
Ages, with, perhaps, an attempt to reproduce portions of the
Eleusinian Mysteries of Ancient Greece. Much of it will be
recognized as extracted from "Morgan's Free-masonry
Expose," by those familiar with that work; and the origin of
this is quite curious. When Smith and Rigdon first began
their work they were in great doubt what to preach; a
furious religious excitement was prevalent in the West, and
portions of argument in regard to all the *isms* of the day
may be found in the *Book of Mormon.* But anti-Masonry was
just then the great political excitement of New York and the
infant Church was easily drawn into that furious and
baseless crusade, which already ranks in history as one of
those unaccountable popular frenzies which occasionally
disturb our politics, rising from no one knows where, and
subsiding as apparently without cause. Smith's "New
Translation" of the Old Testament is full of anti-Masonry;
the fifth chapter of Genesis as he has it, which he has added
to our version, is devoted entirely to the condemnation of
secret societies, and sets forth particularly how they were
the invention of Cain after "he fled from the presence of the
Lord." But the Brighamites declare the time has not yet
come to publish or circulate this Bible; and it is only quoted
by the Josephites, who use this chapter to condemn the
Endowment. Some years after, however, the Mormons all
became Masons, and so continued till they reached Nauvoo;
there Joseph Smith out-Masoned Solomon himself, and
declared that God had revealed to him a great key-word,
which had been lost, and that he would lead Masonry to far
higher degrees, and not long after their charter was revoked
by the Grand Lodge. How much of Masonry proper has

survived in the Endowment, the writer will not pretend to
say; but the Mormons are pleased to have the outside world
connect the two, and convey the impression that this is
"Celestial Masonry."

Appendix B

THE NEGRO IS "FREED" FROM HIS CURSE

The entire world was startled to hear the announcement from the Mormon church headquarters that effective June 9, 1978, Negroes would no longer be denied the Mormon priesthood. The text of the statement issued as a general letter to the LDS priesthood leaders follows:

THE CHURCH OF JESUS CHRIST OF LATTER-DAY SAINTS
OFFICE OF THE FIRST PRESIDENCY
SALT LAKE CITY, UTAH 84150

June 8, 1978

To All General and Local Priesthood Officers of The Church of Jesus Christ of Latter-day Saints Throughout the World

Dear Brethren:

As we have witnessed the expansion of the work of the Lord over the earth, we have been grateful that people of many nations have responded to the message of the restored gospel, and have joined the Church in ever-increasing numbers. This, in turn, has inspired us with a desire to extend to every worthy member of the Church all of the privileges and blessings which the gospel affords.

Aware of the promises made by the prophets and presidents of the Church who have preceded us that at some time, in God's eternal plan, all of our brethren who are worthy may receive the priesthood, and witnessing the faithfulness of those from whom the priesthood has been withheld, we have pleaded long and earnestly in behalf of these, our faithful brethren, spending many hours in the Upper Room of the Temple supplicating the Lord for divine guidance.

He has heard our prayers, and by revelation has confirmed that the long-promised day has come when every faithful, worthy man in the Church may receive the holy priesthood, with power to exercise its divine authority, and enjoy with his loved ones every blessing that flows therefrom, including the blessings of the temple. Accordingly, all worthy male members of the Church may be ordained to the priesthood without regard for race or color. Priesthood leaders are instructed to follow the policy of carefully interviewing all candidates for ordination to either the Aaronic or the Melchizedek Priesthood to insure that they meet the establised standards for worthiness.

We declare with soberness that the Lord has now made known His will for the blessing of all His children throughout the earth who will hearken to the voice of His authorized servants, and prepare themselves to receive every blessing of the gospel.

Sincerely yours,

The First Presidency

Several minor points need to be noted carefully. First is that they were aware that there were "promises made by the prophets and presidents of the church who have preceded us," and alleged that those promises were that the Negro would "sometime" get the priesthood. Second, God heard their earnest and long pleading on behalf of the Negro. Finally, God "confirmed" by "revelation" that now was the appointed time for the curse to be lifted from the Negro. Notice that the word "curse" was not even used in the news release. Yet, from the Mormon perspective, and extending back into the history of the church, a curse it was.

As far as the "promises" made by earlier leaders are concerned, the current leadership has been less than honest about the timing of the removal of the curse. Previous prophets and apostles did talk about it from time to time, but they were consistent on one point in particular—the "curse" against the Negro would not be lifted until after the general resurrection of all mankind. In other words, it would never happen in this life—during the period known to them as "mortality."

Brigham Young made his opinion very clear about the timing. On several occasions, he took time to address himself to the issue. Essentially, his position was that all the other children of Adam would first have to have their opportunity to possess the priesthood (see *Journal of Discourses*, Volume 2, page 143, Volume 7, pages 290-291 and Volume 11, page 272 as examples).

The tenth prophet, Joseph Fielding Smith, believed the same thing. As late as 1958, he said:

> ... the Lord decreed that the children of Cain should not have the privilege of bearing the priesthood until Abel had posterity who could have the priesthood and that will have to be in the far distant future. When this is accomplished *on some other world, then the restrictions will be removed from the children of Cain* ...
>
> Joseph Fielding Smith
> *Answers to Gospel Questions*
> Volume 2, Page 188

Not too much before the Negro "revelation" was announced, a long-ignored manuscript of a discourse of Brigham Young's came to light which bears directly on what happened in June 1978. Because this discourse survived only in the manuscript form, the following quote (which is taken directly from a typed copy of the manuscript) includes all the spelling and other grammatical errors. Addressing the Territorial Legislature early in 1852, President Young boldly declared:

> We know there is a portion of inhabitants of the earth who dwell in Asia that are negroes, and said to be jews. The blood of Judah has not only mingled almost with all nations, but also with the blood of Cain, and they have mingled there seeds together; these negro Jewes may keep up all the outer ordinenances of the jewish releigeon, they may have there sacrifices, and they may perform all the releigeous, seremonies any people on earth could perform, but let me tell you, that the day they consented to mingle their seed with Cannan, the preisthood was taken away from Judah, and that portion of Judahs seed will never get any rule, or blessings of the preisthood until Cain gets it. Let this church which is called the kingdom of God on the earth; we will sommons the first presidency, the twelve, the high counsel, the Bishoprick, and all the elders of Israel, suppose we sommons them to appear here, and here declare that it is right to mingle our seed,

with the black race of Cain, that they shall come in with with us and be pertakers with us of all the blessings God has given to us. On that very day, and hour we should do so, the priesthood is taken from this Church and kingdom and God leaves us to our fate. The moment we consent to mingle with the seed of Cain the Church must go to desstruction—we should receive the curse which has been placed upon the seed of Cain, and never more be numbered with the children of Adam who are heirs to the priesthood untill that curse be removed.

Brigham Young Addresses
Dated Feb. 5, 1852

It seems that Brigham may have "hit the nail upon the head" this time! It does appear (as you will see a little later) that someone did call the leaders together and decided that it was "right to mingle our seed with the black race." It was Brigham who declared that "on that very day and hour we should do so, the priesthood is taken from this church and kingdom and God leaves us to our fate."

As we can see, Brigham had no second thoughts about what would happen if the subsequent leadership ever gave the priesthood to Negroes in this life. As it turns out, Brigham's speculation about the manner in which such an action might take place (i.e., the high officials getting together and making a corporate decision) is *exactly what did happen.*

Personally, as a Christian, I object to the implication made by the Mormon First Presidency that the "fault" lies with God Almighty. They make it appear that God has been the one responsible—when in fact, it is the fault of the racist leaders in the early beginnings of Mormonism. Nobody, least of all the Mormon leadership, has to plead "long and earnestly" on behalf of the Negroes in order for them to be some kind of "full citizen" in the family of God—those Negroes who have trusted in the saving blood of Jesus Christ *are already fully adopted into the family of God* (John 1:12). If anything, for the last 150 years, Negroes have been highly favored of God. He protected them from the spiritual darkness of Mormonism because of the color of their skin! Instead of that black skin being a mark of some alleged curse of God, it was a blessing of God! Actually, after all the Mormon leadership has said about the Negro, their offering the Mormon priesthood to the Negro is nothing more than adding insult to injury.

The real reason for the priesthood being given to the Negro did not come about because of the "long and earnest pleading" on the part of the Mormon prophet, Spencer W. Kimball, but rather, it was no more than a committee decision reached after deliberation and consideration of the top leaders of the church. In fact, the real reason for the change centered around the pressure built up in Brazil (where many, if not all, of the people have some Negro blood in their veins).

In August of 1978, Rev. Wesley Walters and Mr. Chris Vlachos interviewed the oldest living apostle (at that time), LeGrand Richards. Apostle Richards is one of the leading Mormon apologists and theologians. He is the author of *A Marvelous Work and a Wonder,* which is recognized as one of the most important books ever produced for winning converts to Mormonism. This man was privy to all the inner workings of the top leadership, and in this interview he volunteered some rather startling information. Essentially, Mr. Richards stated that the primary reason for the change was the pressure that the church felt in Brazil (where they were about to open their new temple).

Mr. Richards also pointed out that the mechanics of the procedure were centered around several meetings that the apostles held with President Kimball. In those meetings the various pros and cons were discussed, as well as any and all Mormon Scriptures and teachings from earlier authorities. After a consensus was reached, the council voted upon the idea—it passed. Then the other Mormon General Authorities were informed. About a month later the rest of the world was let in on the secret.

The resulting correspondence between Mr. Vlachos and Mr. Richards is reproduced for your information. It is apparent that Apostle Richards had some serious second thoughts about the "leak" that he was responsible for. Even though one of the very last things he said to Mr. Vlachos and Rev. Walters was that he (Richards) could be quoted, he attempted to change that by saying later that the information was intended only for the interviewers'

personal use. (Can you imagine the Apostle Paul saying
something like that?) In the interest of accuracy and
historical truth and to allow you the opportunity to draw
your own conclusions, sets of letters are reproduced for you
below:

```
858 West  170 North
Orem, Utah   84057
11 September 1978
```

```
Elder LeGrand Richards
LDS Church Office Bldg.
47 E. South Temple St.
Salt Lake City, UT   84111
```

Dear Elder Richards,

I wanted to write and thank you for our visits of
August 16th and a week or so ago. Wesley Walters and I ap-
preciated your kindness in spending so much time with us, and
for explaining your experiences with regard to the recent revelation authorizing you to give the LDS Priesthood to Negroes.
Since I did not take any notes at our first meeting, I wanted
to write and verify a few important points which you made before
I forget them.

One of the most interesting items which you mentioned
was that the whole situation was basically provoked by the
Brazilian temple--that is, the Mormon church has had great dif-
ficulty obtaining Priesthood leadership among its South American
membership; and now with this new temple, a large proportion of
those who have contributed money and work to build it would not
be able to use it unless the Church changed its stand with regard
to giving the Priesthood to Blacks.

I believe that you also mentioned President Kimball as
having called each of the Twelve Apostles individually into his
office to hear their personal feelings with regard to this issue.
While President Kimball was basically in favor of giving the Priesthood to Blacks, didn't he ask each of you to prepare some references for and against the proposal as found in the scriptures?

Another thing which stands out in my mind was the prayer
that President Kimball offered in the special prayer circle with
the Apostles and First Presidency on June 1st: Didn't you say he
prayed essentially that God would give you all the inspiration
necessary to do what was pleasing to the Lord and what was best
for the blessing of His children?

```
Elder LeGrand Richards
11 September 1978, p. 2
```

In addition to these details, I have tried to sequentialize
what you told us about the revelation. The Twelve and First Presidency had a special prayer circle in the Salt Lake Temple on June
1st, where President Kimball prayed for guidance and inspiration
in regard to Negroes. Then, one week later on June 8th, you all
met again and the First Presidency presented the letter released
on June 9th to all Church leaders to the Twelve in order to hear
their reactions. A few members of the Twelve offered suggestions

for a few changes in the document. Afterwards, all twelve Apostles
voted in favor of the announcement. When we asked you if there
was a written revelation, you said that the only written document
was the June 9th letter--that it was considered to be sufficient.
The next morning, all other general authorities met and voted in
favor of the announcement. Then it was released to the press.
I feel fairly certain as to the accuracy of these events, but just
wanted to double-verify it with you.

     I recall Wesley asking if the Mormons still believe that
Negroes were less valient in the pre-mortal existence--this being
a reason for their black skin. Didn't you say that the Brethren
decided that the real reasons are still unknown? I do remember
you saying that the Book of Abraham curse doctrine was considered
with the pros and cons, and that you all decided that if Negroes
live good lives, they are entitled to their blessings. I assume
that this means no new interpretation of the Book of Abraham
account?

     When we talked about intermarriage, I got the feeling
that the Mormon Church will not encourage them, but if they occur,
the Church will support them. Is my perception accurate?

     I guess that's about it. We did talk about other things,
but these stick out more in my mind as the important parts. When
you reply, please let me know if this accurately represents what
you told Wesley and I. I really appreciate your personal concern
in answering all our questions.

            Very truly yours,

            Chris Vlachos

            Chris Vlachos

THE CHURCH OF JESUS CHRIST OF LATTER-DAY SAINTS

The Council of the Twelve
47 East South Temple Street, Salt Lake City, Utah 84150

September 12, 1978

Chris Vlachos
358 West 170 North
Orem, Utah 84057

Dear Friend:

    This will acknowledge receipt of your letter of September 11th
and I don't quite understand the purpose of your letter. The
explanations I gave to you when you were here in my office I did not
intend for public use. I thought it would be for your own information.
I don't think there is anything more I need to add to what I told you
at that time.

It wouldn't please me if you were using the information I gave you when you were here in my office for public purposes. I gave it to you for your own information, and that is where I would like to see it remain.

With all good wishes, I remain,

Most sincerely yours,

LeGrand Richards

LR:mb

358 West 170 North
Orem, Utah 84057
15 September 1978

Elder LeGrand Richards
LDS Church Office Bldg.
47 E. South Temple St.
Salt Lake City, UT 84111

Dear Elder Richards,

Thank you for your reply of 12 September. I am writing you again because your response left me very puzzled. After you told Wesley Walters and I the incidents surrounding the recent Negro revelation, we asked you if we could quote what you had said, and you said something to the effect that "Yes, you can quote me, for I have told you exactly what happened." Having been given that permission, I have told many people since our conversation of your personal story. Now you say that it was not intended for public transmission. Of course, I have no intention of publishing any of those events, but having received permission to share the story, I am writing you again to verify the main points. I will continue to share what you told us, and only wish to be sure that what I say is correctly representing what you said.

The basic points of the story as I remember them are:

1. That the whole situation was provoked by the Brazilian temple affair. Apparently, most of the South American members would not have been able to use the temple due to their Negro ancestry.

2. President Kimball personally interviewed each of the Twelve Apostles on the Negro question, and asked you all to prepare references for and against giving Blacks the Priesthood.

3. President Kimball's prayer offered at the June 1st prayer circle was that God would inspire you all to do what was pleasing to Him and what would be best for His children.

4. The letter sent to all Church officials was first presented to the Twelve Apostles by the First Presidency, and voted upon (affirmatively). This occured one week after President Kimball's prayer for guidance.

Elder LeGrand Richards
15 September 1978, p. 2

5. The official letter mentioned in point #4 was the only
   written document involved in the policy change. No written
   revelation or account of inspiration was otherwise produced.

6. No new interpretation of the Book of Abraham "curse" upon
   the descendants of Cain will be offered by the Mormon Church.
   You said that we still do not know why Blacks were cursed,
   and that the lack of valiency in the pre-mortal existence is
   not a doctrine. The general feeling of the Brethren is that
   if Negroes live righteous lives, they are entitled to the
   same blessings as other members of the Church.

7. With reference to intermarriage, the Church does not encourage
   them, but if they occur, the Church will support them and
   allow temple sealings to take place.

As I mentioned in the first paragraph, you originally told
us that we could quote you as having related these facts. This we
will continue to do, but I truly wish to have your verification of
the above seven points so that we do not mis-quote you.

Thank you once again for your personal concern with this
matter.

Sincerely yours,

Chris Vlachos

Chris Vlachos

THE CHURCH OF JESUS CHRIST OF LATTER-DAY SAINTS

The Council of the Twelve
47 East South Temple Street, Salt Lake City, Utah 84150

September 19, 1978

Chris Vlachos
358 West 170 North
Orem, Utah 84057

Dear Mr. Vlachos:

This will acknowledge receipt of your letter of September
15th.

The reason I replied to your last letter as I did was because
some time ago I received a letter from someone down in your area,

complaining about what you were saying. I don't remember just who
the letter was from but I didn't feel that my interview with you was
something that you would want to be publicizing all over. I don't
have any objections to your telling it to a friend, as you have stated
in your letter now of the 15th, I see nothing wrong in your statements
reviewing our interview.

I send my best regards.

Sincerely yours,

LeGrand Richards

LR:mb

APPENDIX C

REFERENCED
MATERIAL

On the following pages are photocopies of the more important quotations used in this book. I have included them as a "back-up" because experience has taught me that many people tend to dismiss some of these quotations as having been taken out of context or misquoted. This reaction is common to Mormon and non-Mormon alike because many of the statements are really quite unbelievable. However, as the photocopies show, these statements *were* made by the Mormon prophets and apostles in all seriousness and they really meant what they said. The reader can judge for himself concerning the contextual accuracy of the quotations.

Except for the quotations from Grandpa Lee's book, each of the photocopies are made from official Mormon publications produced by the LDS church. No material is taken from "anti-Mormon" sources.

In the case of the quotation from *Journal of Discourses*, Volume 1, pages 50-51, rather than photo-reproducing that, I opted to use the reprint from the Millenial Star (see pages 67-68) because that forever eliminates the argument that the "Adam-God" sermon was misquoted. The Millenial Star article was an *exact repetition* (with the same capitalization and emphases) of that earlier printed in the *Journal of Discourses*.

The following table of contents indicates the original source and on which text page and appendix page of this book the quotation is used.

304   HISTORY OF THE CHURCH.   [April 1844

know? Have any of you seen Him, heard Him, or communed with
Him? Here is the question that will, peradventure, from this time
henceforth occupy your attention. The scriptures inform us that
"This is life eternal that they might know thee, the only true God,
and Jesus Christ whom thou hast sent."

If any man does not know God, and inquires what kind of a being
He is,—if he will search diligently his own heart—if the declaration
of Jesus and the apostles be true, he will realize that he has not
eternal life; for there can be eternal life on no other principle.

My first object is to find out the character of the only wise and
true, God, and what kind of a being He is; and if I am so fortunate
as to be the man to comprehend God, and explain or convey the
principles to your hearts, so that the Spirit seals them upon you,
then let every man and woman henceforth sit in silence, put their
hands on their mouths, and never lift their hands or voices, or say
anything against the man of God or the servants of God again.
But if I fail to do it, it becomes my duty to renounce all further pretensions to revelations and inspirations, or to be a prophet; and I
should be like the rest of the world—a false teacher, be hailed as a
friend, and no man would seek my life. But if all religious teachers
were honest enough to renounce their pretensions to godliness when
their ignorance of the knowledge of God is made manifest, they
will all be as badly off as I am, at any rate; and you might just as
well take the lives of other false teachers as that of mine. If
any man is authorized to take away my life because he thinks and
says I am a false teacher, then, upon the same principle, we should
be justified in taking away the life of every false teacher, and where
would be the end of blood? And who would not be the sufferer?*

The Privilege of Religious Freedom

But meddle not with any man for his religion: all governments ought to permit every man to enjoy his religion unmolested.
No man is authorized to take away life in consequence of difference
of religion, which all laws and governments ought to tolerate and
protect, right or wrong. Every man has a natural, and, in our
country, a constitutional right to be a false prophet, as well as a
true prophet. If I show, verily, that I have the truth of God, and
show that ninety-nine out of every hundred professing religious
ministers are false teachers, having no authority, while they pretend
to hold the keys of God's kingdom on earth, and was to kill them
because they are false teachers, it would deluge the whole world
with blood.

* It should be remembered that at the time of this discourse apostates and other
enemies of the Prophet were seeking his life, and open threats were being made
even in his presence. The forces of evil were determined that the Prophet should
be destroyed. It was less than three months following the date of this discourse
when he and his brother Hyrum were martyred.

I will prove that the world is wrong, by showing what God is. I am going to inquire after God; for I want you all to know Him, and to be familiar with Him; and if I am bringing you to a knowledge of Him, all persecutions against me ought to cease. You will then know that I am His servant; for I speak as one having authority.

God An Exalted Man

I will go back to the beginning before the world was, to show what kind of a being God is. What sort of a being was God in the beginning? Open your ears and hear, all ye ends of the earth, for I am going to prove it to you by the Bible, and to tell you the designs of God in relation to the human race, and why He interferes with the affairs of man.

God himself was once as we are now, and is an exalted man, and sits enthroned in yonder heavens! That is the great secret. If the veil were rent today, and the great God who holds this world in its orbit, and who upholds all worlds and all things by His power, was to make himself visible,—I say, if you were to see him today, you would see him like a man in form—like yourselves in all the person, image, and very form as a man; for Adam was created in the very fashion, image and likeness of God, and received instruction from, and walked, talked and conversed with Him, as one man talks and communes with another.

In order to understand the subject of the dead, for consolation of those who mourn for the loss of their friends, it is necessary we should understand the character and being of God and how He came to be so; for I am going to tell you how God came to be God. We have imagined and supposed that God was God from all eternity. I will refute that idea, and take away the veil, so that you may see.

These are incomprehensible ideas to some, but they are simple. It is the first principle of the gospel to know for a certainty the character of God, and to know that we may converse with Him as one man converses with another, and that He was once a man like us; yea, that God himself, the Father of us all, dwelt on an earth, the same as Jesus Christ Himself did; and I will show it from the Bible.

Eternal Life to Know God and Jesus Christ

I wish I was in a suitable place to tell it, and that I had the trump of an archangel, so that I could tell the story in such a manner that persecution would cease forever. What did Jesus say? (Mark it, Elder Rigdon!) The scriptures inform us that Jesus said, as the Father hath power in himself, even so hath the Son power— to do what? Why, what the Father did. The answer is obvious—in a manner to lay down his body and take it up again. Jesus, what are you going to do? To lay down my life as my Father did, and take it up again. Do you believe it? If you do not believe it you do not believe the Bible. The scriptures say it, and I defy all the learning and wisdom and all the combined powers of earth and hell together to refute it. <u>Here, then, is eternal life—to know the only wise and true God; and you have got to learn how to be gods yourselves, and to be kings and priests to God, the same as all gods have done before you, namely, by going from one small degree to another, and from a small capacity to a great one; from grace to grace, from exaltation to exaltation, until you attain to the resurrection of the dead, and are able to dwell in everlasting burnings, and to sit in glory, as do those who sit enthroned in everlasting power.</u> And I want you to know that God, in the last days, while certain individuals are proclaiming His name, is not trifling with you or me.*

The Righteous to Dwell in Everlasting Burnings

These are the first principles of consolation. How consoling to the mourners when they are called to part with a husband, wife, father, mother, child, or dear relative, to know that, although the earthly tabernacle is laid down and dissolved, they shall rise again to dwell in everlasting burnings in immortal glory, not to sorrow, suffer, or die any more, but they shall be heirs of God and joint heirs with Jesus Christ. What is it? To inherit the same power, the same glory and the same exaltation, until you arrive at the station of a god, and ascend the throne of eternal power, the same as those who have gone before. What did Jesus do? Why, I do the things I saw my Father do when worlds came rolling into existence. My Father worked out His kingdom with fear and trembling, and I must do the same; and when I get my kingdom, I shall present it to My Father, so that He may obtain kingdom upon kingdom, and it will exalt Him in glory. He will then take a higher exaltation, and I will take His place, and thereby become exalted myself. So that Jesus treads in the tracks of His Father, and inherits what God did before; and God is thus glorified and exalted in the salvation and exaltation of all His children. It is plain beyond disputation, and you thus learn some of the first principles of the gospel, about which so much hath been said.

When you climb up a ladder, you must begin at the bottom, and ascend step by step, until you arrive at the top; and so it is with

---

* The argument here made by the Prophet is very much strengthened by the following passage: "The Son can do nothing of himself, but what he seeth the Father do; for what things soever he [the Father] doeth, these also doeth the Son likewise. (John 5:19.)

Henry Drummond, for instance (following the Prophet by half a century), in his work, Natural Law in the Spiritual World, in his chapter on growth, has said: "The end of salvation is perfection, the Christ-like mind, character and life. * * * Therefore the man who has within himself this great formative agent, Life [spiritual life] is nearer the end than the man who has morality alone. The latter can never reach perfection, the former must. For the life must develop out according to its type; and being a germ of the Christ-life, it must unfold into a Christ."

the principles of the gospel—you must begin with the first, and go on until you learn all the principles of exaltation. But it will be a great while after you have passed through the veil before you will have learned them. It is not all to be comprehended in this world; it will be a great work to learn our salvation and exaltation even beyond the grave. I suppose I am not allowed to go into an investigation of anything that is not contained in the Bible. If I do, I think there are so many over-wise men here that they would cry "treason" and put me to death. So I will go to the old Bible and turn commentator today.

I shall comment on the very first Hebrew word in the Bible; I will make a comment on the very first sentence of the history of creation in the Bible—*Berosheit*. I want to analyze the word. *Baith*—in, by, through, and everything else. *Roch*—the head, *Sheit*—grammatical termination. When the inspired man wrote it, he did not put the baith there. An old Jew without any authority added the word; he thought it too bad to begin to talk about the head! It read first, "The head one of the Gods brought forth the Gods." That is the true meaning of the words. *Baurau* signifies to bring forth. If you do not believe it, you do not believe the learned man of God. Learned men can teach you no more than what I have told you. Thus the head God brought forth the Gods in the grand council.

I will transpose and simplify it in the English language. Oh, ye lawyers, ye doctors, and ye priests, who have persecuted me, I want to let you know that the Holy Ghost knows something as well as you do. The head God called together the Gods and sat in grand council to bring forth the world. The grand councilors sat at the head in yonder heavens and contemplated the creation of the worlds which were created at the time. When I say doctors and lawyers, I mean the doctors and lawyers of the scriptures. I have done so hitherto without explanation, to let the lawyers flutter and everybody laugh at them. Some learned doctors might take a notion to say the scriptures say thus and so; and we must believe the scriptures; they are not to be altered. But I am going to show you an error in them.

I have an old edition of the New Testament in the Latin, Hebrew, German and Greek languages. I have been reading the German, and find it to be the most [nearly] correct translation, and to correspond nearest to the revelations which God has given to me for the last fourteen years. It tells about Jacobus, the son of Zebedee. It means Jacob. In the English New Testament it is translated James. Now, if Jacob had the keys, you might talk about James through all eternity and never get the keys. In the 21st. of the fourth chapter of Matthew, my old German edition gives the word Jacob instead of James.

The doctors (I mean doctors of law, not physic) say, "If you preach anything not according to the Bible, we will cry treason." How can we escape the damnation of hell, except God be with us and reveal to us? Men bind us with chains. The Latin says Jacobus, which means Jacob; the Hebrew says Jacob, the Greek says Jacob and the German says Jacob, here we have the testimony of four against one. I thank God that I have got this old book; but I thank him more for the gift of the Holy Ghost. I have got the oldest book in the world; but I have got the oldest book in my heart, even the gift of the Holy Ghost. I have all the four Testaments. Come here, ye learned men, and read, if you can. I should not have introduced this testimony, were it not to back up the word *rosh*—the head, the Father of the Gods. I should not have brought it up, only to show that I am right.

A Council of the Gods

In the beginning, the head of the Gods called a council of the Gods; and they came together and concocted [prepared] a plan to create the world and people it. When we begin to learn this way, we begin to learn the only true God, and what kind of a being we have got to worship. Having a knowledge of God, we begin to know how to approach Him, and how to ask so as to receive an answer.

When we understand the character of God, and know how to come to Him, he begins to unfold the heavens to us, and to tell us all about it. When we are ready to come to him, he is ready to come to us.

Now, I ask all who hear me, why the learned men who are preaching salvation, say that God created the heavens and the earth out of nothing? The reason is, that they are unlearned in the things of God, and have not the gift of the Holy Ghost; they account it blasphemy in any one to contradict their idea. If you tell them that God made the world out of something, they will call you a fool. But I am learned, and know more than all the world put together. The Holy Ghost does, anyhow, and he is within me, and comprehends more than all the world; and I will associate myself with him.

Meaning of the Word Create

You ask the learned doctors why they say the world was made out of nothing, and they will answer, "Doesn't the Bible say He *created* the world?" And they infer, from the word create, that it must have been made out of nothing. Now, the word create came from the word *baurau*, which does not mean to create out of nothing; it means to organize; the same as a man would organize materials and build a ship. Hence we infer that God had materials to organize the world out of chaos—chaotic matter, which is element, and in which dwells all the glory. Element had an existence from the time He had. The pure principles of element are principles which can never be destroyed; they may be organized and re-organized, but not destroyed. They had no beginning and can have no end.*

* The view of the Prophet on this subject of creation is abundantly sustained by men of learning subsequent to his time. The Rev. Bader. Powell of Oxford University, for instance, writing for Kitto's Cyclopedia of Biblical Literature, says: "The meaning of this word (create) has been commonly associated with the idea of 'making out of nothing.' But when we come to inquire more precisely into the subject, we can of course satisfy ourselves as to the meaning only from an examination of the original phrase." The learned professor then proceeds to say that three distinct Hebrew verbs are in different places employed with reference to the same divine act, and may be translated, respectively, "create," "make," "form or fashion." "Now," continues the professor, "though each of these has its shade of distinction, yet the best critics understand them as so nearly synonymous that, at least in regard to the idea of making out of nothing, little or no foundation for that doctrine can be obtained from the first of these words." And of course, if no foundation for the doctrine can be obtained from the first of these words—viz., the verb translated "create," then the chances are still less for there being any foundation for the doctrine of creation from nothing in the verb translated "made," "formed," or "fashioned."

Professor Powell further says: "The idea of 'creation,' as meaning absolutely 'making out of nothing,' or calling into existence that which did not exist before, in the strictest sense of the term, is not a doctrine of scripture; but it has been held by many on the grounds of natural theology, as enhancing the ideas we form of the divine power, and more especially since the contrary must imply the belief in the eternity and self existence of matter."

Dr. William Smith's great dictionary of the Bible, (Hackett edition, 1894) has no article on the term "create" or "creation," but in the article "earth," we have reference to the subject, and really an implied explanation as to why this work contains no treatise on "create" or "creation." The act of creation itself, as recorded in the first chapter of Genesis, is a subject beyond and above the experience of man, human language, derived, as it originally was, from the sensible and material world, fails to find an adequate term to describe the act; for our word 'create' and the Hebrew bara, though most appropriate to express the idea of an original creation, are yet applicable and must necessarily be applicable to other modes of creation; nor does the addition of such expressions as 'out of things that were not,' or 'not from things which appear,' contribute much to the force of the declaration. The absence of a term which shall describe exclusively an original creation is a necessary infirmity of language; as the events occured but once, the corresponding term must, in order to be adequate, have been coined for the occasion and reserved for it alone, which would have been impossible."

The philosophers with equal emphasis sustain the contention of the Prophet. Herbert Spencer, in his First Principles (1860), said: "There was once universally current, a notion that things could vanish into absolute nothing, or arise out of absolute nothing. * * * The current theology, in its teachings respecting the beginning and end of the world, is clearly pervaded by it. * * * The gradual accumulation of experiences, has tended slowly to reverse this conviction; until now, the doctrine that matter is indestructible has become a commonplace. All the apparent proofs that something can come of nothing, a wider knowledge has one by one cancelled. The comet that is suddenly discovered in the heavens and nightly waxes larger, is proved not to be a newly-created body, but a body that was until lately beyond the range of vision. The cloud which in the course of a few minutes forms in the sky, consists not of substance that has begun to be, but of substance that previously existed in a more diffused and transparent form. And similarly with a crystal or precipitate in relation to the fluid depositing it. Conversely, the seeming annihilations of matter turn out, on closer observation, to be only changes of state. It is found that the evaporated water, though it has become invisible, may be brought by condensation to its original shape. The discharged

310   HISTORY OF THE CHURCH.   [April 1844

The Immortal Intelligence

I have another subject to dwell upon, which is calculated to exalt
man; but it is impossible for me to say much on this subject. I shall
therefore just touch upon it, for time will not permit me to say all. It
is associated with the subject of the resurrection of the dead,—
namely, the soul—the mind of man—the immortal spirit. Where
did it come from? All learned men and doctors of divinity say that
God created it in the beginning; but it is not so: the very idea lessens
man in my estimation. I do not believe the doctrine; I know better.
Hear it, all ye ends of the world; for God has told me so; and if
you don't believe me, it will not make the truth without effect. I will
make a man appear a fool before I get through; if he does not believe
it. I am going to tell of things more noble.

We say that God Himself is a self-existing being. Who told you
so? It is correct enough; but how did it get into your heads? Who
told you that man did not exist in like manner upon the same principles? Man does exist upon the same principles. God made a tabernacle and put a spirit into it, and it became a living soul. (Refers
to the Bible.) How does it read in the Hebrew? It does not say in
the Hebrew that God created the spirit of man. It says, "God made
man out of the earth and put into him Adam's spirit, and so became
a living body."

The mind or the intelligence which man possesses is co-equal [co-
eternal] with God himself.* I know that my testimony is true; hence,

fowling-piece gives evidence that though the gunpowder has disappeared, there
have appeared in place of it certain gases, which, in assuming a larger volume,
have caused the explosion."

Fiske follows Spencer, of course, and in his Cosmic Philosophy sums up the matter
in these words: "It is now unconceivable that a particle of matter should either
come into existence, or lapse into non-existence."

Robert Kennedy Duncan (1905), in his New Knowledge says: "Governing matter
in all its varied forms, there is one great fundamental law which up to this time
has been ironclad in its character. This law, known as the law of the conservation
of mass, states that no particle of matter, however small, may be created or destroyed.
All the king's horses and all the king's men cannot destroy a pin's head. We may
smash that pin's head, dissolve it in acid, burn it in the electric furnace, employ,
in a word, every annihilating agency, and yet that pin's head perists in being.
Again, it is as uncreatable as it is indestructible. In other words, we cannot create
something out of nothing. The material must be furnished for every existent article.
The sum of matter in the universe is x pounds,—and, while it may be carried through
a myriad of forms, when all is said and done, it is just— x pounds."

"The elements are eternal, and spirit and element inseparably connected receive
a fulness of joy. * * * The elements are the tabernacle of God; yea, man is the
tabernacle of God, even temples." (D. & C. Sec. 93:35.) Notes by Elder B. H. Roberts.

*It is obvious that the word "co-equal" should have been written "co-eternal," for
we know the doctrines of the Church as revealed to, and taught by, the Prophet,
teach us definitely that God "comprehendeth all things, and all things are before
him, and all things are round about him, and he is above all things, and in all
things, and is through all things, and is round about all things; and all things are
by him, and of him, even God, for ever and ever." (D. & C. Sec. 88:41.) Moreover

when I talk to these mourners, what have they lost? Their relatives and friends are only separated from their bodies for a short season: their spirits which existed with God have left the tabernacle of clay only for a little moment, as it were; and they now exist in a place where they converse together the same as we do on the earth,

I am dwelling on the immortality of the spirit of man. Is it logical to say that the intelligence of spirits is immortal, and yet that it has a beginning? The intelligence of spirits had no beginning, neither will it have an end. That is good logic. That which has a beginning may have an end. There never was a time when there were not spirits;** for they are co-equal [co-eternal] with our Father in heaven.

I want to reason more on the spirit of man; for I am dwelling on the body and spirit of man—on the subject of the dead. I take my ring from my finger and liken it unto the mind of man—the immortal part, because it had no beginning. Suppose you cut it in two; then it has a beginning and an end; but join it again, and it continues one eternal round. So with the spirit of man. As the Lord liveth, if it had a beginning, it will have an end. All the fools and learned and wise men from the beginning of creation, who say that the spirit of man had a beginning, prove that it must have an end; and if that doctrine is true, then the doctrine of annihilation would be true. But if I am right, I might with boldness proclaim from the house-tops that God never had the power to create the spirit of man at all. God himself could not create himself.

Intelligence is eternal and exists upon a self-existent principle. It is a spirit from age to age and there is no creation about it.* All the minds and spirits that God ever sent into the world are susceptible of enlargement.

In the Book of Abraham we read that the Lord said to Abraham: "These two facts do exist, that there are two spirits, one being more intelligent than the other; there shall be another more intelligent than they: I am the Lord thy God, I am more intelligent than they all." (Abraham 3:19.)

**It appears to be very clear that the Prophet had in mind the intelligence, when he said "the soul—the mind of man—the immortal spirit," was not created or made, and that there never was a time when there were not spirits for they are co-eternal with God. It is the doctrine of the scriptures, both in the Bible and in the Doctrine and Covenants, that we are the offspring of God. He is our Father; we are begotten sons and daughters unto Him. So Paul taught the Greeks on Mars' Hill. (Acts 17: 26-29.) It was taught by the resurrected Lord to Mary at the tomb, (John 20:17.) and by the Lord to the Prophet and Sidney Rigdon in the great vision (Sec. 76:22-24.) The reader is referred further to the official statement of the First Presidency and the Council of the Twelve Apostles, under the caption, The Father and The Son, in the Improvement Era, August, 1916.

"Man was also in the beginning with God. Intelligence, or the light of truth, was not created or made, neither indeed can be." (D. & C. Sec. 93.)

*It is clear in this statement that the terms "intelligence" and "spirit" are used synonymously and that the intelligent uncreated entity, spoken of as intelligence, is meant.

312   HISTORY OF THE CHURCH.   [April 1844

The first principles of man are self-existent with God. God himself, finding he was in the midst of spirits and glory, because he was more intelligent, saw proper to institute laws whereby the rest could have a privilege to advance like himself. The relationship we have with God places us in a situation to advance in knowledge. He has power to institute laws to instruct the weaker intelligences, that they may be exalted with Himself, so that they might have one glory upon another, and all that knowledge, power, glory, and intelligence, which is requisite in order to save them in the world of spirits.**

This is good doctrine. It tastes good. I can taste the principles of eternal life, and so can you. They are given to me by the revelations of Jesus Christ; and I know that when I tell you these words of eternal life as they are given to me, you taste them, and I know that you believe them. You say honey is sweet, and so do I. I can also taste the spirit of eternal life. I know that it is good; and when I tell you of these things which were given me by inspiration of the Holy Spirit, you are bound to receive them as sweet, and rejoice more and more.

The Relation of Man to God

I want to talk more of the relation of man to God. I will open your eyes in relation to the dead. All things whatsoever God in his infinite wisdom has seen fit and proper to reveal to us, while we are dwelling in mortality, in regard to our mortal bodies, are revealed to us in the abstract, and independent of affinity of this mortal tabernacle, but are revealed to our spirits precisely as though we had no bodies at all; and those revelations which will save our spirits will save our bodies. God reveals them to us in view of no eternal dissolution of the body, or tabernacle. Hence the responsibility, the awful responsibility, that rests upon us in relation to our dead; for all the spirits who have not obeyed the Gospel in the flesh must either

---

**"Behold this is my work and my glory—to bring to pass the immortality and eternal life of man."—(The Lord to Moses, Book of Moses, Chapt. 1:39: Pearl of Great Price)—that is "to bring to pass the immortality and eternal life of man," as man. This passage has reference doubtless to man as composed of spirit and body—a proper soul (see D. & C. Sec. 88:15-16)—"For the spirit and the body is the soul of man; and the resurrection of the dead is the redemption of the soul." In other words, the "work" and the "glory" of God are achieved in bringing to pass the "immortality and eternal life of man," as man, in the eternal union of the spirit and body of man through the resurrection—through the redemption of the soul. This brings into eternal union "spirit and element" declared by the word of God to be essential to a fulness of joy—"The elements are eternal, and spirit and element, inseparably connected, receive a fulness of joy; and when separated man cannot receive a fulness of joy." (D. & C. Sec. 93). Also "Adam fell that man might be: and men are that they might have joy." (2 Nephi 2:25). Indeed, the whole purpose of God in bringing to pass the earth-life of man is to inure to the welfare and enlargement of man as urged in the teaching of the Prophet in the paragraph above. God affects man only to his advantage. Note by Elder B. H. Roberts.

158   CELESTIAL MARRIAGE.

pure, and sublime attributes which are perfected in all their fulness in themselves.

If none but Gods will be permitted to multiply immortal children, it follows that each God must have one or more wives. God, the Father of our spirits, became the Father of our Lord Jesus Christ according to the flesh. Hence, the Father saith concerning him, "Thou art my Son, this day have I begotten thee." We are informed in the first chapter of Luke, that Mary was chosen by the Father as a choice virgin, through whom He begat Jesus. The angel said unto the Virgin Mary, "The Holy Ghost shall come upon thee, and the power of the Highest shall overshadow thee: therefore, also, that holy thing which shall be born of thee shall be called the Son of God." After the power of the Highest had overshadowed Mary, and she had by that means conceived, she related the circumstance to her cousin Elizabeth in the following words: "He that is Mighty hath done to me great things; and holy is His name." It seems from this relation that the Holy Ghost accompanied "the Highest" when He overshadowed the Virgin Mary and begat Jesus; and from this circumstance some have supposed that the body of Jesus was begotten of the Holy Ghost without the instrumentality of the immediate presence of the Father. There is no doubt that the Holy Ghost came upon Mary to sanctify her, and make her holy, and prepare her to endure the glorious presence of "the Highest," that when "He" should "overshadow" her she might conceive, being filled with the Holy Ghost; hence the angel said, as recorded in Matthew, "That which is conceived in her is of the Holy Ghost;" that is, the Holy Ghost gave her strength to abide the presence of the Father without being consumed; but it was the personage of the Father who begat the body of Jesus; and for this reason Jesus is called "the *Only* Begotten of the Father;" that is, the only one in this world whose fleshly body was begotten by the Father. There were millions of sons and daughters whom He begat before the foundation of this world, but they were spirits, and not bodies of flesh and bones; whereas, both the spirit and body of Jesus were begotten by the Father—the spirit having been begotten in heaven many ages before the tabernacle was begotten upon the earth.

The fleshly body of Jesus required a Mother as well as a Father. Therefore, the Father and Mother of Jesus, according to the flesh, must have been associated together in the capacity of Husband and Wife; hence the Virgin Mary must have been, for the time being, the *lawful* wife of God the Father: we use the term *lawful* Wife, because it would be blasphemous in the highest degree to say that He overshadowed her or begat the Saviour unlawfully. It would have been unlawful for any *man* to have interfered with Mary, who was already espoused to Joseph; for such a heinous crime would have subjected both the guilty parties to death, according to the law of Moses. But God having created all men and women, had the most perfect right to do with His own creation, according to His holy will and pleasure: He had a lawful right to overshadow the Virgin Mary in the capacity of a husband, and beget a Son, although she was espoused to another; for the law which He gave to govern men and women was not intended to govern Himself, or to prescribe rules for his own conduct. It was also lawful in Him, after having thus dealt with Mary, to give her to Joseph her espoused husband. Whether God the Father gave Mary to Joseph for time only, or for time and eternity, we are not informed. Inasmuch as God was the first husband to her, it may be that He only gave her to be the wife of Joseph while in this mortal state, and that He intended after the resurrection to again take her as one of his own wives to raise up immortal spirits in eternity.

As God the Father begat the fleshly body of Jesus, so He, before the world began, begat his spirit. As the body required an earthly Mother, so his

190 / Mormonism Mama & Me

The Latter=Day Saints'
MILLENNIAL STAR.

HE THAT HATH AN EAR, LET HIM HEAR WHAT THE SPIRIT SAITH
UNTO THE CHURCHES.—*Rev.* ii. 7.

No. 48.—Vol. XV.   Saturday, November 26, 1853.   Price One Penny.

ADAM, OUR FATHER AND GOD.

(From the Journal of Discourses.)

My next sermon will be to both Saint and sinner. One thing has remained a mystery in this kingdom up to this day. It is in regard to the character of the well beloved Son of God; upon which subject the Elders of Israel have conflicting views. Our God and Father in heaven, is a being of tabernacle, or in other words, He has a body, with parts the same as you and I have; and is capable of showing forth His works to organized beings, as, for instance, in the world in which we live, it is the result of the knowledge and infinite wisdom that dwell in His organized body. His son, Jesus Christ has become a personage of tabernacle, and has a body like his father. The Holy Ghost is the Spirit of the Lord, and issues forth from Himself, and may properly be called God's minister to execute His will in immensity; being called to govern by His influence and power; but *He* is not a person of tabernacle as we are, and as our Father in Heaven and Jesus Christ are. The question has been, and is often, asked, who it was that begat the Son of the Virgin Mary. The infidel world have concluded that if what the Apostles wrote about his father and mother be true, and the present marriage discipline acknowledged by Christendom be correct, then Christians must believe that God is the father of an illegitimate son, in the person of Jesus Christ! The infidel fraternity teach *that*, to their disciples. I will tell you how it is. Our Father in Heaven begat all the spirits that ever were or ever will be upon this earth; and they were born spirits in the eternal world. Then the Lord by His power and wisdom organized the mortal tabernacle of man. We were made first spiritual and afterwards temporal.

Now hear it, O inhabitants of the earth, Jew and Gentile, Saint and sinner! When our father Adam came into the garden of Eden, he came into it with a *celestial body*, and brought Eve, *one of his wives*, with him. He helped to make and organize this world. He is MICHAEL, *the Archangel*, the ANCIENT OF DAYS! about whom holy men have written and spoken—HE *is our* FATHER *and our* GOD, *and the only God with whom* WE *have to do.* Every man upon the earth, professing Christians or non-professing, must hear it, and *will know it sooner or later.* They came here, organized the raw material, and arranged in their order the herbs of the field, the trees, the apple, the peach, the plum, the pear, and every other fruit that is desirable and good for man; the seed was brought from another sphere, and planted in this earth. The thistle, the thorn, the brier, and the obnoxious weed did *not* appear until after the earth was cursed. When Adam and Eve had eaten of the forbidden fruit, their bodies became mortal from *its effects*, and therefore their offspring were mortal. When the virgin Mary conceived the child Jesus, the Father had begotten him

770 SECOND EPISTLE OF ORSON PRATT.

.. his own likeness. He was *not* begotten by the Holy Ghost. And who is the Father? He is the first of the human family; and when he took a tabernacle, it was begotten by *his Father* in heaven, after the same manner as the tabernacles of Cain, Abel, and the rest of the sons and daughters of Adam and Eve; from the fruits of the earth, the first earthly tabernacles were originated by the Father, and so on in succession. I could tell you much more about this; but were I to tell you the whole truth, blasphemy would be nothing to it, in the estimation of the superstitious and over-righteous of mankind. However, I have told you the truth as far as I have gone. I have heard men preach upon the divinity of Christ, and exhaust all the wisdom they possessed. All Scripturalists, and approved theologians who were considered exemplary for piety and education, have undertaken to expound on this subject, in every age of the Christian era; and after they have done all, they are obliged to conclude by exclaiming " great is the mystery of godliness," and tell nothing.

It is true that the earth was organized by three distinct characters, namely Eloheim, Yahovah, and Michael, these three forming a quorum, as in all heavenly bodies, and in organizing element, perfectly represented in the Deity, as Father, Son, and Holy Ghost.

Again, they will try to tell how the divinity of Jesus is joined to his humanity, and exhaust all their mental faculties, and wind up with this profound language, as describing the soul of man, " it is an immaterial substance!" What a learned idea! Jesus, our elder brother, was begotten in the flesh by the same character that was in the garden of Eden, and who is our Father in Heaven. Now, let all who may hear these doctrines, pause before they make light of them, or treat them with indifference, for they will prove their salvation or damnation.

I have given you a few leading items upon this subject, but a great deal more remains to be told. Now remember from this time forth, and for ever, that Jesus Christ was not begotten by the Holy Ghost. I will repeat a little anecdote. I was in conversation with a certain learned professor upon this subject, when I replied, to this idea—" if the Son was begotten by the Holy Ghost, it would be very dangerous to baptize and confirm females, and give the Holy Ghost to them, lest he should beget children, to be palmed upon the Elders by the people, bringing the Elders into great difficulties."

Treasure up these things in your hearts. In the Bible, you have read the things I have told you to night; but you have not known what you did read. I have told you no more than you are conversant with; but what do the people in Christendom, with the Bible in their hands, know about this subject? Comparatively nothing.

EXTRACTS FROM THE SECOND EPISTLE OF ORSON PRATT,

TO THE SAINTS SCATTERED THROUGHOUT THE UNITED STATES AND BRITISH PROVINCES— GREETING.

(*From the Seer, No. 11, Vol.* i.)

Brethren of the Priesthood, keep yourselves pure and unspotted before God; and if you know of any man in the Church who already has a wife, seeking to enter into covenant with any other female, know assuredly that he has transgressed, and unless he repent, let him be cut off from the Church.

*   *   *   *

" Writing Mediums," &c.; for they will darken your minds, and bring you to destruction; they are the spirits of darkness let loose upon this generation because of their wickedness; and they will increase more and more upon the earth until the coming of Christ, as the Scriptures predict.

*   *   *   *

if it is only to the extent of a hair's breadth. And if he cannot keep a person this side the Gospel line, he will walk with that individual on the line and strive to push him over.

That is so invariably the case that people need eyes to see, and understanding to know how to discriminate between the things of God and the things that are not of Him. Will this people learn? I am happy and joyful, I am thankful, and can say of a truth, brethren and sisters, that the manifestations of goodness from this people are not to be compared, in my opinion, with those from any other people upon the face of the whole earth since the days of Enoch.

Old Israel, in all their travels, wanderings, exercises, powers, and keys of the Priesthood, never came nigh enough to the path this people have walked in to see them in their obedience that was and is required by the Gospel. Yet there are thousands of weaknesses and overt acts in some of this people, which render us more or less obnoxious to each other.

Still, you may search all the history extant of the children of Israel, or that of any people that ever lived on the face of the earth since the days of Enoch, and I very much doubt, taking that people with their traditions, and comparing them with this mixed multitude from the different nations now in the world with our traditions, whether you would find a people from the days of Enoch until now that could favorably compare with this people in their willingness to obey the Gospel, and to go all lengths to build up the kingdom of God.

I have said a great many times, and repeat it now, and whether I am mistaken or not I will leave for the future to determine, and though, as I do, Joseph when living reproved the people, that I believe with all my heart that the people who gathered around Enoch, and lived with him and built up his City, when they had travelled the same length of time in their experience as this people have, were not as far advanced in the things of the kingdom of God.

Make your own comparisons between the two people, think of the traditions of the two. How many nations were there in the days of Enoch? The very men who were associated with him had been with Adam; they knew him and his children, and had the privilege of talking with God. Just think of it.

Though we have it in history that our father Adam was made of the dust of this earth, and that he knew nothing about his God previous to being made here, yet it is not so; and when we learn the truth we shall see and understand that he helped to make this world, and was the chief manager in that operation.

He was the person who brought the animals and the seeds from other planets to this world, and brought a wife with him and stayed here. You may read and believe what you please as to what is found written in the Bible. Adam was made from the dust of an earth, but not from the dust of this earth. He was made as you and I are made, and no person was ever made upon any other principle.

Do you not suppose that he was acquainted with his associates, who came and helped to make this earth? Yes, they were just as familiar with each other as we are with our children and parents.

Suppose a number of our sons were going to Carson Valley to build houses, open farms, and erect mills and workshops, and that we should say to them that we wish them to stay there five years, and that then we will come and visit them, when I go there will they be afraid of me? No, they would receive me as their father, just as Adam received his Father.

INTELLIGENCE, ETC.

289

and be prepared to receive glory, immortality, and eternal life, that when they go into the spirit-world, their work will far surpass that of any other man or being that has not been blessed with the keys of the Priesthood here.

Joseph Smith holds the keys of this last dispensation, and is now engaged behind the vail in the great work of the last days. I can tell our beloved brother Christians who have slain the Prophets and butchered and otherwise caused the death of thousands of Latter-day Saints, the priests who have thanked God in their prayers and thanksgiving from the pulpit that we have been plundered, driven, and slain, and the deacons under the pulpit, and their brethren and sisters in their closets, who have thanked God, thinking that the Latter-day Saints were wasted away, something that no doubt will mortify them—something that, to say the least, is a matter of deep regret to them—namely, that no man or woman in this dispensation will ever enter into the celestial kingdom of God without the consent of Joseph Smith. From the day that the Priesthood was taken from the earth to the winding-up scene of all things, every man and woman must have the certificate of Joseph Smith, junior, as a passport to their entrance into the mansion where God and Christ are—I with you and you with me. I cannot go there without his consent. He holds the keys of that kingdom for the last dispensation—the keys to rule in the spirit-world; and he rules there triumphantly, for he gained full power and a glorious victory over the power of Satan while he was yet in the flesh, and was a martyr to his religion and to the name of Christ, which gives him a most perfect victory in the spirit-world. He reigns there as supreme a being in his sphere, capacity, and calling, as God does in heaven. Many will ex-

No. 19.]

claim—"Oh, that is very disagreeable! It is preposterous! We cannot bear the thought!" But it is true.

I will now tell you something that ought to comfort every man and woman on the face of the earth. Joseph Smith, junior, will again be on this earth dictating plans and calling forth his brethren to be baptized for the very characters who wish this was not so, in order to bring them into a kingdom to enjoy, perhaps, the presence of angels or the spirits of good men, if they cannot endure the presence of the Father and the Son; and he will never cease his operations, under the directions of the Son of God, until the last ones of the children of men are saved that can be, from Adam till now.

Should not this thought comfort all people? They will, by-and-by, be a thousand times more thankful for such a man as Joseph Smith, junior, than it is possible for them to be for any earthly good whatever. It is his mission to see that all the children of men in this last dispensation are saved, that can be, through the redemption. You will be thankful, every one of you, that Joseph Smith, junior, was ordained to this great calling before the worlds were. I told you that the doctrine of election and reprobation is a true doctrine. It was decreed in the counsels of eternity, long before the foundations of the earth were laid, that he should be the man, in the last dispensation of this world, to bring forth the word of God to the people, and receive the fulness of the keys and power of the Priesthood of the Son of God. The Lord had his eye upon him, and upon his father, and upon his father's father, and upon their progenitors clear back to Abraham, and from Abraham to the flood, from the flood to Enoch, and from Enoch to Adam. He has watched that family and that blood as it has circulated from its fountain to the

RESTORATION—RESURRECTION, &c.

Remarks by President BRIGHAM YOUNG, *made in the Bowery, Great Salt Lake City, October* 21, 1860.

REPORTED BY G. D. WATT.

We wish the Saints to distinctly understand that the remarks just made by brother Hyde do not pertain to doctrine, are not commandments, and have nothing to do with the ordinances of the house of God. He has given us some of his views and reflections. Suppose them to be true, and what of them? Suppose they are not true, and what of it? They have nothing to do with the doctrines and faith of this people. Whether they are true or not is about as immaterial as to know whether it is going to rain to-morrow or next week. If it rains, all we can do is to say, Let it rain; if it does not rain, all we have to do is to prepare to do the best we can with the dust: that is all there is of it. It is no matter whether those views and reflections are true or false.

According to the Scriptures, as they have come to us, we most assuredly believe that the measure we receive at the hands of our enemies will be measured to them again. But whether the wicked seek to corrupt the Church of God or not, the Saints will inherit every good thing. This is not saying that we are Saints. I have not yet come to that, though I firmly believe that we are trying to be Saints. Those that overcome and sit down with Jesus in his Father's kingdom will possess all things: no good thing will be withheld from them.

Man is the lord of this earth, not woman. It is frequently told you that all the creatures of God, except man, will abide and honour the law under which they are placed. The vegetable, mineral, and animal kingdoms, except man, will abide the law by which they were made, and will be prepared to dwell on the new earth, in the midst of the new heavens that will be re-organised—the earth that we now inhabit. Man is the transgressor. Eve was the first to partake of the forbidden fruit, and the man was disposed to follow her, and did follow her; consequently, sin is in the world, and when redemption comes it must come by man. When we speak of law and the transgression of law, we refer to the law of God to man.

I doubt whether it can be found, from the revelations that are given and the facts as they exist, that there is a female in all the regions of hell. We are complained of for having more wives than one. I don't begin to have as many as I shall have by and by, nor you either, if you are faithful. I am not the one that will dispose of them, but the Almighty to whom they belong; and it is His right to dispose of us and of all his creatures and creations.

I assuredly believe that all brother Hyde has said in regard to the restoration of the Saints to their inheritances, &c., will come to pass. And I believe, furthermore, if the men who have driven us—the counties, States, and the General Government of the United States, proffer to take

MAN THE HEAD OF WOMAN, ETC.   259

teousness sake? None! They claimed
that they did it on account of their
wickedness; and if they never have
made this acknowledgement, do you
think they ever will? No! With a
blind and maddened zeal against the
Saints, strengthened by the eternal
hatred and jealousy of the fallen
angels, will they fill the cup of their
iniquity and ripen in the glare of their
oppression for the judgments of Almighty God.

Are we everywhere spoken against?
Is almost every newspaper and journal, with a thousand and one anony-
mous letter writers, pouring forth
their spleen, animadversions, and ma-
ledictions upon the Saints in Utah?
Do they wish and intend to blow up a
storm—a tempest to burst upon our
heads with all the fury of the combined elements to sweep us from the
face of the earth? Or secretely and
under cover, do they intend to rig a
purchase to prey upon the peace and
happiness of the Saints who have fled
from the face of the " serpent," unprotected and unredressed, to this
desolate land, to which no other people would come until after we came
and killed the snakes, built the brid-
ges, proved the country, raised bread
and built houses for them to come to,
a land where no other people can or
will dwell, should the Mormous leave
it!

Why this hatred and ill-will against
you? What have you done to pro-
voke it? We have rebuked iniquity;
and, in some instances, in rather high
places. But the real cause is explained by our Saviour: " Ye are not
of the world, but I have chosen you
out of the world, therefore the world
hate you."

Remember that God not only rules
the storm, but visits the secret chambers. He can hush the storm, and
say to the winds, " Peace, be still,"
and catch the fowler in his own snare.

The professed purity of this generation will not allow the institutions
of Utah to exist undisturbed, if they
can devise any scheme to disturb
them. It is true that the people of
Utah believe in and practise polygamy. Not because our natural desires lead us into that condition and
state of life, but because our God
hath commanded it, and wishing to
comply with that as well as with all
others of His commands, we are as we
are. We also wish to be counted
Abraham's children, to whom the promises were made, and also with whom
the covenants were established; and
being told that if we are the children of Abraham, we will do the
works of Abraham, we are not a little
anxious to do as he did. Among other
things that he did, he took more than
one wife. In this he was not alone,
for this example was copied by most of
the ancient worthies and others who
succeeded him under the same everlasting covenant. Even the wisest
and best men—men after God's own
heart, entered the most deeply into
this practice. Nor was this practice
limited to the days of the Old Testament.

It will be borne in mind that once
on a time, there was a marriage in
Cana of Galilee; and on a careful
reading of that transaction, it will be
discovered that no less a person than
Jesus Christ was married on that
occasion. If he was never married,
his intimacy with Mary and Martha,
and the other Mary also whom Jesus
loved, must have been highly unbecoming and improper to say the best
of it.

I will venture to say that if Jesus
Christ were now to pass through the
most pious countries in Christendom
with a train of women, such as used to
follow him, fondling about him, combing his hair, anointing him with precious
ointment, washing his feet with tears,
and wiping them with the hair of their
heads and unmarried, or even mar-

ried, he would be mobbed, tarred, and feathered, and rode, not on an ass, but on a rail. What did the old Prophet mean when he said (speaking of Christ), "He shall see his seed, prolong his days, &c." Did Jesus consider it necessary to fulfil every righteous command or requirement of his Father? He most certainly did. This he witnessed by submitting to baptism under the hands of John. "Thus it becometh us to fulfil all righteousness," said he. Was it God's commandment to man, in the beginning, to multiply and replenish the earth? None can deny this, neither that it was a righteous command; for upon an obedience to this, depended the perpetuity of our race. Did Christ come to destroy the law or the Prophets, or to fulfil them? He came to fulfil. Did he multiply, and did he see his seed? Did he honour his Father's law by complying with it, or did he not? Others may do as they like, but I will not charge our Saviour with neglect or transgression in this or any other duty.

At this doctrine the long-faced hypocrite and the sanctimonious bigot will probably cry, blasphemy! Horrid perversion of God's word! Wicked wretch! He is not fit to live! &c., &c. But the wise and reflecting will consider, read, and pray. If God be not our Father, grandfather, or great grandfather, or some kind of a father in reality, in deed and in truth, why are we taught to say, "Our Father who art in heaven?" How much soever of holy horror this doctrine may excite in persons not impregnated with the blood of Christ, and whose minds are consequently dark and benighted, it may excite still more when they are told that if none of the natural blood of Christ flows in their veins, they are not the chosen or elect of God. Object not, therefore, too strongly against the marriage of Christ, but remember that in the

last days, secret and hidden things must come to light, and that your life also (which is the blood) is hid with Christ in God.

Abraham was chosen of God for the purpose of raising up a chosen seed, and a peculiar people unto His name. Jesus Christ was sent into the world for a similar purpose, but upon a more extended scale. Christ was the seed of Abraham, so reckoned. To these, great promises were made; one of which was, that in Abraham and in his seed, which was Christ, all the families of the earth should be blessed. When? When the ungodly or those not of their seed should be cut off from the earth, and no family remaining on earth except their own seed. Then in Abraham and in Christ, all the families and kindreds of the earth will be blessed—Satan bound, and the millenium fully come. Then the meek will inherit the earth, and God's elect reign undisturbed, at least, for one thousand years.

Is there no way provided for those to come into this covenant relation who may not possess, in their veins, any of the blood of Abraham or of Christ? Yes! By doing the works of Abraham and of Christ in the faith of Abraham and of Christ; not in unbelief and unrighteousness, like the wicked world who have damned themselves in their own corruption and unbelief. If thou wilt believe on the Lord Jesus Christ, and repent of thy sins, and put them all away, and forsake them for ever, and turn unto the Lord our God, and serve Him with all thy might, mind, and strength, the Holy Ghost will change thy vile body, quicken and renew thy spirit and natural system, so that thou shalt lay off or overcome that fallen nature which is in the body with its sins, and be created anew in Christ Jesus, with a new heart and a new spirit, even the Holy Ghost; this will cause your spirits to cry, Abba, Father. Your

prove? Do you want to prove that an old apostate, who has been cut off from the Church thirteen times for lying, is anything worthy of notice?

I heard that a certain gentleman, a picture maker in this city, when the boys would have moved away the wagon in which this apostate was standing, became violent with them, saying, Let this man alone, these are Saints that are persecuting (sneeringly.) We want such men to go to California, or anywhere they choose. I say to those persons, you must not court persecution here, lest you get so much of it you will not know what to do with it. Do NOT court persecution. We have known Gladden Bishop for more than twenty years, and know him to be a poor, dirty curse. Here is sister Vilate Kimball, brother Heber's wife, has borne more from that man than any other woman on earth could bear; but she won't bear it again. I say again, you Gladdenites, do not court persecution, or you will get more than you want, and it will come quicker than you want it. I say to you Bishops, do not allow them to preach in your wards. Who broke the roads to these valleys? Did this little nasty Smith, and his wife? No, they staid in St. Louis while we did it, peddling ribbons, and kissing the Gentiles. I know what they have done here—they have asked exorbitant prices for their nasty stinking ribbons. [Voices, "that's true."] We broke the roads to this country. Now, you Gladdenites, keep your tongues still, lest sudden destruction come upon you.

I will tell you a dream that I had last night. I dreamed that I was in the midst of a people who were dressed in rags and tatters, they had turbans upon their heads, and these were also hanging in tatters. The rags were of many colors, and, when the people moved, they were all in motion. Their object in this appeared to be, to attract attention. Said they to me,

"We are Mormons, brother Brigham." "No, you are not," I replied. "But we have been," said they, and they began to jump, and caper about, and dance, and their rags of many colors were all in motion, to attract the attention of the people. I said, "You are no Saints, you are a disgrace to them." Said they, "We have been Mormons." By and bye, along came some mobocrats, and they greeted them with, "How do you do, sir, I am happy to see you." They kept on that way for an hour. I felt ashamed of them, for they were in my eyes a disgrace to "Mormonism." Then I saw two ruffians, whom I knew to be mobbers and murderers, and they crept into a bed, where one of my wives and children were. I said, "You that call yourselves brethren, tell me, is this the fashion among you?" They said, "O, they are good men, they are gentlemen." With that, I took my large bowie knife, that I used to wear as a bosom pin in Nauvoo, and cut one of their throats from ear to ear, saying, "Go to hell across lots." The other one said, "You dare not serve me so." I instantly sprang at him, seized him by the hair of the head, and, bringing him down, cut his throat, and sent him after his comrade; then told them both, if they would behave themselves they should yet live, but if they did not, I would unjoint their necks. At this I awoke.

I say, rather than that apostates should flourish here, I will unsheath my bowie knife, and conquer or die. [Great commotion in the congregation, and a simultaneous burst of feeling, assenting to the declaration. Now, you nasty apostates, clear out, or judgment will be put to the line, and righteousness to the plummet. [Voices, generally, "go it, go it."] If you say it is right, raise your hands. [All hands up.] Let us call upon the Lord to assist us in this, and every good work.

TO KNOW GOD IS ETERNAL LIFE, ETC.

wisdom could devise, this people stroll into the swamp, get into the woods among the brambles and briars, and wander around until night overtakes them, I say, shame on such people.

I am ashamed to talk about a reformation, for if you have entered into the spirit of your religion, you will know whether these things are so or not. If you have the spirit of your religion and have confidence in you, walk along and continue to do so, and secure to yourselves the life before you, and never let it be said, from this time henceforth, that you have wakened out of your sleep, from the fact that you are always awake.

We talk about the reformation, but recollect that you have only just commenced to walk in the way of life and salvation. You have just commenced in the career to obtain eternal life, which is that which you desire, therefore you have no time to spend only in that path. It is straight and narrow, simple and easy, and is an Almighty path, if you will keep in it. But if you wander off into swamps, or into brambles, and get into darkness, you will find it hard to get back.

Brother Cummings told you the truth this morning with regard to the sins of the people. And I will say that the time will come, and is now nigh at hand, when those who profess our faith, if they are guilty of what some of this people are guilty of, will find the axe laid at the root of the tree, and they will be hewn down. What has been must be again, for the Lord is coming to restore all things. The time has been in Israel under the law of God, the celestial law, or that which pertains to the celestial law, for it is one of the laws of that kingdom where our Father dwells, that if a man was found guilty of adultery, he must have his blood shed, and that is near at hand. But now I say, in the name of the Lord, that if this people will sin no more, but faithfully live their

religion, their sins will be forgiven them without taking life.

You are aware that when brother Cummings came to the point of loving our neighbours as ourselves, he could say yes or no as the case might be, that is true. But I want to connect it with the doctrine you read in the Bible. When will we love our neighbour as ourselves? In the first place, Jesus said that no man hateth his own flesh. It is admitted by all that every person loves himself. Now if we do rightly love ourselves, we want to be saved and continue to exist, we want to go into the kingdom where we can enjoy eternity and see no more sorrow nor death. This is the desire of every person who believes in God. Now take a person in this congregation who has knowledge with regard to being saved in the kingdom of our God and our Father, and being exalted, one who knows and understands the principles of eternal life, and sees the beauty and excellency of the eternities before him compared with the vain and foolish things of the world, and suppose that he is overtaken in a gross fault, that he has committed a sin that he knows will deprive him of that exaltation which he desires, and that he cannot attain to it without the shedding of his blood, and also knows that by having his blood shed he will atone for that sin, and be saved and exalted with the Gods, is there a man or woman in this house but what would say, " shed my blood that I may be saved and exalted with the Gods?"

All mankind love themselves, and let these principles be known by an individual, and he would be glad to have his blood shed. That would be loving themselves, even unto an eternal exaltation. Will you love your brothers or sisters likewise, when they have committed a sin that cannot be atoned for without the sheding of their blood? Will you love that man or woman well enough to shed their blood?

That is what Jesus Christ meant. He never told a man or woman to love their enemies in their wickedness, never. He never intended any such thing; his language is left as it is for those to read who have the Spirit to discern between truth and error; it was so left for those who can discern the things of God. Jesus Christ never meant that we should love a wicked man in his wickedness.

Now take the wicked, and I can refer to where the Lord had to slay every soul of the Israelites that went out of Egypt, except Caleb and Joshua. He slew them by the hands of their enemies, by the plague, and by the sword, why? Because He loved them, and promised Abraham that He would save them. And He loved Abraham because he was a friend to his God, and would stick to Him in the hour of darkness, hence He promised Abraham that He would save his seed. And He could save them upon no other principle, for they had forfeited their right to the land of Canaan by transgressing the law of God, and they could not have atoned for the sin if they had lived. But if they were slain, the Lord could bring them up in the resurrection, and give them the land of Canaan, and He could not do it on any other principle.

I could refer you to plenty of instances where men have been righteously slain, in order to atone for their sins. I have seen scores and hundreds of people for whom there would have been a chance (in the last resurrection there will be) if their lives had been taken and their blood spilled on the ground as a smoking incense to the Almighty, but who are now angels to the devil, until our elder brother Jesus Christ raises them up—conquers death, hell, and the grave. I have known a great many men who have left this Church for whom there is no chance whatever for

exaltation, but if their blood had been spilled, it would have been better for them. The wickedness and ignorance of the nations forbid this principle's being in full force, but the time will come when the law of God will be in full force.

This is loving our neighbour as ourselves; if he needs help, help him; and if he wants salvation and it is necessary to spill his blood on the earth in order that he may be saved, spill it. Any of you who understand the principles of eternity, if you have sinned a sin requiring the shedding of blood, except the sin unto death, would not be satisfied nor rest until your blood should be spilled, that you might gain that salvation you desire. That is the way to love mankind.

Christ and Belial have not become friends; they have never shaken hands; they never have agreed to be brothers and to be on good terms; no, never; and they never will, because they are diametrically opposed to each other. If one conquers, the other is destroyed. One or the other of them must triumph and utterly destroy and cast down his opponent. Light and darkness cannot dwell together, and so it is with the kingdom of God,

Now, brethren and sisters, will you live your religion? How many hundreds of times have I asked you that question? Will the Latter-day Saints live their religion? I am ashamed to say anything about a reformation among Saints, but I am happy to think that the people called Latter-day Saints are striving now to obtain the Spirit of their calling and religion. They are just coming into the path, just waking up out of their sleep. It seems as though they are nearly all like babies; we are but children in one sense. Now let us begin, like children, and walk in the straight and narrow path, live our religion, and honour our God.

With these remarks, I pray the

in His great fulness, that men might be brought unto repentance and good works, that they might be restored unto grace, for grace according to their works. And I would that all men might be saved. But we read that in that great and last day, there are some who shall be cast out; yea, who shall be cast off from the presence of the Lord ; yea, who shall be consigned to a state of endless misery, fulfilling the words which say, they that have done good, shall have everlasting life ; and they that have done evil, shall have everlasting damnation. And thus it is. Amen."

REBUKING INIQUITY.

Remarks by President J. M. Grant, Delivered in the Bowery, Great Salt Lake City, September 21, 1856.

I feel that the remarks which we have heard this morning are true, and they apply directly to you who are now present, and to the inhabitants of this city and of the Territory generally, and we do not excuse any of you.

If the arrows of the Almighty ought to be thrown at you we want to do it; and to make you feel and realize that we mean you. And although we talk of the old clay's being ground in the mill, we do not mean it to apply to some other place, for we have enough here who have been dried ever since their baptism, and many of them are cracked and spoiling.

Some have received the Priesthood and a knowledge of the things of God, and still they dishonor the cause of truth, commit adultery, and every other abomination beneath the heavens, and then meet you here or in the street, and deny it.

These are the abominable characters that we have in our midst, and they will seek unto wizards that peep, and to star-gazers and soothsayers, because they have no faith in the holy Priesthood, and then when they meet us, they want to be called Saints.

The same characters will get drunk and wallow in the mire and filth, and yet they call themselves Saints, and seem to glory in their conduct, and they pride themselves in their greatness and in their abominations.

They are the old hardened sinners, and are almost—if not altogether—past improvement, and are full of hell, and my prayer is that God's indignation may rest upon them, and that He will curse them from the crown of their heads to the soles of their feet.

I say, that there are men and women that I would advise to go to the President immediately, and ask him to appoint a committee to attend to their case ; and then let a place be selected, and let that committee shed their blood.

We have those amongst us that are full of all manner of abominations, those who need to have their blood shed, for water will not do, their sins are of too deep a dye.

You may think that I am not teaching you Bible doctrine, but what says the apostle Paul? I would ask how many covenant breakers there are in this city and in this kingdom. I believe that there are a great many; and if they are covenant breakers we need a place designated, where we can shed their blood.

Talk about old clay; I would rather have clay from a new bank than some that we have had clogging the wheels for the last nineteen years. They are a perfect nuisance, and I want them cut off, and the sooner it is done the better.

We have men who are incessantly finding fault, who get up a little party spirit, and criticise the conduct of men of God. They will find fault with this, that, and the other, and nothing is right for them, because they are full of all kinds of filth and wickedness.

And we have women here who like any thing but the celestial law of God; and if they could break asunder the cable of the Church of Christ, there is scarcely a mother in Israel but would do it this day. And they talk it to their husbands, to their daughters, and to their neighbors, and say they have not seen a week's happiness since they became acquainted with that law, or since their husbands took a second wife. They want to break up the Church of God, and to break it from their husbands and from their family connections.

Then, again, there are men that are used as tools by their wives, and they are just a little better in appearance and in their habits than a little black boy. They live in filth and nastiness, they eat it and drink it, and they are filthy all over.

We have Elders and High Priests that are precisely in this predicament, and yet they are wishing for more of the Holy Ghost, they wish to have it in larger doses. They want more revelation, but I tell you that you now have more than you live up to,

more than you practise and make use of.

If I hurt your feelings let them be hurt. And if any of you ask, do I mean you? I answer, yes. If any woman asks, do I mean her? I answer, yes. And I want you to understand that I am throwing the arrows of God Almighty among Israel; I do not excuse any.

I am speaking to you in the name of Israel's God, and you need to be baptized and washed clean from your sins, from your backslidings, from your apostacies, from your filthiness, from your lying, from your swearing, from your lusts, and from every thing that is evil before the God of Israel.

We have been trying long enough with this people, and I go in for letting the sword of the Almighty be unsheathed, not only in word, but in deed.

I go in for letting the wrath of the Almighty burn up the dross and the filth; and if the people will not glorify the Lord by sanctifying themselves, let the wrath of the Almighty God burn against them, and the wrath of Joseph and of Brigham, and of Heber, and of high heaven.

There is nothing to prevent you from being humble and doing right, but your own little, foolish, and wicked acts and doings. I will just tell you that if an angel of God were to pass Great Salt Lake City, while you are in your present state, he would not consider you worthy of his company.

You have got to cleanse yourselves from corruption, before you are fit for the society of those beings. You may hear of people in other cities being baptized and renewing their covenants, but they are not sinners above all others; and except the inhabitants of Great Salt Lake City repent, and do their first works, they shall all likewise perish, and the wrath of God will be upon them and round about them.

You can scarcely find a place in this city that is not full of filth and abominations ; and if you would search them out, they would easily be weighed in the balances, and you would then find that they do not serve their God, and purify their bodies.

But the course they are taking leads them to corrupt themselves, the soil, the waters, and the mountains, and they defile everything around them.

Brethren and sisters, we want you to repent and forsake your sins. And you who have committed sins that cannot be forgiven through baptism, let your blood be shed, and let the smoke ascend, that the incense thereof may come up before God as an atonement for your sins, and that the sinners in Zion may be afraid.

These are my feelings, and may God fulfil them. And my wishes are that He will grant the desires of my brethren, that Zion may be purified, and the wicked purged out of her, until God shall say I will bless the rest ; until He shall say I will bless your flocks, your herds, your little ones, your houses, your lands, and all that you possess; and you shall be my people, and I will come and take up my abode with you, and I will bless all those that do right; which may He grant, in the name of Jesus. Amen.

THE PEOPLE OF GOD DISCIPLINED BY TRIALS—ATONEMENT BY THE SHEDDING OF BLOOD—OUR HEAVENLY FATHER—A PRIVILEGE GIVEN TO ALL THE MARRIED SISTERS IN UTAH.

A Discourse by President Brigham Young, Delivered in the Bowery, Great Salt Lake City, September 21, 1856.

Before I sit down, I shall offer a proposition to the congregation ; though I will first say a few words concerning our religion, our circumstances, and the circumstances of the brethren and people generally that inhabit these valleys, but more especially of those that have the privilege of assembling at this Tabernacle from Sabbath to Sabbath.

If they will rightly consider their situation, they will believe for themselves that they are in a place, in a country, where they can be Saints as well as in any other place there is on the face of this earth.

True, we hear some complaints from those who lose the spirit of their religion, who turn away from us. They think that this people will suffer here. I will give you my feelings upon the subject.

There is not a hardship, there is not a disappointment, there is not a trial, there is not a hard time, that comes upon this people in this place, but that I am more thankful for than I am for full granaries.

We have been hunting during the past twenty-six years, for a place where we could raise Saints, not merely wheat, and corn. Compara-

were destroyed by the Indians. That unfortunate affair has been laid to the charge of the whites. A certain judge that was then in this Territory wanted the whole army to accompany him to Iron county to try the whites for the murder of that company of emigrants. I told Governor Cumming that if he would take an unprejudiced judge into the district where that horrid affair occurred, I would pledge myself that every man in the regions round about should be forthcoming when called for, to be condemned or acquitted as an impartial, unprejudiced judge and jury should decide; and I pledged him that the court should be protected from any violence or hindrance in the prosecution of the laws; and if any were guilty of the blood of those who suffered in the Mountain Meadow massacre, let them suffer the penalty of the law; but to this day they have not touched the matter, for fear the Mormons would be acquitted from the charge of having any hand in it, and our enemies would thus be deprived of a favorite topic to talk about, when urging hostility against us. "The Mountain Meadow massacre! Only think of the Mountain Meadow massacre!!" is their cry from one end of the land to the other. "Come, let us make war on the Mormons, for they burnt government property." And what was the government doing there with their property? They were coming to destroy the Mormons, in violation of every right principle of law and justice. A little of their property was destroyed, and they were left to gnaw, not a tile, but dead cattle's bones. I was informed that one man brought five blood hounds to hunt the Mormons in the mountains, and that the poor devil had to kill them and eat them before spring to save himself from starving to death, and that he was fool enough to acknowledge it

afterwards in this city. This is the kind of outside pressure we have to meet with. Who wanted the army of 1857 here? Who sent for them? Liars, thieves, murderers, gamblers, whoremasters, and speculators in the rights and blood of the Mormon people cried to government, and government opened its ears, long and broad, saying, "I hear you, my children, lie on, my faithful sons Brocchus, Drummond and Co.," and so they did lie on until the parent sent an army to use up the Mormons. Now I say, for the consolation of all my brethren and sisters, they cannot do it; and that is worse to them than all the rest; they cannot do it.

The rank, rabid abolitionists, whom I call black-hearted Republicans, have set the whole national fabric on fire. Do you know this, Democrats? They have kindled the fire that is raging now from the north to the south, and from the south to the north. I am no abolitionist, neither am I a proslavery man; I hate some of their principles and especially some of their conduct, as I do the gates of hell. The Southerners make the negroes, and the Northerners worship them; this is all the difference between slaveholders and abolitionists. I would like the President of the United States and all the world to hear this.

Shall I tell you the law of God in regard to the African race? If the white man who belongs to the chosen seed mixes his blood with the seed of Cain, the penalty, under the law of God, is death on the spot. This will always be so. The nations of the earth have transgressed every law that God has given, they have changed the ordinances and broken every covenant made with the fathers, and they are like a hungry man that dreameth that he eateth, and he awaketh and behold he is empty.

The following saying of the prophet is fulfilled: "Now also many nations

of? And she said, An old man cometh up, and he is covered with a mantle. And Saul perceived that it was Samuel, and he stooped with his face to the ground and bowed himself." (1 Sam. 28 : 12-14.) It will be perceived that the form of Samuel's spirit was that of " an old man," "covered with a mantle." Now this could not have been Samuel's body, for that was mouldering in the grave ; therefore it must have been his spirit. From the form which this spirit had, Saul was enabled to "*perceive that it was Samuel.*" Saul, after bowing down to the ground with reverence before Samuel, entered into conversation with him ; and Samuel prophesied unto him, and told him what should befal Israel, and that he and his sons should be slain the next day and come into the spiritual world with him.

When the three Hebrews were cast into the fiery furnace, Nebuchadnezzar was astonished, "and said, lo! I see four men loose, walking in the midst of the fire, and they have no hurt ; and the FORM of the fourth is like unto the Son of God." (Dan. 3 : 25.) This fourth personage walking in the fire must have been the spiritual body of the Son of God, or some other spiritual body resembling him in form. The form of this spiritual body resembles also the form of man, hence he exclaimed, " I see four men loose."

The revelator, John, saw the spirits of the martyrs, which he describes as follows : " And when he had opened the fifth seal, I saw under the altar the souls of them that were slain for the word of God and for the testimony which they held ; and they cried with a loud voice saying, How long, O Lord, holy and true, dost thou not judge and avenge our blood on them that dwell on the earth ? And white robes were given unto every one of them ; and it was said unto them that they should rest yet for a little season until their fellow servants and their brethren, that should be killed as they were, should be fulfilled." (Rev. 6 : 9-11.) These

spirits must have had form, or John could not have seen them : they were capable of speaking with a loud voice and of wearing white robes. If a spirit have no form, it could neither speak nor wear clothing. We have already seen that the spirit of Samuel was clothed with a mantle, while those that John saw, had white robes given to them. These passages prove that the spirits of men are in the shape or image of the fleshly tabernacle, and that the spirit of the Son of God, before he took upon himself flesh, did resemble man, and was in the likeness or shape of his fleshly body, into which he afterwards entered.

The shape or form of the spirits of beasts is in the image of their natural bodies. When Elijah was escorted to heaven, he had the honor of riding in a chariot drawn by horses. (2 Kings 2: 11, 12.) When the king of Syria sent horses and chariots, and a great host, to take Elisha, the prophet, and carry him a prisoner into the Syrian army, the servant of the prophet, seeing his master surrounded by such a formidable host, was very much alarmed for his safety, and cried out, "Alas, my master ! how shall we do ? And he answered, Fear not : for they that be with us are more than they that be with them. And Elisha prayed, and said, Lord, I pray thee open his eyes that he may see. And the Lord opened the eyes of the young man, and he saw ; and, behold, the mountain was full of HORSES and chariots of fire round about Elisha." (2 Kings 6 : 15-17.) These horses shone with the brilliancy of fire. They were spiritual horses, under the management and control of an army of spirits riding in chariots. These spirits of horses must have been in the same shape as the natural bodies of horses, or else they would not have been recognised as belonging to that species of animals. They were exceedingly numerous, so that "*the mountain was full*" of them.

John says, "I saw Heaven opened, and behold a WHITE HORSE;

and He that sat upon him was was called Faithful and True, and in righteousness He doeth judge and make war." "And the armies which were in Heaven followed Him upon WHITE HORSES, clothed in fine linen white and clean."—Rev. 19 : 11, 14. Thus, we perceive, that the Son of God, himself, and all the armies of Heaven, occasionally ride on horseback ; and, therefore, there must be thousands of millions of horses in Heaven ; and as no horses, pertaining to this earth, had then received a resurrection, these, doubtless, were the spiritual bodies of horses whose natural bodies had returned to the dust.

As we have proved, that the spirits of men, and of horses, and of all manner of beasts, and of creeping things, and of birds, are in the shape of their mortal tabernacles, it is reasonable to infer, analogically, that the spirits of grass, of herbs, and of trees, are in the form of the natural bodies of the respective vegetables which they once inhabited ; and that those vegetables which are now living, are inhabited by living spirits in the form of themselves.

All spirits have *magnitude*, as well as form, which can be clearly shown from the Scriptures. Those passages, that have been already quoted, proving that spirits have form, also prove that they have magnitude. The Spirit of Samuel, as seen by Saul, and the spirit of the Son of God, walking in the fiery furnace, were, both, of the size of men. The spirits of horses, beasts, birds, and creeping things, were, not only of the shape of their respective natural bodies, but were evidently of the same size as those bodies when full grown ; otherwise they would have been represented, as infants instead of men, as colts instead of horses, &c.

The tabernacles of both animals and vegetables continue to grow or increase in size, until they attain to the original magnitude of their respective spirits, after which the growth ceases. When the spirit first takes possession of the vegetable or animal seed or embryo, it contracts itself into a bulk of the same dimension as the seed or tabernacle into which it enters : this is proved from the fact, that the spiritual body of the Son of God, seen by Nebuchadnezzar, was of the size of man, and yet this same spiritual body was afterwards sufficiently contracted to enter into, and to be wholly contained within an infant tabernacle. In like manner, every other spirit, whether vegetable or animal, is of the full size of the prospective tabernacle, when it shall have attained its full growth ; and, therefore, when it first enters the same, it must, like the spiritual body of the Son of God, be greatly diminished from its original dimensions. Spirits, therefore, must be composed of substances, highly elastic in their nature, that is, they have the power to resume their former dimensions, as additional matter is secreted for the enlargement of their tabernacles. It is this expanding force, exerted by the spirit, which gradually developes the tabernacle as the necessary materials are supplied.

When the limb of a tree or of an animal is severed from the main body, the spirit, occupying that limb, is not severed from the other parts of the spirit, but immediately contracts itself into the living portions of the body, leaving the limb to decay. The contraction of spiritual bodies is still further proved, from the fact, that a legion of wicked spirits actually huddled themselves together in the tabernacle of one man. These wicked spirits, being fallen angels, were actually in the shape and size of the spirits of men ; therefore, they must have been exceedingly contracted to have all entered one human body.

23. The celestial beings who dwell in the Heaven from which we came, having been raised from the grave, in a former world, and having been filled with all the fulness of these eternal attributes, are called Gods, because the fulness of God dwells in each. Both the males and the females enjoy this fulness. The celestial vegetables and fruits which grow out of the soil of this redeemed Heaven, constitute the food of the Gods. This food differs from the food derived from the vegetables of a fallen world: the latter are converted into blood, which, circulating in the veins and arteries, produces flesh and bones of a mortal nature, having a constant tendency to decay: while the former, or celestial vegetables, are, when digested in the stomach, converted into a fluid, which, in its nature, is spiritual, and which, circulating in the veins and arteries of the celestial male and female, preserves their tabernacles from decay and death. Earthly vegetables form blood, and blood forms flesh and bones; celestial vegetables, when digested, form a spiritual fluid which gives immortality and eternal life to the organization in which it flows.

24. Fallen beings beget children whose bodies are constituted of flesh and bones, being formed out of the blood circulating in the veins of the parents. Celestial beings beget children, composed of the fluid which circulates in their veins, which is spiritual, therefore, their children must be spirits, and not flesh and bones. This is the origin of our spiritual organization in Heaven. The spirits of all mankind, destined for this earth, were begotten by a father, and born of a mother in Heaven, long anterior to the formation of this world. The personages of the father and mother of our spirits, had a beginning to their organization, but the fulness of truth (which is God) that dwells in them, had no beginning; being "from everlasting to everlasting." (Psalm 90: 2.)

25. In the Heaven where our spirits were born, there are many Gods, each one of whom has his own wife or wives which were given to him previous to his redemption, while yet in his mortal state. Each God, through his wife or wives, raises up a numerous family of sons and daughters; indeed, there will be no end to the increase of his own children: for each father and mother will be in a condition to multiply forever and ever. As soon as each God has begotten many millions of male and female spirits, and his Heavenly inheritance becomes too small, to comfortably accommodate his great family, he, in connection with his sons, organizes a new world, after a similar order to the one which we now inhabit, where he sends both the male and female spirits to inhabit tabernacles of flesh and bones. Thus each God forms a world for the accommodation of his own sons and daughters who are sent forth in their times and seasons, and generations to be born into the same. The inhabitants of each world are required to reverence, adore, and worship their own personal father who dwells in the Heaven which they formerly inhabited.

26. When a world is redeemed from its fallen state, and made into a Heaven, all the animal creation are raised from the dead, and become celestial and immortal. The food of these animals is derived from the vegetables, growing on a celestial soil; consequently, it is not converted into blood, but into spirit which circulates in the veins of these animals; therefore, their off-spring will be spiritual bodies, instead of flesh and bones. Thus the spirits of beasts, of fowls, and of all living creatures, are the off-spring of the beasts, fowls and creatures which have been redeemed or raised from the dead, and which will multiply spirits, according to their respective species, forever and ever.

27. As these spiritual bodies, in all their varieties and species, become

numerous in Heaven, each God will send those under his jurisdiction to take bodies of flesh and bones on the same world to which he sends his own sons and daughters. As each God is "The God of the spirits of all flesh," pertaining to the world which he forms; and as he holds supreme dominion over them in Heaven, when he sends them into a temporal or terrestrial world, he commits this dominion into the hands of his sons and daughters, which inhabit the same.

28. When the world is redeemed, the vegetable creation is redeemed and made new, as well as the animal; and when planted in a celestial soil, each vegetable derives its nourishment therefrom; and the fluid, thus derived, circulates in the pores and cells of the vegetable tabernacle, and preserves it from decay and death; this same fluid, thus circulating, forms a spiritual seed, which planted, grows into a spiritual vegetable; this differs from the parent vegetable, in that it has no tabernacle. This is the origin of spiritual vegetables in Heaven. These spiritual vegetables are sent from Heaven to the terrestrial worlds, where, like animals, they take natural tabernacles, which become food for the sustenance of the natural tabernacles of the animal creation. Thus the spirits of both vegetables and animals are the offspring of male and female parents which have been raised from the dead, or redeemed from a fallen condition, with the world upon which they dwelt.

29. The number of the sons and daughters of God, born in Heaven before this earth was formed, is not known by us. They must have been exceedingly numerous, as may be perceived, by taking into consideration the vast numbers which have already come from Heaven, and peopled our planet. during the past six thousand years. The amount of population now on the globe, is estimated in round numbers at one thousand million. If we take this estimation for the average number per century, during the seven thou-

sand years of its temporal existence, it will amount to seventy thousand millions. During the early age of the world, there were many centuries in which the amount of population would fall short of this average; but during the Millennium, or the last age of the world, the population will, probably, far exceed this average. Seventy thousand million, therefore, is a rough approximation to the number of inhabitants which the Lord destined to dwell in the flesh on this earth. It will be seen, from this estimation, that about seventy thousand million sons and daughters were born in Heaven, and kept their first estate, and were counted worthy to have a new world made for them, wherein they were permitted to receive bodies of flesh and bones, and thus enter upon their second estate.

30. It must be remembered, that seventy thousand million, however great the number may appear to us, are but two-thirds of the vast family of spirits who were begotten before the foundation of the world: the other third part of the family did not keep the first estate. Add to seventy thousand million, the third part which fell, namely, thirty-five thousand million, and the sum amounts to one hundred and five thousand million which was the approximate number of the sons and daughters of God in Heaven before the rebellion which broke out among them.

31. If we admit that one personage was the Father of all this great family, and that they were all born of the same Mother, the period of time intervening between the birth of the oldest and the youngest spirit must have been immense. If we suppose, as an average, that only one year intervened between each birth, then it would have required, over one hundred thousand million of years for the same Mother to have given birth to this vast family. The law, regulating the formation of the embryo spirit, may, as it regards time, differ considerably from the period required for the formation of the infant tabernacle

of flesh. Should the period between each birth, be one hundred times shorter than what is required in this world, (which is very improbable,) it would still require over one thousand million of years to raise up such a numerous progeny. But as heavenly things are, in many respects, typical of earthly, it is altogether probable that the period required for the formation of the infant spirit, is of the same length as that required in this world for the organization of the infant tabernacle.

32. If the Father of these spirits, prior to his redemption, had secured to himself, through the everlasting covenant of marriage, many wives, as the prophet David did in our world, the period required to people a world would be shorter, within certain limits, in proportion to the number of wives. For instance, if it required one hundred thousand million of years to people a world like this, as above stated, it is evident that, with a hundred wives, this period would be reduced to only one thousand million of years. Therefore, a Father, with these facilities, could increase his kingdoms with his own children, in a hundred fold ratio above that of another who had only secured to himself one wife. As yet, we have only spoken of the hundred fold ratio as applied to his *own* children; but now let us endeavor to form some faint idea of the multiplied increase of worlds peopled by his *grandchildren*, over which he, of course, would hold authority and dominion as the Grand Patriarch of the endless generations of his posterity. If, out of the whole population of the first redeemed world, only one million of sons were redeemed to the fulness of all the privileges and glory of their Father, they, in their turn, would now be prepared to multiply and people worlds the same as their Father, being made like him and one with him. While their Father, therefore, was peopling the second world, these million of redeemed sons would people one million of worlds. Each of these worlds would be redeemed and glorified, and

become celestial worlds or heavens. Thus there would be the "Heaven of Heavens" inhabited by the Grand Patriarch and those of the same order with him; secondly, there would be the two redeemed worlds or heavens inhabited by his children; and, thirdly, there would be the one million of heavens inhabited by his grandchildren. We have only estimated, as yet, the second generation of worlds. If the estimate be carried still further in the same ratio, it will be found that the number in the third generation amounts to one billion three million and three worlds. The fourth generation would people over a trillion, and the fifth over a quadrillion of worlds; while the one-hundredth generation would people more worlds than could be expressed by raising one million to the ninety ninth power. Any mathematician who is able to enumerate a series of 595 figures, will be able to give a very close approximation to the number of worlds peopled by the descendants of one Father in one hundred thousand million of years, according to the average ratio given above. Now this is the period in which only one world could be peopled with one wife. While the Patriarch with his hundred wives, would multiply worlds on worlds, systems on systems, more numerous than the dust of all the visible bodies of the universe, and people them with his descendants to the hundredth generation of worlds; the other, who had only secured to himself one wife, would in the same period, just barely have peopled one world.

33. Each father gives laws to his family, adapted to the degree of knowledge which they possess. The laws given to impart the ideas of right and wrong to infant spirits, are of a more simple nature than those ordained for the government of spirits after they have acquired this knowledge. Each law has its appropriate penalty affixed, according to the nature of the law and the amount of knowledge possessed by the beings whom it is intended to govern. The

INDEX

Abraham:
  Became a god, 87
  Concubines and children accounted for righteousness, 87
  Faith accounted for righteousness, 87
Adam (and Adam-God):
  Announced by Brigham Young, 68, 190, 191
  Begat Jesus in the flesh, 68, 73, 190, 191
  Begat Jesus in the spirit, 73
  Comes from another planet, 70, 192
  Does not come from another planet, 68, 190, 191
  Doctrine comes from God, 70, 71, 192
  Father of our spirits, 67, 68, 71, 73, 190, 191
  Holds the keys of salvation, 71
  Mormons reject doctrine, 70, 73
  A polygamist, 68, 73, 190
  Resurrected before this life, 73
  Required male and female to make, ix
  Sin of, a blessing and necessity, 6
Animals:
  Horses in heaven, 204, 205
    Jesus and armies in heaven ride, 204
    Resurrected, spirits of, 204, 205
Babies:
  Born in heaven, 51, 59, 68, 69
  Diapers must be furnished in heaven, 50, 51
  God born a, 2, 8, 51, 53
Baptism:
  For the dead, 47, 96
  Rebaptism for Grandpa Lee, 146
Bible:
  "Inspired" Version, 17, 18, 92
  Insufficient guide, 17, 18, 40
  Plain parts taken away, 17, 91
Blood Atonement:
  Defined, 100-101, 197
  Destroying Angels carried out, 108-111
  Denied today, 127
  Is a "Biblical" doctrine, 104, 200-202
  Jesus' atonement insufficient, 106, 107, 123, 125
  Judas died by, 114
  Nearest of kin must kill relative's seducer, 121
  Necessary, 102-103, 106
  Of Joseph Smith pleads unto heaven, 15
  Offenses qualifying for:
    Apostasy, 101, 102, 105, 118, 120-122, 197, 203
    Adultery, 103, 117-118, 119, 200-202
    Fornication, 106
    Lying, 120

Man:
  Began as "intelligence", coequal with God, 55-56
  Begins life innocent and pure, God's children, 44
  Can become a God himself, 47, 54, 56
    By becoming an "Adam", 69
    Through polygamy, 87, 94
    Through sexual increase, 46, 94, 95
  Emasculation of, 108
  God in embryo, 56
  Innate goodness of, 44, 45
  Must tithe, 43
  Naturally opposed to God, 44
  Not naturally opposed to God, 44
  Offspring of God, 46
  Resurrects wives and children, 43, 58
  Self-existent with God, 55, 56
  Spirits of begotten in heaven, 206
  To be married, procreate children in heaven, 47
  To become an "Adam", 69
Matter:
  Is eternal, 55
Meridian of Time:
  Jesus born in, head of, 17, 20
Mormons:
  More noble, more intelligent spirits in heaven, 3, 12
  Most righteous people on earth, 12
  Spirits of choice, superior, sent to
    white L.D.S. parents, 2, 3
Mothers in Heaven:
  Adoration of, 14, 59
Mountain Meadows Massacre:
  And Mormon war against U.S., 135-126
  Booty of, sent to Mormon tithing office, 139
  Brigham Young incites Indians to aid in, 135-136
  General references to, Chapter 10
  John D. Lee is scapegoat for, 139-142
Negroes:
  Denied priesthood, 171, 172
  Given priesthood, 170
    Reason why, 174ff
  Have "degraded" parentages, 12
  Marriage to results in death, 122
  Preexistent life determined lineage, 3
Paradise:
  Is third heaven, 144
Paul the Apostle:
  A polygamist, 90, 195, 196
People's Temple Cult:
  Relationship to Mormonism, 99, 100
Polygamy (Plural Marriage):
  Abraham, a god because of, 87
  Correct, great, ennobling, 79
  Doctrine and Covenants still commands, 87-88
  Enter into and be saved by, 88
  God's preferred plan for man, 79
  Insures virility, 82
  Jesus and God practiced, 61, 89, 90, 92, 195, 196
  Men become gods by, 87, 94
  One of the most important doctrines ever revealed, 94
  Still a valid doctrine, 94-96
  To be reinstituted, 95
Priesthood L.D.S.:
  Authority to "act for God", 21
  Emasculation and murder of gentiles ordered by, 108

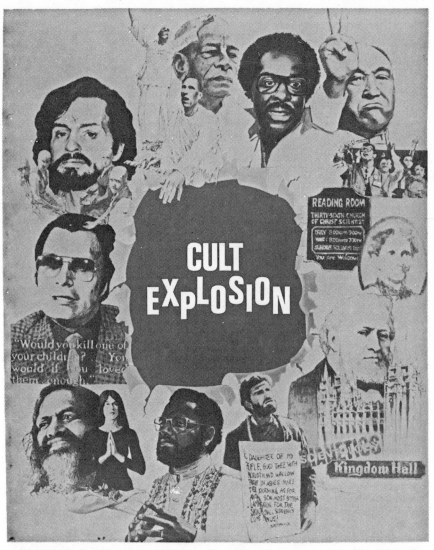

CULT EXPLOSION

Untold millions today are in spiritual bondage in the cults and the occult. Throughout the world, there is truly a *CULT EXPLOSION*. Many cults are growing rapidly because they *seem* so much like true Christianity. They sound like Christianity and they claim to have the truth. They use this "front" to draw people in.

The *CULT EXPLOSION* begins with the tragedy of Jonestown, graphically depicting the heartache and desperation that come from false prophets and manmade religions. Viewers are startled at the similarity of Jim Jones' People's Temple and the other eleven major American cults, and are made to realize that all have the same basic doctrines and approaches. The film features former leaders of many cult groups explaining the secret inner core of such groups, and how they found freedom and eternal life in the *real* Jesus. It is a valuable teaching tool for the church and should be seen by everyone.

The motion picture is produced and distributed by New Liberty Films, Burbank, California.

REORDERING INFORMATION

Additional copies of *Mormonism, Mama and Me* may be obtained by writing to:

Calvary Missionary Press
P.O. Box 13532
Tucson, Arizona 85732

1-4 copies	3.95 ea.
5-9 copies	3.55 ea.
10-24 copies	3.15 ea.
over 24 copies	2.75 ea.

Add 15 percent for postage and handling. Please enclose check with your order.